The Basics *of*
Self-Inquiry

Enlightened Lifestyles, Book One

The Basics of Self-Inquiry: Living Life Forward With Perfect Vision

Printed in Spain, 2024

ISBN-13: 978-1-7367044-4-8

Cover and book design: Robert Grey, Brooks+Grey Design.

Cover painting *Standing as Awareness* by Amy Falstrom.

ENLIGHTENED LIFESTYLES | BOOK ONE

The Basics of
Self-Inquiry

LIVING LIFE FORWARD WITH
PERFECT VISION

ISABELLA VIGLIETTI-SWARTZ

SHINING
WORLD

ShiningWorld.com

By Isabella Viglietti-Swartz:

The Enlightened Lifestyles series:

Book One, *The Basics of Self-Inquiry: Living Life Forward With Perfect Vision*
Book Two, *Lifestyle Solutions*
Book Three, *What Is the Body?*

The Yoga of Relationships: Non-Duality in Life

Dedication

THIS SERIES OF books would not have been possible without the guidance of my beloved friend, husband and teacher
James Swartz.

I am eternally grateful.

✦

Isabella Viglietti-Swartz

Contents

Contents

Contents

Foreword

SHININGWORLD, A NOT-FOR-PROFIT charity, is happy to present a trilogy unfolding the non-dual wisdom of Vedanta, written by Isabella Viglietti, my wife and best friend for the last twelve years. During that time Isabella has assimilated the essence of Vedanta that was handed down to me by my teachers, Swami Chinmayananda and Swami Dayananda, two renowned sages in the great tradition of Vedanta. She will continue the lineage, and it is our hope that this trilogy will bless you with freedom and unconditional non-dual love for the benefit of yourself, the world and the teaching itself.

ShiningWorld is dedicated to the dissemination, realization and actualization of the timeless non-dual wisdom of Vedanta, a means of knowledge for whole and complete unborn Existence shining as Consciousness/Awareness, popularly known as the non-dual Self.

~ James Swartz

"You are what your deep driving desire is.

As your desire is, so is your will.

As your will is, so is your deed.

As your deed is, so is your destiny."

~ Brihadaranyaka Upanishad

Chapter 1

Why Am I Unhappy?

THIS TRILOGY COVERS all the aspects that relate to an enlightened lifestyle, starting with the psychological and spiritual factors in the first book of the series. Book two progresses to the main lifestyle issues, such as relationships, sex, money, work, etc. The third book covers the body and taking care of it. I begin with a condensed version of the methodology of Vedanta with reference to Self-inquiry as a helpful addition to the complete methodology of the teachings of Vedanta. These are unfolded in more detail in James Swartz's books *How to Attain Enlightenment: The Vision of Non-Duality* and *The Essence of Enlightenment: Vedanta, the Science of Consciousness* and many other books by him and other teachers in the great lineage of Vedanta. There is no need to rewrite what has already been perfectly written. If you are committed to Self-inquiry, you need to make sure to read all the texts recommended in the three stages of Self-inquiry as outlined in the next two chapters of this first volume of Enlightened Lifestyles.

Though Self-inquiry is not essential to an enlightened lifestyle, there is no way to make effective changes to our quality of life without understanding what drives us. While there are other therapeutical ways to understand what conditions and motivates us, the non-dual teachings of Vedanta get to the underlying problem: understanding who and what we are in relation to the big picture of life and beyond it, and it gives us the tools to apply that knowledge directly to our life. So, let's begin with the fundamental question of life for most of us: Why I am so seldom truly happy?

What Causes Unhappiness?

Though everyone wants to be happy however we define it, many of us do not find happiness. Even if our lives are relatively stress-free and harmonious, we still feel an underlying nagging sense of dissatisfaction. No matter how much therapy we subject ourselves to, meditation we do or self-help books we read, nothing really seems to make our baseline dissatisfaction go away. We may be able to sublimate it to an extent, and there are ways that help, such as spiritual practices, religion, work, exercise and entertainment, to name a few.

The non-dual teachings of Vedanta are different in that they do not depend on anything we do, and they are not a belief system. Assuming we are ready to hear the teachings, they unfold the logic of existence which makes very clear what happiness is and isn't and why we seek it. Vedanta proposes one simple but powerful answer to our lack of happiness, otherwise called the hypnosis of duality. The pervasive and persuasive idea that I am a body-mind separate from everyone and everything, that I am small, incomplete, limited and need something to complete me, veils my mind.

Under the spell of duality means I live in a world in which everything is always changing and is fundamentally uncertain. There is always something I do not know and cannot control. I am always worried I will not get what I want or avoid what I do not want. The people and things my happiness depends upon are not in my control either, and there is the ever-present fear of losing them. Worst of all, I believe I am born and will die. Duality effectively blinds me to the counter-intuitive possibility that nothing is separate from me, that I am not my body-mind, and that I am unlimited and need nothing to make me whole, because I am the only factor that is always present and unchanging: non-dual Consciousness. Therefore, though my body is born and will die, I cannot be born or die, because I am never not "here."

The hypnosis of duality is so deep that it causes complete ignorance of our true nature. Deluded by it, we seek happiness outside of ourselves, in others, things or experiences, hoping to end the dissatisfaction we feel as a limited, needy person, the victim of our life circumstances or fate, trying to find something that will give our life meaning. But sadly, the happiness we get from getting what we want or avoiding what we don't want does not prevent the deep-seated dissatisfaction from returning. Trying to make the world give us what we think we need to be happy just does not work for long, because happiness does not reside outside of us. The "gnaw" of desire begets more desire. We do not find fulfilment by either running away from the world or towards it.

The Hedonic Treadmill

The majority live in pursuit of a notion of happiness that is subjective and generally acquisitive. Psychologists call it the "hedonic treadmill," a term that describes a happiness set point or adaptation. It's a theory that proposes people return to their level of happiness (or lack of it) regardless of what happens to them, whether it is winning the lottery, finding or losing a loved one or anything else. I realized early in life that I would never be any happier than I am right now, and that nothing good or bad in my life essentially changes this. This fact may seem hopelessly negative and dooms us to a life of existential meaninglessness. If getting what we want does not make us happy, why get out of bed in the morning? Why bother to do anything?

Is "Doing Happiness" Being Happy?

The copious amount of advice on the topic of reaching our full potential to be happy, with its obsession with longevity and productivity, often focuses on "happy life" happiness, what we need to do or gain to be happy, like working hard to get a degree, promotion, the best job/partner/place to live, entertainment or that much-desired vacation. But working hard to arrange for a happy life requires continued effort, which is hard to sustain, especially when the realization dawns that subjective happiness responds to circumstances and seems caused by them, but basically it is internal. We can be unhappy in very positive circumstances, and happy in very negative ones. We can experience temporary happiness when it happens to come upon us; we can induce it with practices, entertainment, travel or drugs. But object-dependent "happiness" is a fickle guest whose company we pursue and whose visits are rare and fleeting. We cannot make lasting subjective happiness "happen." It is not in our control, because it depends on various factors out of our control.

Two Important Existential Questions

Few people stop to ask two simple existential questions, both of which point to obvious (but unexamined) conclusions:

1. Am I full of desire, agitated and chasing happiness because of the unavailability of desirable objects (like a relationship, love, money, security/better car/home/job/whatever)? Or am I chasing happiness by running away from unwanted objects (relationships, jobs, houses, etc.), looking for more, better or different? If this is true for me, I must believe that I am incomplete, that the desirable or undesirable objects/experiences are separate from me, and I

believe happiness resides in them or away from them, in something better or different.

2. Why do I believe that gaining and/or avoiding anything is going to give me something I don't already have? Is it not clear in my own experience (if I am honest and really think about it) that the joy obtained from gaining or avoiding objects vanishes, though it may give me temporary happiness and take away my dissatisfaction for a while, and my dissatisfaction always returns?

The Unexamined Logic of the Wheel of Desire

The unexamined logic of these two questions creates what Vedanta calls "the wheel of desire and action," and most people are like little hamsters running endlessly in one spot on this wheel, thinking they are getting somewhere, helplessly pushed and pulled by desires, compelled to act out the same tendencies, like robots, in the hope of a different result. We are absolutely convinced that we need to act to gain the "right" object or avoid the "wrong" object (both of which are always changing) that will do the job of making us happy and complete. And as soon as we get the right object or escape the wrong object, we are after the next right object or run away from the most recent wrong object, puppets on a string dancing to the tune of forces beyond our control, a recipe for madness and a futile endeavour, because no object has the power to make us happy. It's no wonder the world is full of depressed, anxious people. Most of us do not investigate why the bliss from gaining or avoiding objects we desire does not offer lasting happiness; we just accept that this is the way things are. Yet this is what everyone wants. Temporary happiness is fine, but it is never enough.

What or where is lasting happiness, and why does it seem so impossible to achieve?

Duality Creates Dissatisfaction

The deluding power of duality (*Maya*) makes us, unchanging Consciousness, appear to change. It keeps us bound to the wrong idea about what happiness is and where to find it. From this perspective, we do not know for sure what the truth is and are not equipped with the means to be certain about anything, like ships adrift in a tempestuous and threatening ocean. The only thing we can be sure of is the uncertainty about everything, except for the certainty of change. The reason is that in duality our only means of knowledge of anything, the five senses, is restricted to perception and inference. The senses are limited and limiting, because perception and inference are subject to interpretation, which makes them unreliable as a measure of truth. Within the perception of the world as a duality, everything is potentially true or false; nothing can be completely known, because nothing is what it appears to be. This fact makes philosophers and scientists uneasy and nervous, and like a shadow, duality dogs all systems of scientific, worldly and even religious thought. And that means the way I interpret what is happening in my life is never the whole truth.

Yesterday's truth is today's fallacy. What I felt strongly about in the morning I am completely unclear about and in doubt of by dinner time. Some scientists in their delusion still believe that one day science will be able to explain everything. Science is not capable of stepping out of duality without knowledge of what Consciousness is. We cannot measure or quantify Consciousness, because it is the measure and knower of all things measurable and quantifiable, including the scientist. So the scientist, like everyone else, remains limited to perception and inference gained from the five senses. Non-duality, or Self-knowledge, is counter-intuitive because it is not in duality nor is it limited to the senses. Vedanta removes the blindfold of duality to reveal the non-dual, whole and complete, unchanging, ever-present Self as our true nature. But the blindfold is not easy to remove, because duality is so tenacious and convincing.

Happiness Is Peace of Mind

The teachings of Vedanta are essentially about happiness and well-being, what stands in its way and what creates or maximizes the conditions for it to flourish. Living life well is a complex business and means different things to different people; Vedanta is not pre-scriptive or proscriptive, because everyone's life *karma* is different. It has one agenda: happiness is good and suffering is not necessary, and the only way to actualize it is through knowledge, not experi-ence. But if we cannot tell the difference between duality and non-duality, we will not understand our true identity, nor the nature of the Field of Existence and the natural laws that run it, and we will suffer. So, if peace of mind and freedom from suffering is what motivates you, you may be ready for Self-inquiry into your state of mind, the factors that condition it and how that relates to an iden-tity you never considered you have: that of the non-dual unlimited knower or witness of the limited personal identity you have thus far taken to be the truth about you.

What Is Non-Duality?

Non-duality means you recognize the Self (Consciousness) as the only reality, non-separate from you, but independent of the person and the world you live in. It is very important to register this part: *non-separate from but independent of the person and its world.* It is not the denial of the individual or the world; it is a perspective that includes everything yet stands free of everything. A non-dual perspective requires re-evaluation of your world view, stepping out of duality by submitting the mind through Self-inquiry to a different means of knowledge: Self-knowledge. Self-knowledge is not like object-knowledge, because it is not an object of knowledge. It is the subject, and the subject can never be known by the object. Self-knowledge must be correctly taught or the mind will interpret it according to its filters. A commitment to Self-inquiry requires maintaining eternal vigilance, because duality is insidious and insinuates itself into everything like a thief in the night, robbing us of our most precious possession, peace of mind and true happiness.

Happiness Is Permanent Perfect Satisfaction

Vedanta contends that happiness is not the product of something you do, gain or feel, but a state of perfect uncaused satisfaction. And it is quite possible to experience it permanently, regardless of what you are or are not feeling or doing. In fact conditions in life could seem most unconducive to happiness, yet you are still perfectly satisfied because happiness depends on that which never changes, the Self. It does not depend on objects or favourable external conditions, i.e. any experience. Perfect satisfaction depends on Self-knowledge, meaning whether you are Self-referenced as opposed to object-referenced.

Self-Referenced or Object-Referenced?

An object is anything other than you, be it a material object or a subtle experience like a thought or a feeling such as bliss, joy, delight, gladness, etc. If you know there is nothing to add to yourself that augments who you are, there is nothing wrong with enjoying objects for the temporary happiness they offer. But most of us chase objects because we expect them to bring lasting happiness. And if you are chasing happiness, you had better be a marathon runner, because you will never catch it. You may end up in a deep chasm of despair and loss, and never find your way out. Depression sets in as hopes and dreams are laid waste, becoming bitterness and cynicism. It does not have to be that way if you stop to realize that you cannot gain something you already have. You are what you seek.

"Object-referenced" means you believe that happiness comes from something or someone outside of you. "Self-referenced" means you have realized that joy is never outside of you, but resides permanently and *exclusively* in you. While the joy from objects is impermanent and fleeting, the joy of being Self-referenced is not rare, even when outside circumstances don't seem conducive to it, like when the body is ill or our lives are threatened in some way. And seeing as our lives are always under threat because the body is on loan to us, finding permanent satisfaction is the most important factor if we want to be happy while "in" a body.

Desire Is Duality

As long as we are alive, we desire something, even if it is just to live. No matter what our desires are, whether we are aware of them or not, everything we do is an attempt to be happy. People who kill themselves are trying to be happy by escaping what makes them unhappy. Criminals, murderers and even child molesters are looking for happiness, no matter how depraved the search is. Most desires are a sign that happiness is absent or we are dissatisfied with what we have, don't have or with who we are. Even positive desires, like being a good person, spiritual seeking or living intelligently, are a sign that we are seeking happiness and need to make corrections to our life to experience it. If we had found what we were looking for, we would not desire or seek it.

Something is missing, so we focus our attention on getting our desire fulfilled. We don't realize it, but what we are really after is the release from desire itself, not the object of our desire. We act to remove driving desire, because it is painful, which is why we focus on getting what we want as quickly as possible. Desire is another word for time, because we are painfully aware of time when driven by desire. We want what we want when we want it the way we want it, and we suffer until we get it, which is why there is invariably great urgency around most desire. We think getting what we want will make us happy. And it does, for a short while.

Desire Has No Rest

So we focus on doing actions for results. But there is a small problem: because we are not in charge of the results, this builds up a lot of emotional and mental agitation. Oscar Wilde thought that the only way to get rid of driving desire was to yield to it. Well, we know how that works. It just strengthens existing desires or builds stronger ones, which is fine if those desires are beneficial and are satiated. But it is not difficult to see that the *raison d'être* of most desire is not to be satisfied but to expand. Desire by its nature does not want to end, it wants to want more. Seventeenth-century scholar Robert Burton put it admirably: "A true saying it is, 'Desire hath no rest.'" In the Hindu tradition, a rat symbolizes desire because rats are always gnawing on something. Rats have no choice but to keep eating or their teeth will grow into their skulls and kill them. This is a very apt metaphor for how desire manages our lives. Desire exhausts everyone eventually; it just wears us out.

Duality Consumes

Has it ever been any different since we emerged from the cave, learned how to farm and adopted the idea of ownership? Not much. Only the objects of desire change, but desire is desire. Reality as it is known for most is experienced as a duality. By its nature, it is fear- and lack-based, which creates the illusion of separation and incompleteness. The world of duality is an imperfect place and always will be, where we are all endlessly consuming experiences trying to find satisfaction. How then do we manage what drives us to consume so that we can be happy and live shame- and guilt-free?

More objects do not equal more happiness, but all too often the moral poverty and corruption that unbridled affluence can bring rob us of authenticity and mental peace. Does authenticity depend on personal truth as the famous philosopher Søren Kierkegaard put it, "The crucial thing is to find a truth which is truth for me"? Will foregoing the trappings of civilization and heading for a cave in India do the job as so many spiritual wannabes have attempted? Not if you think the cave in India will bring you happiness, because it will not. You take your world with you, wherever you go. There is no place to hide from the unconscious mind.

Everything in life is forever changing, and so are our desires and the objects of our desire. Think about a past all-consuming desire that possessed your mind in a vice-like grip, one you would have given almost anything to have fulfilled. Whether fulfilled or not, where is it now? Just a distant memory, if not forgotten. The power of a driving binding desire is like a fierce electrical storm soon spent as it runs out of fuel to sustain itself. No matter the collateral damage in getting what we want, desire sated brings enormous relief. We feel "on top of the world," which sadly wears off all too soon; another desire appears and off we go on another Mad Hatter chase!

Chasing Happiness Leads to Apathetic Resignation

We are like those crazy people who chase tornadoes, the adrenaline junkies who get their thrills from danger, because chasing happiness often leads to disappointment and injury. This is why sooner or later, in self-preservation if not despair or depression, we give up on happiness and resign ourselves to "getting by." It seems that half the people in the so-called "developed" world manage to keep going thanks to antidepressants. The majority have normalized apathetic resignation to the vicissitudes of life within a few decades of life, if not sooner.

Many of us live our lives walking the tightrope between the deep abyss of despair and the hope for a better life. It's a fine line. Whenever despair wins, we walk in darkness, cankered and craven. Then the world is a fearsome place. When love is victorious and defeats despair, we reach the path of grace, contentment and self-confidence. All is well with the world and life is good, while it lasts. The lucky ones realize that there must be something wrong with their thinking, not that happiness is a fiction.

In our dualistic society, we often revere desire as a sign of vitality and life. Marketing of all sorts admonishes us to "obey your thirst"!

Most people believe it is the fulfilment of their desires that equals happiness, and it is having desires that give direction and meaning to their lives. And it's true, we all need something to motivate us in life, so goals are important and give us purpose. There are natural desires, like eating when hungry and sleeping when tired, physical contact, and some positive desires, like Self-inquiry, which are not contrary to peace of mind. But the problem with most gratuitous desires is that when we get what we want, we are happy, but it never lasts, so back under the whip of desire we go. The Buddha taught that desire is the root of suffering and we must end all of it to be happy, which is just not possible. There is nothing inherently wrong with desire, and we can never stop ourselves from feeling some desire, no matter how full or happy we are. What we need to ask ourselves then is not how to get rid of desire, but what is desire, and where does it come from?

Desire Itself Is Not the Problem

The defining question is: What is behind desire? Who is the one that desires, what do you desire most, and is the desire binding? A binding desire is anything that creates bondage, positive or negative. Ultimately, we want to be free of all desires, but the worst are binding desires contrary to our true nature that break *dharma* (personal and universal laws). These are a mask for fear, because desire and fear go hand in hand. Desire is a positive fear, and fear is a negative desire. We cannot get rid of all desire, nor do we need to, but we can sublimate negative binding desires so that our petty fears and injurious gratuitous addictions do not enslave us.

An addiction is any desire we cannot satiate. A negative binding desire is something we cannot resist and harms us, but without which we cannot be happy. I am sure it is unnecessary to give examples, because there are so many addictive desires that obviously cause suffering: for sex, alcohol, food, drugs and tobacco, a few that come to mind; as well as those that break universal laws: like hatred, violence, prejudice, perversion and greed; whereas not so obvious negative binding desires are for love, acceptance, validation, etc. A positive binding desire is one in keeping with our nature and universal laws, such as a balanced non-obsessive desire for order, competence and simplicity; a desire to eat healthily; to always be honest, fair and kind; a desire for Self-inquiry, as mentioned; or for a devotional practice that honours the Self. These are just a few positive binding desires.

Vedanta Gives Us the Tools to Manage Life

In the next chapter, I unfold in more detail the two main tools that Vedanta offers us to manage our mind: *karma yoga* and *triguna yoga*. Briefly, *karma yoga* is the tool we use in the transactional reality. It supplies the understanding that we can act appropriately but are not in charge of results, ever. We may take the right action at the right time and not get what we want, something all of us are painfully aware of. *Karma yoga* requires surrendering our desire for a particular result to the Field of Existence, the universe, or God, in an attitude of gratitude, taking the results as a gift, whatever they are. Far from easy to do, but it is actually common sense if we think about it. Burning ourselves out with the burden of existential doership is a guarantee of suffering. Sadly, this is not obvious to most.

Triguna yoga is the tool to manage the inner world of the mind run by its fears and desires. *Guna* is a Sanskrit word that means "rope" because the *gunas* bind us to objects we desire or fear. The *gunas* are the psychological components of what drives us from within, our inborn nature and conditioning. I expound on the teaching of the *gunas* in forthcoming chapters, but briefly, the three energies are *sattva*, the energy of revelation, clarity, intelligence, knowledge, beauty and truth. *Rajas* is the energy of projection, action, desire and passion. *Tamas* is the energy of physical matter, sleep, ignorance, dullness, endurance and sloth.

The Three Energies That Make Up the Field

The *gunas* are known (or somewhat known) to us in the form of thoughts and feelings which morph into repetitive behavioural patterns in the form of actions or inaction. They are unknown to us in the form of unconscious programming (what we call likes and dislikes, or desires and fears) which give rise to our thoughts, feelings and our *karma*, or life story. Furthermore, these conscious or unconscious drives are conditioned by forces usually even less known to us, what psychologists refer to as the "collective unconscious" and what we refer to as the "macrocosmic causal body," or "total mind," the repository and seed state of all the factors that influence, condition and shape our destiny. Secular people call this the universe, or the field of life. Religious people call this God. Vedanta calls it *Isvara*, but it does not matter what you call it as long as you understand how the causal body affects your life.

Unfortunately, most people are totally identified with their conscious mind, to the extent that they believe they *are* their conscious mind and the story it spins about their identity. The reality our mind constructs is influenced by its inbuilt subjective filters and biased memory; it is an aggregate or amalgam of ideas it has about "what happened." However, the conscious mind without knowledge of the far more powerful unconscious mind from which it arises is like a very tiny little cog in a great big machine, oblivious to anything but itself, deluded as to its importance or station in life, whereas the macrocosmic unconscious, or total mind, is totally impersonal. It is a huge reservoir of information that interacts constantly with the Field of Existence, which is made up of all sentient objects: the microcosmic unconscious and conscious minds of individuals, the sentient minds of all other living beings, whether plant or animal, as well as all insentient objects.

Human individual minds are not apart from the Field but immersed in it; the microcosmic and macrocosmic are one Field. However, how we interpret the data coming from this vast Field determines our experience of the world. Our interpretation guides us, like an inner GPS as we chart our course, for better or worse. We overlay all sensory data with emotional significance according to our own filters in a constant stream of sensations, impulses, judgments and desires. And we suffer the consequences, because reality does not always match up. Other sentient beings, from animals to microbes, do not evaluate what happens in them or around them, so they do not suffer "their" *karma*, which is not interpreted and therefore impersonal. Life forms that cannot deviate from their program have no problem with their lot. Humans, on the other hand, while also programs, have the added function of self-reflection and "free will." We can chase objects and make choices; we can deviate from our program, which may or may accord with our highest good. Though it is true that the macrocosmic unconscious is infinitely more powerful than our conscious minds, it is possible to effect a change in the macrocosmic mind with Self-knowledge.

Self-knowledge Is the Only Elixir

Self-knowledge is the only knowledge capable of making a permanent change in the unconscious and conscious mind. It is the hard and fast knowledge of our true identity as Consciousness, the Self. It is also the complete knowledge of the three factors in the Field of Existence that govern everything in it, mentioned above. It makes this claim because Self-knowledge is always true in all circumstances and states of mind. It stands independent of my experience, beliefs and time. It is the knowledge that we cannot negate with any other knowledge, be it scientific, philosophical or religious. No logic can refute this, because there must be Consciousness present to know, to not know, accept or deny anything. No object exists without knowledge of it. And knowledge depends on Consciousness, but Consciousness does not depend on objects to exist. It makes existence and knowledge possible; this is based on fact, not belief. Do you exist minus all objects? That depends on who you think you are. If you identify with your body-mind, you will probably say no. But how can you be your body or mind if they are known to you?

If an object is anything known to you, something is known to you, the subject, and cannot be you. No object knows you. Ask yourself, do your thoughts and feelings or does your body know you? No, they don't. Maybe you think another person knows you, but do they? Who is it they know? Consider the hypothesis that other people do not really exist as we perceive them, that for each of us the magnitude of our isolation is profound. The possibility of a true bond of love or friendship may be remote. We are all born and die alone, no matter how many people we love or love us, a fact that brings much grief to those who believe happiness comes from anything external.

The *Sine Qua Non* of Life

All we ever know are our thoughts about other objects/people. The subject is the only "knower." Who is the subject? Consciousness, the Self with a capital "S," the ever-present, ever-full, unchanging witness of your life and everything in it, that by which all is known to you, the *sine qua non* of life itself, a succinct Latin term that literally translated means "without which nothing." Without knowledge of our true Self, we have nothing. And without the Self, nothing exists.

David and Goliath

Because it is so difficult to escape duality, and although everyone knows what it feels like to be happy, very few of us know what it means to be the source of happiness, irrespective of what is going on in our lives or state of mind. Even if you are not identified with the body-mind, it is no small feat to render negative binding desires or addictions non-binding. Think of David and Goliath. The only way to make a permanent change in the powerful unconscious mind is to understand and manage the forces that condition the conscious mind and retrain it to sublimate binding desires into the desire for the Self. To become Self-referenced instead of object-referenced is a complete reversal of the way most people live, and hugely counter-intuitive.

Real and permanent happiness, being Self-dependent, is never given or taken away from you, because the Self is an intrinsic factor. Sadly, the relentless search for temporary happiness outside of us is the norm. Songs, advertising and marketing ploys of every description which sell the notion that happiness is "out there" – somewhere – are all-pervasive, as is the tendency to negativity.

The Binding Tendency to Negativity

Neuropsychologists say our brains are like Teflon for positive experiences and Velcro for negative ones. If this sounds like a recipe for unhappiness, it is, and it's one reason that depression and anxiety are epidemics in the modern world. It is a human tendency, it appears, to focus more on negativity. Maybe it served us well in our caveman days when being too positive may have cost us our lives. But it no longer applies to most of us, as our survival is assured. Here's the good news: we can rewire our brains. Neuroplasticity proves that we can change the structure and function of our brain throughout our lives, and that our thoughts, emotions and behaviour are the primary means of doing that. We can overcome our inherent negativity bias and rewire our brains to pay more attention to the positive experiences we have.

The catch, which neuroscientists don't point out, is that unless we work really hard to manipulate our psyche to overcome our conditioning, these changes are extremely difficult to maintain unless they are based on Self-knowledge. If our mind/emotion management is based on Self-knowledge, the changes that take place bring us to a deeper understanding of who we are and closer to a permanent state of equilibrium. While life is woven fine with vanity and suffering as well as great joy and endless beauty, Self-knowledge can bring permanent peace of mind and freedom from suffering regardless of what life throws at us. Self-knowledge is the only true disaster insurance. And to be maintained, this must include a lifestyle that conforms to eternal truth, not one that tries to make eternal truth conform to it.

We all want a good life and do our best to achieve that, given what we know and our life *karma*. Our investigation into what makes us happy reveals that what we believe and how objective we are about what motivates us to do or want anything has a great deal to do with how happy our lives are. Without some idea of our internal world, what's going on for us below surface appearances and "pushing our buttons," we can mistakenly believe we are in control, autonomous beings that "create our own reality." But if we don't understand the forces that govern the way we think and feel, we are very far from being in control of our mental/emotional state. The way we live life is like sitting in the back seat of a car while a mad stranger is in the driver's seat, who takes us wherever they want to go. As the philosopher Kierkegaard said, perhaps one of the greatest tragedies of life for many is that it "can only be understood backwards, but must be lived forwards." And as my husband's father said to him before he died, "Too soon old, too late smart."

Living Life Forward With Perfect Vision

Self-knowledge offers a powerful alternative: to live life with your eyes wide open, fully aware of what is going on in the moment, always looking forward with 20/20 vision, never backwards, free of the past, unafraid of the future, cleaning up your *karma* as it arises, at peace, not chasing, waiting for or needing anything to make us happy. If this sounds too good to be true, it is not. But it's not easy. You may very well have to stop making excuses and give up your comfort zones. Self-inquiry requires examining our psychological make-up, especially the things about ourselves we don't want to see, by facing the unseen factors that run the mind and the Field of Life, our environment.

In the next chapter, we cover the steps to Self-inquiry and what it entails.

Chapter 2

The Background *to* Self-Inquiry

What Is Self-Inquiry?

SELF-INQUIRY IS NOT seeking, it is about becoming a finder. It is not about adding anything to you, perfecting or changing you as a person. The teachings of Vedanta basically state that there is nothing wrong with you except the way you think, in particular who you think you are. Self-inquiry is about the removal of what stands in the way of appreciating your true and unlimited nature as the non-dual Self, or Consciousness. Vedanta contends that it is far from beyond us to understand exactly who we are, what drives us and why. It provides a commonsensical and logical set of proven principles that work to simplify the complexities of the mind and prepare it to assimilate the knowledge that sets us free of suffering.

Vedanta is simply the truth about you, not your truth or my truth or anyone's truth: the Truth. The non-dual precepts of Vedanta are not based on belief, and they unfold the whole *mandala* of life with impeccable logic. While there is no requirement to abandon whatever you believe in to undertake Self-inquiry, you do need to at least be prepared to investigate your beliefs in a new light. While everything in this world is up for interpretation according to our conditioning and opinions, including "logic," Vedanta contends that logic only stands if it is completely independent of all personal beliefs, options and interpretations. If it doesn't, no matter how good your thinking is, it is a subjective interpretation of the truth.

Vedanta Is the Science of Consciousness

Vedanta is called the "science of Consciousness," and although it originates from Vedic culture, the basic teaching is universal in that its fundamental principle is that reality is non-dual as opposed to dual. It is as rigorous and uncompromising as any science, an objective and scientific analysis of the true nature of reality (and your experience) based on non-negatable facts. These facts are delivered in proofs called *prakriyas*. They are arrived at, not with empirical proof, but by negating all non-essential variables, leaving the one essential invariable fact: that you are conscious. You can never deny this, as to do so you must be conscious. The point is, how does being conscious relate to your identity, and how does knowledge of this set you free of suffering? Therein lies all the teaching of Vedanta.

Like any other science, Vedanta is not personal and has a methodology, which if followed with great dedication and commitment will provide irrefutable knowledge that is freedom from limitation and suffering, *moksa*, or Self-knowledge, if the student is qualified. "Qualified" means the mind is purified and prepared (more on this further on). If you are ready to hear the teachings and they are correctly and consistently applied to your life, the means of knowledge produce the most elusive kind of happiness that is free of dependence on objects, referred to as "perfect satisfaction." There are many teachings that claim to offer enlightenment, but there is nothing else available to us that compares with Vedanta, if you understand what it reveals about the true nature of your existence and of all existence.

Historical Background of Vedanta

Before unfolding what Self-inquiry entails, and though it is not essential to Self-inquiry, it really helps to understand some of the history of Vedanta and its scriptural texts in order to fully grasp and value their import. *Veda Anta,* Vedanta, is a doctrinal teaching at the end of the *Vedas,* which are the sacred, impersonal and eternal scriptures of Hindu tradition. There are four Vedas; the first three pertain to the person living in the world, cover different aspects of physical life, and are for obtaining desired results in the world. They are the *Rig Veda, Yajur Veda, Sama Veda* and, lastly, the *Atharva Veda.* The last section of the fourth and last Veda deals exclusively with the true nature of reality as a non-duality and is called *Vedanta,* which literally means "the knowledge that ends the quest for knowledge." Its main teachings are unfolded in the *Upanishads,* the *Brahma Sutras* and the *Bhagavad Gita.*

The Vedas form the ancient tradition called the *Sanatana Dharma* (the Eternal Way), which originated in what is now called India but was once called Bharat, meaning the "Land of Light," or "The People Who Uphold Righteousness," between 6,000 and 7,000 years ago. This point has been argued by many scholars, but most agree that the Vedas are at least 3,500 old, making Vedanta the oldest scriptural teaching on the planet. But in truth, Vedanta has no age, because it is not in time; it is the eternal truth of existence, so has no beginning or end.

Vedanta in essence is not specific to any culture, race or religion, as Consciousness does not "belong" to anyone. It is who we are. The methodology or means of knowledge Vedanta uses to unfold the eternal unchanging non-dual teachings was developed and perfected by the Indian culture, most recently updated by Sri Adi Shankaracharya in the eighth century AD. The methodology is accredited to the Hindu religion, but Vedanta is nonetheless not part of any religion or philosophy. Many Indian people of today or long ago are and were as ignorant of the non-dual teachings of the

Vedas as any Westerner. The focus of most people on the planet is about making life work with as much ease as possible, which is why the first three Vedas teach exclusively how to do that. Only at the very end of the last Veda does Vedanta emerge for those who have realized that life is a zero-sum game and are ready for the ultimate teaching.

Though many Indians are Moslems, in general the big difference between the Indian and Western cultures is that the former is culturally steeped in and guided by a devotional attitude to the idea of God as universal and omnipresent, symbolized in any form or no form, hence the Hindu pantheon of many God-symbols and ubiquitous devotional rituals. Vedanta may be only for the qualified, but nonetheless, the non-dual teachings spread throughout the East and West, influencing the spiritual traditions of the whole world. It is the truth that underpins all truth, whether you are aware of it or not. The Sanatana Dharma, or Eternal Way, is alive and well, and always will be.

Vedanta Is Independent of Any Person

Vedanta is taken to be a philosophy by many, but it predates all known religious or philosophical paths because it is independent of any person or path. It is a *sruti*, which means "that which is heard," and it was originally transmitted orally. The reason it is a *sruti* is that it is *apauruseya jnanam*, meaning "not the philosophy, belief or experience of one person like a prophet or a mystic," as in the Buddha, Jesus or Abraham. Religions and philosophical teachings are the personal fabrications, beliefs and contentions of people, be they great thinkers or not.

They are thus subject to the contamination of personal views, and of change. Vedanta is neither subject to change nor contaminated by personal views, though it can be taught or understood incorrectly.

If the ego co-opts the teachings, what we call "enlightenment sickness," they will definitely become corrupted. But that does not change the teachings. It only means that they will not work for their intended purpose, which is to end suffering by removing ignorance of your true nature.

The Truth, Self-knowledge

Unlike object-knowledge, Self-knowledge stands on its own and is always true because it is true to the Self/Consciousness, meaning it cannot be dismissed or negated by any other knowledge. It is the only non-negatable factor present in every situation and time frame, past, present or future. You know this is true because if it were not, the you that you identify with as a body-mind would be six feet under. Self-knowledge is different from knowledge of objects, which is object-based, not subject-based. Knowledge of objects is not knowledge unless it is true to the object. If I am looking at a dog, and my eyes and mind are functional, I will not see a cat. If it is "my" knowledge, then it is my subjective interpretation of an object (*pratibasika*), which is not necessarily knowledge.

Ignorance (or my point of view) causes me to see or experience objects in a certain way because of "my" conditioning, or premature cognitive commitments. People believe that what they experience and think they know is knowledge. It may be knowledge, and it may be ignorance which can be negated. But Self-knowledge is neither confirmed nor negated by anyone's opinions or experience, because it is free of experience.

Vedanta Is Revealed Knowledge

Because Vedanta is revealed to the mind of man, not thought up by man, nor is it the result of any action on anyone's part, you can trust it. So what do we mean by "revealed"? Don't all religions claim this? What Vedanta means by revealed is simple. A good example of revealed knowledge is Einstein's "discovery" of the law of relativity and gravity or the ancient Greek "discovery" of electricity. To "discover" means to "uncover something that was there but previously unknown." Relativity, gravity and electricity describe how the world works according to the laws of physics, not according to Einstein or any researcher in particular. Gravity, relativity and electricity do not care if you believe in them. They operate the same way whether you understand what they are or not.

It is the same with Consciousness; it does not care if you have realized your true nature or not, because it is unaffected by knowledge or ignorance. You are the Self whether you know it or not. Liberation from ignorance is for the apparent person who lives in the apparent reality. As Consciousness, you have always been free, which is why *moksa*, or freedom from limitation and suffering, entails discrimination of you, the Self, from the objects that appear in you. This includes "your" body-mind. In other words, disidentification with the person you take yourself to be as your primary identity AND knowing what that means so that Self-knowledge translates into all areas of life. Vedanta is freedom *from* the person and *for* the person.

The Main Texts *of* Vedanta

The *Upanishads,* the *Brahma Sutras* and the *Bhagavad Gita (Puranas)*

1. The Puranas

The *Puranas* form the basis of the Hindu religion, and are mythological ideas or stories taught in the way of forms such as symbols and rituals. They were originally intended for people who were not sophisticated enough to understand or worship the formless. The reason for this was that unqualified people could gain Self-knowledge by implication from the form to the formless. All Puranas are really the Vedas in code. There are many important Puranas, and the most important of all is the *Bhagavad Gita,* which is told in the form of an allegory (some schools of Vedic thought do not consider it a Purana). If properly understood and taught (which is often not the case), the *Gita* unfolds the whole methodology of Vedanta.

The *Bhagavad Gita* – the "Song of God" – is one of the world's most important spiritual documents insofar as it is the essence of the *Upanishads,* humanity's most ancient extant texts on the science of life. It provides a timeless solution to the existential crises that we all face at some point in our lives. The *Gita* is part of the *Mahabharata* (ostensibly inscribed by the sage Vedavyasa) and was written about 300 years before the birth of Christ. It is believed by some to be historical and to have actually happened, but there is no actual proof.

2. The Upanishads

The *Upanishads* are revealed texts. The meaning of the word "Upanishad" is "Self-knowledge" and these scriptures are generally for advanced inquirers because none of them contains the whole methodology of Vedanta. While the stories contained in the *Upanishads* seem simple, if the background and meaning of the symbols is not properly unfolded, it is easy to get confused. There are more than 200 *Upanishads,* the first ten being the most important. Some of the *Upanishads* are referenced by author, but authorship has no bearing on what they impart, because it is the timeless and impersonal knowledge of the Self, Consciousness. The authorship is in the form of commentaries (*karikas*) which unfold the meaning of the texts. The essence of all the *Upanishads* is the core teaching of Vedanta, which is:

> *Knowing that because of which everything is as good as known.*
> *It addresses the value of inference in accepting*
> *your identity as Awareness.*

3. The Brahma Sutras

The last scriptural text included in the Vedanta *pramana* ("means of knowledge") is the *Brahma Sutras*, which is a collection of intellectual discourses regarding very subtle issues compiled and published by Badarayana. They are complicated discussions that are not necessary for Self-inquiry but are useful for teachers of Vedanta to understand the finer details of the Vedanta doctrine.

The Texts Suggested for Each Stage of Self-Inquiry

BEGINNER

1. *Tattva Bodh* by Shankara: Explains the basic terminology and language used in Vedanta. Vedanta is a means of Self-knowledge through words called a *sabda pramana*. It gives you direct knowledge of your eternal nature through the implied meaning of words when they are unfolded through a specific methodology called the *sampradaya*. But because all languages are inherently dualistic, the use of words and

terms is influenced by many factors, both in the speaker and the one listening. Most people speak the language of experience (duality), but Vedanta speaks the language of identity – that of the Self (non-duality). However, it is still confined to using words to teach, and all words are open to interpretation. So for Self-inquiry to work, where the ostensible meaning does not work (the ostensible meaning is the meaning stated but not necessarily true), Vedanta teaches with the implied meaning based on logic. It is extremely careful with the use of words and terminology, and *Tattva Bodh* explains this well.

2. *The Value of Values* by Swami Dayananda: The importance of this text and how absolutely essential this topic is in preparation for and to succeed at Self-inquiry cannot be overemphasized (more on this further on).

3. *The Essence of Enlightenment* and/or *How to Attain Enlightenment* by James Swartz: Essential for Self-inquiry, as they unfold the whole methodology of the teachings for beginners to advanced inquirers. All you need to succeed at Self-inquiry is found in these two books. For beginners, the first five chapters of either book explain the foundations of Vedanta: motivations, values, *dharma*, qualifications and, very importantly, *karma yoga*.

4. *Bhagavad Gita*, chapters one to five: Explains the foundations for *moksa* and Self-inquiry.

5. *The Yoga of Love* by James Swartz: Explains the importance of devotional practice, *bhakti yoga*, required to succeed at Self-inquiry.

6. *Vedanta: The Big Picture* by Swami Paramarthananda: Offers another concise overview of the whole teaching methodology of Vedanta.

INTERMEDIATE

1. *Bhagavad Gita*, chapters six to ten, and *The Essence of Enlightenment*, chapters six to ten, and/or *How to Attain Enlightenment* by James Swartz: Unfold *jnana yoga*, the teachings on the identity between *Isvara* and *jiva*, and the *gunas*, which are the three psychological forces behind everything in Creation (explained below).

2. *Aparokshanubhuti* by Shankara: Explains the difference between knowledge and experience.

3. *Vivekachudamani* by Shankara: Unfolds discrimination between the Self and the three bodies, or five sheaths.

4. *The Yoga of the Three Energies* by James Swartz: Essential to unfold the teaching on the three *gunas*.

ADVANCED

1. *Bhagavad Gita*, last five chapters: Explains what it means to be Self-realized and Self-actualized.

2. *The Essence of Enlightenment*, chapters eleven to thirteen, and/or *How to Attain Enlightenment* by James Swartz, last five chapters: same as above.

3. *Inquiry into Existence* (commentaries on *Panchadasi* by James Swartz): Essential to unfold the identity between the person (*jiva*), the Creation (*jagat*) and the Creator (*Isvara*).

4. *Mandukya Upanishad and Gaudapada's Karika* (commentaries by James Swartz): Explains the important difference between cause-and-effect and the non-origination teaching.

A Word of Caution: You Cannot Study Vedanta

Vedanta, or non-duality, is not a theory in practice. Though it is imperative that you apply your mind to the teachings and commit them to memory, ultimately you cannot study and memorize Vedanta like you would to earn a university degree. Many inquirers get stuck in the belief that if they can parrot the teachings or learn Sanskrit, they are Self-realized. But even though all teachings require an intellectual understanding, the difference with Vedanta is that it is not a philosophical or scientific thought system or hypothesis.

Vedanta requires a certain kind of intellect — one that is refined, purified and surrendered so that it is capable of assimilating the meaning of the teachings, which are extremely subtle and therefore very counter-intuitive. Some inquirers are in love with their ability to think, and have a lot of ego around their own ideas and intelligence, so it is harder for them to put their thinking aside. Self-inquiry requires training the intellect to think differently and to want different things.

While we need an intellect, it is not the intellect that removes ignorance. The intellect is just an object known to you, the Self. You cannot "think your way to enlightenment," because it is the ego, the doer, doing the thinking. The ego must surrender to a qualified teacher and the teachings and trust Self-knowledge to scour the mind of ignorance. And lastly, it is not necessary to have more than a very rudimentary knowledge of some basic Sanskrit terms to undertake Self-inquiry (most are mentioned in this book). Only a very few Sanskrit terms have no good English equivalents, but most do.

Why Do I Need Self-Inquiry?

In trying to understand ourselves and life, if we are looking for more than scientific validation, philosophical inspiration or something to believe in, we have two basic options: psychotherapy and Self-inquiry. Vedanta encourages psychotherapy, though it is not equal to Self-inquiry. Self-inquiry is investigating how your "small" (or individual) self and the Field it lives in relates to your "big" Self (capital "S"). But it is extremely difficult to seriously undertake Self-inquiry if you are dragging around a huge burden of unresolved psychological detritus. A balanced, mature and healthy mind is a non-negotiable prerequisite for Self-inquiry. Though Self-inquiry is far superior to psychotherapy, psychotherapy can be very useful, as it helps to develop the qualification required for Self-inquiry.

As stated in the previous chapter, we suffer because we identify with the body-mind, and so believe we are flawed, inadequate, incomplete and separate from everything. We do not understand why or how we are programmed to want what we want or the forces that compel us to act. We chase objects (an object is defined as anything known to me, which includes my body-mind or thoughts and feelings) in the attempt to make ourselves whole. But no object can make us happy for long, because all objects are value-neutral, are always changing and therefore not under our control.

We live in fear of loss and death, worry about the future and regret the past. And the reason for this is that we are deluded by *Maya,* or the hypnosis of duality. Vedanta reveals that duality is a mirage, an apparition, or a superimposition onto non-duality. It is only apparently real, or *mithya,* "that which is not always present and always changing," real defined as *satya,* "that which is always present and unchanging," i.e. Consciousness. It gives us the tools to apply to our lives in order to understand and manage our mind so that we can discriminate between what is real and apparently real, and thus live peaceful, happy, worry-free lives.

If you are already a happy satisfied person and your life is meaningful and fulfilling, even if you are identified with your body-mind, you do not need Self-inquiry. But most people are not happy or satisfied with their lives, even those who have no worldly worries of any kind. Most people's lives are chronicles of endless suffering, thanks to the power of *Maya* which deludes and fragments the mind. And the lucky ones are those whose suffering has turned the mind inwards towards the Self in search of answers that last.

No Fast Track

We live in a world where we are accustomed to and expect fast results, and the spiritual world is no different. In fact, in many ways, a lot of spiritually-driven people are even more materialistic and egotistical than purely materialistic worldly people. But with

Vedanta, you must accept that you are not the boss. If you cannot surrender to the teachings and follow the methodology because you are goal-oriented, lack motivation or qualifications, Self-knowledge will just not obtain; there is no fine print to this. Even if you are a mature person and your mind is highly qualified and dedicated to it, slow and steady is the only sure way to succeed at Self-inquiry.

It does not work to rush, because you will invariably skip or miss building a good foundation which will hold you up at some point. So be warned: Vedanta is not for those with major psychological problems, the egotistical, those in a hurry, the lazy or faint of heart, nor the unqualified. It is the most rigorous and challenging teaching available for the mind and will challenge everything you thought you knew. It will force you to face the less-than-fabulous aspects of your personality, but not to fix them, only to understand and negate them as not-me so as to be free of them. Freedom is not something you "get" overnight, which is why Vedanta appeals to so few people. Only a mature and pure mind is capable of assimilating Self-knowledge, hence the necessity for qualifications (see below).

Vedanta Is Not Exclusive

The teachings of Vedanta are not exclusive to Vedanta. They are to be found wherever there is a non-dual teaching that is independent (stands alone) and capable of revealing what it means to be the Self. But the problem with other teachings, such as Buddhism or Neo-Advaita (and some religions), is that they do not teach the whole methodology of non-duality, nor do they offer the tools to help you translate the non-dual teachings in a practical way into your life, such as karma yoga, to name just one. Worse, while they may have aspects of non-duality, ignorance is woven fine with knowledge. Unless you understand the difference between duality (*mithya*) and non-duality (*satya*), you will not be able to discriminate between knowledge and ignorance, so freedom will not obtain.

Buddhism and much of the spiritual teachings outside of Vedanta are based on *yoga,* whose primary aim is to improve the person and get rid of the mind. They teach that it is in ending desire through meditation and good deeds that we "attain enlightenment." It's all about doing something to gain something. But Vedanta explains that we cannot improve the person, nor get rid of the mind, because they are not real; they are duality (*mithya*), and not the problem.

Identification with the person, the doer, i.e. ignorance of your true nature as *satya,* is the real problem, not the mind. It is neither possible nor necessary to get rid of the mind (ego); it can only be understood to be not-Self through the removal of ignorance by Self-knowledge. Freedom from ignorance cannot be obtained by doing, because you cannot gain something you already have; the Self is not an object of experience. It is impossible to objectify the Self for this reason. As the Self, you are the subject and that which you seek.

Once the true nature of the mind is known to be the Self, binding tendencies (*vasanas*) are rendered non-binding by Self-knowledge, and the sense of doership is negated. Doership is the mistaken idea that you are the author of your life and "make things happen." It ignores the fact that the Field of Existence determines results at all times, and you have no control over all the factors involved. When doership goes, the mind remains — and no longer troubles the individual person (*jiva*) anymore. You can live free of the person as the Self, while also living free as a person, and never confuse the two again. However, purely cognitive understanding does not remove suffering.

Many people who have realized their true identity as the Self do not realize that a subtle unconscious belief that the Self is something other than them, something to gain, remains. There is still an identification with the person, so they personalize the Self, thinking that by "the Self" we mean the reflection of the Self, the *jiva*, or the person. The Self is the source of the reflection, which is caused by *Maya*. To break the spell of *Maya* and take your primary identity as Consciousness, we need a means of knowledge capable of deconstructing who or what the *jiva* is, what *Isvara* (God, or the creative principle) refers to and why, and what is the same and what is different about both.

For Self-knowledge to translate into the life of the *jiva*, *mithya* must be understood in the light of Self-knowledge, not in light of our own subjective or limited understanding. *Mithya* may not be real, but it is not going to disappear just because you have realized your true nature to be the Self, Consciousness, the source of all. Self-realization is where the "work" of Self-inquiry begins. Self-actualization is quite another other matter. To succeed at Self-inquiry means thinking in a whole new context – that of non-duality – and this is far from easy. Your *jiva* conditioning is hardwired in duality. So go slowly. You need to assimilate and understand the logic every step of the way to get the "big picture" and for Self-knowledge to stick.

Where to Begin?

Most inquirers (even mature ones) who come to Vedanta have a ton of indoctrination from other teachings to work through. It's not that there is anything wrong with other teachings, but most other teachings are unclear about what the Self is, nor are they able to explain the apparent reality with reference to the Self other than through personal experiences or beliefs. As stated, Self-inquiry involves an analysis of what makes up and governs the Field of Existence, which includes the individual, with the aim of negating our dependence on objects for happiness. It is to discriminate between non-duality and duality, i.e. between experience (the object/effect) and Consciousness (the subject/cause). There is a world of difference between these two perspectives, and the ability to discriminate is called non-dual vision, which is permanent freedom from limitation, because it is not only about understanding our conditioning and the world we live in, it is freeing ourselves of both.

Before beginning Self-inquiry, ask yourself: What are my true values and motivations? Am I genuinely interested in improving the quality of my life? If you are, then it is reasonable to assume that if you could improve it on your own, you would already have done so by now. In this case, put aside what you think you know, refrain from reading through the filters of your existing beliefs and opinions, and remain willing to be ignorant, wrong or misinformed. You can always take your opinions back if you like them so much better. But if in cherry-picking ideas you discard what you don't like or agree with, confirmation bias will operate (among other biases) and you will waste your time.

To succeed at Self-inquiry, you must commit yourself to follow the logic and methodology of the steps as they are presented in the scripture. If you try to fit the teachings into your own ideas or try to tailor them to fit in with your beliefs, Self-inquiry will not work to remove ignorance. The teachings are extremely methodical. Vedanta is a progressive teaching designed to answer every doubt. Sign on to the logic and don't skip ahead until you know you have understood and assimilated each step. If you rush through the steps because you think you know better, you will defeat the purpose and are clearly more invested in your own ideas. Apply the steps to your thinking and see how this affects your life. Self-inquiry is about applied knowledge, so if it does not translate into your life and you see no benefit, it is never the teaching at fault.

There are three main reasons the teachings do not assimilate, thus Self-inquiry may fail for you. The first is either a lack of qualifications and unaltered thinking or a lack of motivation in putting the teachings into practice. The second is that there are remaining binding tendencies and doership. The last is that your lifestyle must be cleaned up. For a simple and peaceful life, healthy lifestyle habits in eating, sleeping, working, relationships, sex, money, recreational habits, etc. must be cultivated in accordance with the scripture, not the other way around. Everything that is not in line with the teachings must be renounced. This is covered in great detail in volumes two and three of the Enlightened Lifestyles trilogy.

Being Properly Taught Is Imperative

Apart from the three factors mentioned above, you must be properly taught, because the mind is conditioned to think in a certain way. Non-duality is counter-intuitive – it is a provocative teaching designed to give rise to doubts, which it also answers. Unguided, the mind will interpret what it hears or reads according to its conditioning and Self-knowledge will not obtain. You may "get it" for a while and then "unget it" for the reasons mentioned above, basically because the mind has not been sufficiently purified. Also, there are apparent contradictions within the teachings that are not real contradictions and need to be resolved by a qualified teacher. And there is one more factor to consider: grace. It is only by the grace of God that anything happens – and grace is earned.

The Three Non-Negotiable Factors
to Begin Self-Inquiry

1. **Motivation:** You need to be so tired of suffering that you are ready to commit to understanding what causes it.

2. **Qualifications:** All the qualifications noted below are essential to succeed at Self-inquiry. But if they are not all present when you start inquiry, you can develop them. To begin Self-inquiry, you need at the very least the entry-level qualification, which is the realization that it is pointless to try to find happiness in objects, i.e. you have seen the futility of chasing your desires or trying to avoid your aversions. You know there must be something more to this life.

3. **Faith:** You need enough faith in the teachings to sign on to Self-inquiry and stick with it. If you do not trust the teachings, they will not work for you.

Qualifications Required

To assimilate what Vedanta teaches, qualifications are necessary for discrimination between the Self, or *satya* (that which is always present and unchanging), and the objects that appear in it, that which is apparently real, meaning the *jiva* and the world, *mithya* (that which is always changing and not always present). Therein lies the rub. It is one thing to understand what freedom is, but that does not set you free necessarily. To live free as the Self requires the hard and fast full assimilation of what it means to be the Self and not the *jiva*, plus all three steps of Self-inquiry completed.

We need qualifications to succeed at anything in the world. So it stands to reason that there should be qualifications for Self-inquiry as well. Although not all the qualifications need to be present to begin with, they must be understood and developed.

THE MOST IMPORTANT QUALIFICATIONS ARE:

1. The burning desire for liberation from bondage to objects, meaning one has understood that there is nothing to gain through objects, that there is no joy inherent in them. I desire above all to understand my true nature and have stopped chasing objects.

2. Faith in the teachings, not blind faith, but faith pending the outcome of your investigation. If you cannot check your beliefs "at the door," Self-inquiry will not work for you. You must be prepared to forego your attachment to other teachings, at least temporarily.

3. Dispassion, non-attachment to outcome, i.e. *karma yoga*,

surrendering the results of actions to *Isvara*, or the Field of Existence, with an attitude of gratitude.

4. Discrimination, the ability to discriminate what is changeless, or real (Consciousness), from that which is changing, or only seemingly real (all objects, which include the mind and body, thoughts and emotions, in other words, anything other than Consciousness, the real you).

5. Control of the senses and of the organs of action. This includes thought/emotion management, speaking and all activities, especially sensory ones like eating and sex.

Further Requirements *and* Pointers *for* Self-Inquiry

1. You Are Not the Boss

Many inquirers do not understand what Self-inquiry entails, and that if you commit to it, you need to relinquish control, because you are locked into a predetermined process, or *sadhana*. You are no longer the boss. The whole point of Self-inquiry is to investigate your binding tendencies and sense of doership to bring that wilful self-centred ego into line with scripture, or Self-knowledge. If the ignorance/duality tail is still wagging the dog, it is important to accept that fact and follow the program of Self-inquiry to the letter.

2. Self-Inquiry Is Your Priority

First and most important, Self-inquiry should be the most

important part of your day, not incidental to it if you truly want freedom from existential suffering caused by duality. If Self-inquiry does not translate into your life, it will have minimal benefit to you. For the mind to assimilate Self-knowledge, all three stages of inquiry outlined below must be completed methodically and thoroughly, not necessarily in a linear fashion. Most inquirers will weave in and out of the stages as their doubts arise and get dispelled by the teachings. Vedanta is taught in a very specific way for a very good reason: the mind is very conservative and ignorance is hardwired and tenacious.

3. You Cannot Do Your Way to Freedom

You are not going to "achieve" enlightenment. Every inquirer is different and thus has different needs, but the only thing that is a standard requirement for each inquirer is that they are sufficiently qualified, surrendered to the teachings with *karma yoga*, dedicated to *moksa* and properly taught. If you have the required faith in the teachings and are truly committed, grace is the deciding factor on whether *moksa* obtains. No teacher of Vedanta however good can enlighten you or remove your ignorance, only facilitate the teachings. Nothing the individual or doer "does" is going to achieve freedom, because the doer is the problem. There are no guarantees and no goals to achieve, because you are already the Self. All Vedanta can do for you is give you the tools to apply to your mind so that Self-knowledge can do the work of removing the ignorance that is preventing you from appreciating this fact, setting you permanently free of duality and suffering.

The doer does not get enlightened, nor can it "do" its way to enlightenment. Yes, you must be very dedicated to your *sadhana*, no doubt about that. And that is a kind of doing, but a very different doing because it involves *karma yoga,* which means it is a doing surrendered to the teachings. Self-inquiry is not easy; there are no shortcuts. But *karma yoga* and trust in *Isvara* will get you "there" where you are already, if it is *Isvara's* will. Only Self-knowledge can remove ignorance, not the ego.

PLEASE NOTE

If you want Self-inquiry to succeed, you must read the texts in the order they are presented in this chapter. To help with your inquiry, *ShiningWorld.com* offers a wide range of other texts and articles, videos on all the teachings and, very importantly, thousands of pages of questions and answers in our *satsang* section. The Q&A operates with a search function using keywords to facilitate your search. Make sure you avail yourself of this, as it answers any questions or doubts you could have. If none of this helps, feel free to write to us, as we are happy to assist you with your Self-inquiry.

Chapter 3

The Steps *to* Self-Inquiry

The First Four Steps *in* Self-Inquiry Are *the* Preparations *for* It

THE FOUR IMPORTANT *yogas* for Self-inquiry mentioned below are essential in preparation for Self-inquiry, and continue throughout the duration. When Self-knowledge is firm and you are no longer an inquirer, they change from applied knowledge to automatic knowledge, i.e. though all four *yogas* continue, they are no longer practices as such, as there is no longer any need to purify the mind, because it rests in the Self.

Preparation for Self-Inquiry 1: Fearless Moral Inventory

There are four basic human motivations, and they work in a predictable progression from security to pleasure, then virtue and, lastly, freedom from limitation. Depending on what you value most, your values will be very different. For Self-inquiry to work, your primary value needs to be freedom from limitation. All values need to be in line with the scripture as well as the personal and universal laws of life (*dharmas*), which are based on non-injury in thought, word and deed. Therefore the place to start Self-inquiry is a fearless moral inventory of my main motivations in life. If I have never investigated my motivations or the values that underpin them, I am only motivated by what serves me, my likes (desires) and dislikes (fears). I live my life like a spoiled child. I want what I want the way I want it when I want it, and I get very upset when I don't get what I want.

If I do not value non-injury and freedom, my mind is under the spell of duality, so I believe I am separate and incomplete. I live in constant anxiety that I will not get what I want or lose what I have. I am unaware of the natural laws that run the Field of Life, which cannot be broken without consequence. Oblivious to what my purpose is or what the Field requires from me, I fail to act appropriately. I manipulate or break the universal laws of life to get what I want, even though breaking *dharma* robs me of self-confidence, self-esteem, peace of mind and trust.

Dharma is complex, and it is impossible for one person to tell another what their personal *dharma* is or what is right for them in any situation; what is right for you will not be right for me on a personal level. Generally, when you feel happy and at peace with what you are doing, you are following what is right for you and true to your relative nature. When there is a nagging, unhappy or guilty voice in your head, you are most likely contravening *dharma*, either by what you are doing or not doing.

PLEASE NOTE

Essential reading on values is Swami Dayananda's *The Value of Values*. Do not skip it! It explains simply and clearly all the values to develop and to avoid for Self-inquiry to work.

Preparation for Self-Inquiry 2: *Karma Yoga*

The importance of *karma yoga* cannot be overstated; you simply will not make progress without it. It is our most powerful tool with which we manage the mind with reference to our transactional reality. For Self-inquiry to work, *karma yoga* means dedication of every thought, word and deed to God/*Isvara*, or the Field of Existence, in an attitude of gratitude and consecration. It means knowing that you are not in charge of results, and taking whatever results that come as a gift. *Karma yoga* is a giving, not a getting, attitude. It is the appropriate response to life's demands. It breaks the hold of binding desires and converts an extroverted emotional mind into a peaceful introspective mind. In essence, *karma yoga* is *bhakti* (devotional) *yoga*.

Secular Karma Yoga

Secular *karma yoga* is *karma yoga* with desire, which can also work for worldly people not qualified for Self-inquiry and not going for *moksa*. A secular *karma yogi* applies *karma yoga* to accomplish things in the world and get what they want or avoid what they don't want. But assuming you have realized the futility of chasing objects in the world and are serious about Self-inquiry, secular *karma yoga* is the preparation for entry-level inquirers to minimize the pressure of likes and dislikes.

The next chapter unfolds the whole teaching on the three stages of *karma yoga*; make sure you understand it and apply it.

Preparation for Self-Inquiry 3: Meditation, or *Upasana Yoga*

Upasana yoga entails reflection on your values, conduct of a fearless moral inventory, understanding the qualifications required for Self-inquiry and a start on development of the ones that are lacking. It requires practices such as meditation to purify and prepare the mind for Self-inquiry, and clean up any lifestyle issues that are not in keeping with a peaceful mind. Cultivate meditation and the extroverted mind will gradually turn inwards. You do not need to take a course on how to meditate, though that may help. Ultimately meditation is just being present with the Self, with you. Breathing helps, as does sitting in silence. Silence is not the absence of sound. It is the presence of the Self. You can be in silence no matter what is happening around you because "silence" is a word for "you," the silent ever-present impartial witness.

Preparation for Self-Inquiry 4: Devotional Practice

A devotional practice is essential to manage the childish wilful ego. Like gratitude, it is a gift we give ourselves, not something required of us from the Field, or God. All the elements were worshipped, deified and given great homage in the Vedic tradition. If you do not have a place of devotional focus, an altar, make one. It is a place in your life where you show up *for* God, not to *find* God, but a place of worship that reflects the love that is your true nature. Put beautiful things on it as symbols of the Self: photos of your teachers, your loved ones, a candle, maybe some incense. Any symbol will do.

The Hindu religion has so many religious idols because they know that everyone has their own take on the Divine, and any take will do because you can't miss. God is Life. And the God of Vedanta shares your identity in the Self. Worship of God in any form is worship of Self. Most modern spiritual people have abandoned religion because so much suffering has been foisted on humanity in its name. But the religious impulse, the Self loving itself, is hardwired. So it is incumbent on a *karma yogi* to choose a symbol of the Self that is attractive and uplifting, and worship it regularly.

Chanting and rituals can be helpful for energetic *rajasic* types who need to be occupied with something worthwhile instead of wasting time in gratuitous egoic pursuits – such as an addiction to social media, for instance. Chants are also great for *tamasic* types to lift *tamas* into balance with *sattva*. We love to chant and do so several times daily. Find one that works for you or make one up.

Chanting *mantras* is the same as praying and a great way to keep the mind on the Self. As Vedantins, we chant what are called "identity *mantras*" and we understand the meaning of the words. We chant *mantras* because we enjoy the bliss of the Self, but we know that the bliss is who we are. We do not chant or perform any other ritual to gain anything. The purpose of the *mantra* is to deliver knowledge, not to have a blissful experience, and though it can do that too, it is not the aim.

Rituals as a devotional practice of some kind are also an important way to show appreciation for the great gift of life, as an homage to *Isvara*, to the Self. They become an obstacle when you think you are a doer doing good deeds for reward or it makes you more "spiritual" to carry out elaborate rituals or you see yourself as apart from the ritual.

The Four Stages *of* Self-Inquiry

Self-Inquiry Stage 1:
Sravanna, Listening and Hearing the Scriptures

Assuming the inquirer has understood the importance of the preparations mentioned above and is practising all of them, and has at least entry-level qualifications, the first stage of Self-inquiry is about hearing the teachings. It requires that you start at the beginning to make sure that you understand the terminology used in Vedanta. Sign on to the logic and stick with it, along with diligently applying *karma yoga*. Vedanta is taught in a progressive and methodical way to answer all doubts that arise at each level of understanding. It is very important not to rush in search of instant answers (which is often what spiritual types are after), because that will not work. Ignorance is highly tenacious and resistant to removal, so patience and dedication are vital requirements, along with a realistic view that rejects the need for instant solutions to problems.

If you are too attached to your desires, your ideas, beliefs and opinions acquired and developed from your exposure to multiple teachings, Self-inquiry will not work. It requires that you admit to yourself that you are the problem and that what you think you know has not worked thus far, so there must be something you don't know, the knowledge of which could make all the difference. If you are still chasing objects (such as a relationship/sex/money, etc.), trying to get the world to give you what you think you lack or even chasing a life-changing spiritual experience, Vedanta is not for you. In that case, it is best that you immerse yourself in worldly pursuits until you are thoroughly convinced the world cannot satisfy your desires and give you what you are seeking.

Self-Inquiry Stage 2:
Manana, Reasoning, Contemplation

The second stage of Self-inquiry requires thought about what the scripture is saying, examination of the unexamined logic of your own experience and starting to apply the teachings to your life. At this point, you look at your beliefs and opinions in the light of what the scripture says, not the other way around. This stage requires that you have established the qualifications required for Self-inquiry, so check if they are in place, strengthen the ones that are not and track yourself on them on a moment-to-moment basis. Make and implement necessary lifestyle changes that you stick to. There is no way to skip this; Self-inquiry is very simply not compatible with a mind that is not purified and prepared, in addition to practise of *karma yoga*. The purpose of *karma yoga* is to cultivate devotion for the scripture, develop your understanding and gain a contemplative disposition so that you can assimilate the meaning of the teachings.

You should not think that you will start inquiry one fine day when you are contemplative. You should set aside at least half an hour or an hour a day or more for study of Vedanta, preferably in the morning when the mind is fresh. Pick a text, read a verse or a few pages each morning and contemplate what you read throughout the day. You don't become contemplative all at once. You have contemplative moments throughout the day and insights all along. If you are not dedicated to Self-inquiry, have not developed the qualifications for Self-inquiry, are not practising *karma yoga* or find yourself making excuses for the way you live because you are in denial about binding *vasanas*, you will not make progress. Even if Self-realization does occur, it will not stick. You will not actualize Self-knowledge unless you surrender to the teachings and address every aspect of your life.

Even though this stage is about contemplation of the scriptures, it overlaps the last and final stage, *nididhyasana*, so discrimination of *satya* (the unchanging Self) from *mithya* (the ever-changing person), *karma yoga* and *guna* management are vital. *Karma yoga* will eventually destroy the notion of "doer-ship" if properly understood and faithfully adhered to in every thought, word and deed. In the *manana* stage, it is meant to clear the mind of enough likes and dislikes until it becomes composed enough for sustained Self-inquiry.

TRIGUNA VIBHAVA YOGA

The next stage of *karma yoga* only applies in the third and final stage of Self-inquiry, *nididhyasana*. But before we get to that, there is no chance of making progress with Self-inquiry or effectively discriminating between what belongs to you as the Self and what belongs to you as the *jiva* without at least a basic understanding of the forces that condition the mind, the *gunas: sattva* (clarity, revelation), *rajas* (action/desire) and *tamas* (matter/dullness). This is called *triguna vibhava yoga,* or *jnana yoga* (knowledge *yoga*), also called *guna* management.

Guna management is essential for managing thoughts and feelings that dominate the mind. *Guna yoga* is also understanding the Creator and ordainer of the Field (*Isvara*, or God), the identity between you as an individual and the Field, why they are the same and what is different. Without this understanding it is impossible to negate the egoic doer and all its fear/desire programs, so you will not progress to the last and final stage of inquiry. Many people do realize the Self at this stage, but that is really where the "work" of Self-inquiry begins. To progress to the final stage requires full and complete faith in and compliance with the scripture – it alone is the boss of your life, not the *jiva*, and it requires the final stage of *karma yoga*, Self-actualization. In the next stage, sacred *karma yoga* applies.

The teaching is unfolded in more depth in James Swartz's book *The Yoga of the Three Energies*, a must for serious inquirers. I will explain all three *gunas* and mind management in detail in the next four chapters.

Self-Inquiry Stage 3: Nididhyasana, Self-Actualization

Self-realization is not Self-actualization, which is the final "stage." Self-actualization is not actually a stage, because all stages are objects known to the Self, but "getting there" comes only after all the previous stages mentioned so far are completed. And the process of Self-actualization, *nididhyasana*, is also the hardest. It usually takes the longest. The knowledge that you are the Self has obtained, but complete freedom from the personal program has not; there are still some binding mental/emotional patterns to purify, hence the need for *guna yoga*. For most people who have realized the Self but not actualized it, this stage in a way is like "requalifying" – re-examination of qualifications and strengthening those that are still weak. It requires the final negation of the idea of yourself as an individual, a *jiva*. Up until now, *karma yoga* went from relinquishing results of actions to the Field and taking given results as a gift to the next level, renunciation of the idea of doer-ship and desire.

SACRED KARMA YOGA: KARMA YOGA WITHOUT DESIRE

In the last stage of Self-inquiry, *karma yoga* becomes a different kind of mind management: *karma yoga* without desire, or sacred *karma yoga.* It is for more advanced inquirers. It is the transformation of our remaining binding mental/emotional conditioning into devotion to the Self. At this stage, you have given up the need for anything. You are not after God's "stuff." You are after God, period. It's not that you no longer have desires; all desires are not contrary to *dharma*, and moreover directed to the Self. Self-actualization is management of the mind's involuntary habitual thoughts and feeling patterns, which are bedrock duality and often survive Self-realization. Until this stage is complete, Self-actualization has not taken place and discrimination can be lost, if not permanently at least temporarily. You are not free, because limiting thoughts/feelings like fear, smallness, need, shame, confusion, low self-esteem, etc. can still limit access to Self-knowledge and destroy peace of mind.

Sacred *karma yoga* is explained in more detail in the next chapter on the three stages of *karma yoga.*

Self-Inquiry Stage 4: The Final Renunciation

For Self-actualization to take place, the final and most subtle renunciation must occur. It is renouncing the idea of seeking liberation, because you ARE free and always have been. As the Self, you have never been bound. This is the toughest stage, because if there are still some binding mental/emotional patterns, it can prevent the inquirer from attaining actualization. It is not a case of what is missing, but what is still there: the idea that the doer still needs to "do" something to perfect the *jiva.* Or there remains a very subtle thought that there is still some amazing experience that must take place to prove you are the Self.

But there is no proof, because you *are* the proof. No experience can prove that. There comes a time when practise of the teachings of Vedanta no longer works its magic, because it's time to move beyond it. You are no longer a seeker but a finder, and you need to answer the question: Are you doing the knowledge or *are* you the knowledge? Vedanta is not about accumulating or perfecting Self-knowledge or any practice as such, because to the Self, you, even knowledge is a known object. And freedom is not about perfecting the *jiva*, it is freedom from and for it. The *jiva* is what it is, and it is as good as non-existent if Self-knowledge is firm.

FREEDOM FROM THE KNOWER OF KNOWLEDGE

Strangely, for many the toughest part of Self-inquiry is giving up being an inquirer (which is just another comforting identity) and throwing Vedanta away. It is a means to an end, and when it has served its intended purpose, you no longer need it. Vedanta as a means of knowledge is meant to remove ignorance, that is all. When you are Self-knowledge, the means of knowledge must disappear. If the knowledge remains, you have the knowledge, but you also still have ignorance. Freedom is the absence of ignorance, not the gain of knowledge. It is freedom from the knower of knowledge.

It is BEING the knowing, not knowing the knower, Existence shining as Awareness. No maintenance is required. Hanging on to knowledge is hanging on to the *jiva*, which keeps the doer, seeker, knower and ignorance alive. So at this stage, you must cut the lifeline and live as the Self, no buts. From here on there are no rules for you or things you should or should not do, apply or inquire into. There is no *nididhyasana* for the Self. How can there be? You are the Self, period. You follow *dharma* by default, but the *jiva* is free to be what it is, without censure. However, if there are still binding *vasanas* for an inquirer who prematurely claims they are the Self, and thus believes that *nididhyasana* does not apply to them, Self-actualization cannot take place. Unfortunately, this is quite common, and the result is either the Advaita Shuffle or enlightenment sickness, which is when the ego co-opts the knowledge.

To Be Fully Self-Actualized Means:

1. That you have **fully discriminated the Self** (Consciousness/Awareness) from the objects that appear in you (all objects, meaning all gross objects as well as one's conditioning, thoughts and feelings – all experience), and do so spontaneously, 24/7. You are not the Self and the *jiva*, or person. You are the Self, period.

2. Self-knowledge has (a) rendered the binding desires non-binding and (b) negated your sense of doership completely. In other words, the ego program is understood and fully negated. The individual still exists with its inborn nature and operates in the world, but its program is like a burnt rope – it no longer has the power to bind. It is as good as non-existent and rests in the fullness of the Self. The world neither attracts nor repels it. There is nothing left to identify with other than the Self.

3. Therefore, once Self-knowledge is permanent, you never think of yourself as a person again. You also don't think of yourself as the Self. You just are the Self. Your primary iden-

tity is fully established as the Self. And you are totally fine with the apparent person as they are and their role in the world. All desires from here will not be opposed to dharma; they are preferences, nothing more. You are fine with and fine without. *Karma yoga* is just common-sense knowledge. It can be said that this stage never really ends even when Self-actualization obtains, because though desires are no longer binding, the person is still a constantly changing entity due to the gunas, because it lives in the Field, which is also always constantly changing. Thus, though the mind may no longer condition to the *gunas*, mind management continues. But here Self-knowledge works spontaneously and instantly to nullify any effects, because there is no iden-tification with the person and the Field of experience.

Though there are no rules for a Self-actualized person because they are free of all limitations, nonetheless, one automatically fol-lows *dharma* because you still honour the natural laws that run the Field of Existence. Non-injury in thought, word and deed is the highest priority. You know there is nothing to gain or lose in the world, and it is all you. Your lifestyle will be fully in accordance with Self-knowledge in every respect.

An Enlightened Lifestyle

It is not necessary to complete all the stages of Self-inquiry to create an enlightened lifestyle, but you will not progress with Self-inquiry without one. Spiritual growth requires it, and since the value for this is not available in materialistic societies, you must create a simple peaceful lifestyle yourself. A clear understanding of the Field of Existence brings the individual into a relationship with the whole that creates a satisfied, contented mind. Without this connection we cannot express our God-given positive qualities. A happy life is a life in harmony with the whole. The second and third books in this trilogy are devoted to investigation of all the major aspects of life in light of living an enlightened lifestyle.

I define an unenlightened lifestyle as a neurotic, emotional, dissatisfied, self-indulgent, messy, desire-based, stress-filled life. I define an enlightened lifestyle as a simple, orderly, considerate, content, emotionally balanced, knowledge-based, intelligent and relatively stress-free life. This applies to every single area of your life: sex, money, relationships, work, home, nutrition and health of the body, no fine print, no excuses. We all want an enlightened *sattvic* lifestyle, and we can all achieve that no matter our life *karma*. But very few people do, and the reason for that is simple: *rajas* and *tamas* are out of whack with *sattva*.

A commitment to Self-inquiry as explained above, with the help of a qualified teacher and the necessary qualifications present, will remove ignorance and therefore end our existential suffering on all levels. But there is not a one-size-fits-all formula for a peaceful life. While we are all one in the Self, the way we appear as individuals expresses differently in everyone. Ignorance is universal, but our personal ignorance is unique to us; to remove this involves understanding both what drives us personally and the impersonal factors behind our life story (*Isvara*/the *gunas*/unconscious drives, or causal body), but it is not about our life story. The truth is always impersonal and cannot be adapted to suit us, assuming we want freedom from limitation more than anything else. Therein lies the "work" of Self-inquiry.

Checklist for Self-Inquiry Not Working

Though all four stages of Self-inquiry must be completed if *moksa* is your main motivation, most inquirers will cycle through each stage as the knowledge assimilates. Very often, after years, sometimes even decades, an inquirer in the last stage of Self-inquiry, the *nididhyasana* stage, must go back to the beginning to requalify because something is holding them back. Usually, it is related to unconscious *jiva* patterns, some qualification that is still missing or some part of the teaching that was not fully assimilated.

If you are a totally dedicated inquirer, are not interpreting the scriptures and have been properly taught, but your inquiry is not working and you find yourself stuck or there is no change at all in the quality of your life, it will be due to one or a combination of these issues:

1. Check that preparations required for Self-inquiry are in place and practised throughout inquiry: *karma yoga*, meditation and devotional practice.

2. Conduct a fearless moral inventory of your values and make sure you have read *The Value of Values*. There are no shortcuts to Self-inquiry if you are serious about freedom from suffering.

3. Make a checklist of your likes and dislikes. Understand

your *jiva* programming, its "fault lines" or repetitive patterns. If there is a remaining subtle sense of doership, a binding tendency or more likely an unconscious deeply buried conglomeration of tendencies (*samskara*), this will keep you stuck.

4. One or more qualifications is missing. All are important, so make sure they all are present, and if they are not, develop the ones that are missing or lacking. Track yourself on all of them thought by thought.

5. Make sure you have a solid foundation in the terminology used by Vedanta and the meaning of the most important terms. You may have skipped ahead and missed some important parts of the methodology of Self-inquiry. If so, start at the beginning, read *Tattva Bodh* and progress to the other texts recommended for Self-inquiry.

6. You are not applying the teachings diligently enough, particularly *karma yoga* and *triguna vibhava yoga*. Self-inquiry requires assimilation of the teachings and, very importantly, application to your life. It's a thought-by-thought, 24/7 commitment. Discrimination between the Self and the not-Self at all times and management of the mind's emotional and thinking patterns only works with the application of *karma yoga* and *guna yoga* to every thought, word and action, as does taking a stand in Awareness as Awareness and thinking the opposite thought.

7. You have not been properly taught and are interpreting the teachings.

8. There is something in your lifestyle that does not conform to *dharma* and keeps you distracted from Self-inquiry, which blocks access to the assimilation of Self-knowledge.

9. You have not completed the last stage, the final renunciation of the means of knowledge itself, and are still hanging on to the teachings.

Chapter 4

Karma Yoga

Karma Yoga

As explained in the previous chapters, Self-inquiry requires investigation into how the "small" personal self relates to its primary and impersonal identity, the Self. *Karma yoga* is an essential part of inquiry because it works on the part of the mind that acts to enjoy results, that owns actions and their results. When you act for results, you incur stress before, during and after the action. *Karma yoga* is burnout insurance because it removes stress by exhausting the fears and desires that produce it and allows the immature self-centred inner child, or ego, to develop an objective view of itself and the world. We have a name for that inner child, and it is the egoic doer.

The doer believes it can do its way to getting whatever it wants, and such an ego does not register that everything is given to it – parents, shelter, food, education, clothing, a partner, entertainment, etc. It does not see the infinite actions that had to take place for anything to "happen" which make it impossible for personal actions alone to be the cause of results. Our sense of control is just an illusion, because no action takes place without the blessing of all things in the Field, not even our ability to make decisions. Just ask yourself how much control you have over your own thoughts.

Karma yoga is a straightforward no-nonsense and common-sense solution to this problem. But it is a little-understood practice in the spiritual world, and even less so outside of it. What it boils down to is that I have emotional problems because life is not giving me what I want, meaning my primary instrument (mind) is dominated by projection and denial (*rajas* and *tamas*). If my primary instrument is predominately clear (*sattvic*), it would serve me well and I would accomplish my goals without much trouble. Unfortunately, this is seldom the case. *Karma yoga* transforms a dull (*tamasic*) and/or an excessively active (*rajasic*) mind into a clear, peaceful, efficient (*sattvic*) mind.

Karma Yoga and Vulnerability

Vulnerability requires the resilience to take risks, and that builds self-esteem. To qualify as vulnerability, three things are required: (1) acceptance that the outcome is out of your control and unknown (uncertainty); (2) emotional exposure (if only to yourself); and (3) risk. Vulnerability is the cornerstone of courage, creativity, innovation, self-esteem, authenticity, belonging, worthiness, laughter and joy. Vulnerability is acceptance of the fear of failure, and failing but never giving up. Likewise, it is acceptance of the vulnerability of success and what that brings with it. The interesting thing about *karma yoga* is that it is the only thing that neutralizes fear, risk and vulnerability, because it is based on the understanding that you are not the doer. All risk is relative because all results occur thanks to the Field. Once you surrender the idea of doership, you take vulnerability out of the equation because the responsibility for the outcome (good or bad) is out of your hands. You hand over responsibility to the Field, to whom it belongs.

Born to Control Is Not Karma Yoga

Karma yoga sounds simple, but is not easy to practise consistently, because the ego does not like to relinquish the idea of control, even though it is not in control of results in the first place. Why should we not want to have control over our future experiences? Knowledge is power, and the main reason why our brains insist on simulating the future to get what we want is that our brains find it gratifying to exercise control, not just for the future it (seems) to buy us, but for the exercise itself. Being effective – changing things, influencing things, making things happen – is one of the fundamental needs with which human brains are naturally endowed. Much of our behaviour from infancy onwards is simply an expression of this penchant for control. Take a cursory look at any baby and you will see who has everyone dancing to meet their every need. If we were properly looked after and loved as babies, we will never have it so good again!

Born Wired to Control

We are born wired to control a world that is beyond our control. This fact is not obvious to us, however, and "civilization" is our species' attempt to reign over the intractable forces of nature. While we can argue that we have come a long way since our caveman days, we could also argue the opposite – as much as things change for better or worse, they stay the same. For most of us, no matter how much the evidence to the contrary presents itself, we steadfastly believe our desires will prevail and fortune will favour us. Those who subsidize fortune-telling industries do not want to know what is likely to happen just for the joy of anticipation, but to do something about it, to ensure we get what we want or avoid what we don't want.

But not having desires or not trying to game the future requires that we convince our frontal lobe, the part of our brain wired to plan and control, not to do what it was designed to do. Like trying to tell our heart not to beat is futile, desire in the form of mental simulations of the future arrives in our mind regularly and unbidden, often occupying every corner of our mental lives. Unfortunately for us, our brains are programmed this way. Studies show that most people think about controlling the future far more than they think about the past or present. The desire for control is intricately linked to time and usually involves gain of something we do not currently have or wish to be rid of. It makes us residents of tomorrow and absentees of the now, incapable of appropriate response to what life presents us.

Fantasizing About the Future Is More Pleasurable Than Living It

Why do our brains stubbornly insist on projecting us into the future to get what we want? The reason is simple: we like to fantasize about the future because reality seldom matches our expectations. To try to control the future can be more pleasurable than acutely living it. It is something we find hard to admit, but a fulfilled desire rarely matches the energy required to fulfil it. And even less acknowledged is the reason we do feel good when we get the desired result is not the object of desire itself, but the removal of the pressure of desire, which is painful.

As nothing in the Field stays the same, and nothing is really what it appears to be, our desire to control is so powerful and the feeling of being in control so rewarding that we act as though we can control the uncontrollable. Perhaps the strangest thing about this illusion of control is not that it happens but that it seems to confer many of the psychological benefits of genuine control. A strange fact is that the one group of people who seem generally immune to the illusion of control (not hounded by desire) are clinically depressed people. They are less inclined to overestimate the degree to which they can control events in most situations, which is probably why they are depressed in the first place!

These and other findings have led some researchers to conclude that the feeling of control – whether real or illusory – is one of the wellsprings of mental health. Research suggests that if we lose our ability to control things, we become unhappy, helpless, hopeless, depressed and, occasionally, dead. Many suicides are the result of this feeling of utter hopelessness, as are many illnesses. Some philosophers have stated that over and beyond any other human need is the need for order and control.

Impact Is Rewarding

Having an impact is rewarding. And when we get what we want, it makes us feel safe and successful, that we matter. To be important or significant makes us happy. The act of steering one's boat down the river of time is a source of pleasure, regardless of one's port of call. And success is possible in this world with timely and appropriate action. But there is one small problem with this kind of happiness: ultimately, we don't have control. Life is a zero-sum game, we lose as much as we win, and sooner or later this is what brings everyone down. If we have not developed some equanimity or found a way to live with the vicissitudes of life, we are most likely to end up sad and depressed.

The only solution to this conundrum is *karma yoga* – even if it goes against how the brain is made and how society is programmed, the need to win at all costs, not only to make a difference but to survive. *Karma yoga* is not good news for the ego. It sees no benefit to this practice and resists it tenaciously, as though its existence depends on it. And it does. Giving up control is tantamount to giving up identification with the small, limited self, the one who acts for results and to own things. It is totally counter-intuitive, which is why it is so important and the only way to negate the doer. When Self-knowledge makes it clear that it is Awareness apparently experiencing the ego and not the ego experiencing Awareness, the ego gets on board with the idea of freedom from the limitation of doership, the small ego identity. It is not about denying the existence of the ego, perfecting the ego or banishing the ego. It is about understanding that the ego is not real, meaning it is not who you are.

The Three Main Aspects of Karma Yoga

Karma Yoga Step 1: Appropriate and Timely Action

We can definitely maximize the chances of getting a positive result with appropriate and timely actions. Life works in mysterious ways, and because the Field of Existence runs on natural and consistent laws that apply to everyone, the results of action depend not only on the nature of the Field but also on the nature of the action taken. It should be obvious that if I do not take the appropriate action at the appropriate time, I cannot complain about not getting what I want. However, the results of action do not necessarily depend on the state of mind of the doer, because one can achieve a negative result with positive actions or vice versa. It is possible to take the right action with the right attitude and still get a result we do not want, because the Field of Existence considers the needs of the whole before it takes our individual needs into account.

Here is a great saying about desire and karma yoga from the

Brihadaranyaka Upanishad:

> "You are what your deep driving desire is. As your desire is, so is your will. As your will is, so is your deed. As your deed is, so is your destiny."

As far as the doer goes, there are appropriate actions you can take that are pretty likely (but not guaranteed) to give you what you want. We do have relative free will in that we can make choices to succeed. If this were not possible, it would not be possible to achieve anything in the apparent reality. If we take an action with the *karma yoga* attitude halfheartedly – but really, we know that deep down our likes and dislikes are making the choices – there is no escape from ignorance, and there will be no peace of mind. There is no fooling reality; though it requires vulnerability and honesty, without boundaries we may try to apply *karma yoga* in situations that we know are not healthy for us and require us to take action we are avoiding. For *karma yoga* to work, you must be totally committed and convinced that if you could have solved your problems, you would have done so by now.

Karma Yoga Step 2: Renunciation or Surrender of Results

We will never stop acting for results, and there is nothing wrong with that. But the most important step of *karma yoga* is the understanding that we can act for a desired result, but we are never in charge of the outcome. The results of any action are not up to the individual, but the law of *karma* in the form of the Field of Existence, my immediate environment. Basically, the Field for me is the people with whom I have *karma*, but it includes the whole world. My primary instrument (mind) generates actions that affect the Field, a conscious matrix of laws. The actions I do return to me in various, not always obvious, ways. My life is nothing but the results of the actions I have done before, delivered to me by the Field. The Field is impersonal and delivers the result of the actions of individuals based on the needs of the Field itself. It doesn't care what I want unless what I want serves the Field in some way. Most of us know this is true, because if it were not, we would all have what we want all the time, but we don't.

In terms of my happiness, the Field is all-powerful. My dependence on it causes suffering. I cannot just walk away from it, because there isn't anywhere else to go. My desires command me to act, and even if I run off to a cave in India, they will follow and torture me there. There is no escape, so better to work them out in such a way that they don't come back. And they come back because the needy attitude that motivates them doesn't disappear when I get what I want. As soon as I get one thing, I want something else. *Karma yoga* is an attitude with reference to action that removes unnecessary desire.

ACTION NEVER FAILS, IT ONLY PRODUCES RESULTS

An action itself can never fail us, it only produces results. A given expectation may be said to have failed, but the one with the expectation has not failed. That I have failed or that the action has failed is the wrong conclusion; the expectation is the problem. Understanding this is particularly important for people who feel the need to do things perfectly or feel they have failed. Nobody fails. It is only a matter of wrong judgment, because we are not omniscient and cannot have knowledge of all the factors that shape the results of our actions. Action can produce likes and dislikes only if the result is looked upon as a success or failure.

When the result is looked upon as a function of the invariable laws of action or, what is even better, if it is looked upon as the grace of the Field of Existence, no new likes and dislikes are created, and peace of mind is maintained. With this attitude towards results, actions born of likes and dislikes become the means of elimination of the likes and dislikes. The mind becomes free from the agitations of elation (*rajas*) and depression (*tamas*). Such a mind is tranquil and contemplative.

If peace of mind is the aim, taking whatever results do come as a gift will be the attitude one brings to everything. The sameness of mind (towards success and failure) with respect to action is another definition of *karma yoga* and is the essence of peace of mind, *sattva*. In cultivating the right attitude towards life, one performs one's duty by conforming to the pattern and harmony of the Creation, thus one becomes alive to the beauty of the cosmic order. When the mind becomes clear, we can see the natural order. At the beginning of our spiritual practice, *karma yoga* is an attitude we must cultivate, but eventually it is simply knowledge because it is obvious that the Field runs this way, so it becomes the default position of the mind.

No Bad Result

If you understand what *karma yoga* really is, you will know it always works no matter what result you get. There are no bad results. This is because life is not about getting what you want; it is about the one who does not want. If control is what you are after, you do not understand this. If practised correctly, *karma yoga* takes the existential burden of doership off the shoulders of the limited person and puts it squarely where it belongs, onto the Field, onto *Isvara*. The point of *karma yoga* is to clear the mind of enough likes and dislikes so that it becomes composed enough for sustained Self-inquiry. Only inquiry removes the problem of doership because it shows that you, the Self, cannot be the ego (doer) that is known to you. When that is clear, the doer can appear in you, but you do not identify with it.

Karma Yoga Step 3: Consecration and Gratitude

Karma is an identity issue, fundamentally. It does not mean not acting. It is an attitude one takes towards actions and their results, which is a giving, not a getting, attitude. It is the appropriate response to life's demands and breaks the hold of *rajasic* and *tamasic* desires, converting an extroverted, emotional mind into a peaceful, introspective, *sattvic* mind. With *karma yoga*, I act in the spirit of gratitude and renunciation, of loving consecration based on the understanding that life is a great gift that requires reciprocation. Because I value life more than anything, I reciprocate by taking *dharma* into account, and before acting or speaking I offer the actions/words to the Field. When results come, which they do every minute, I take them as a gift, even if they aren't what I want, in which case I see them as instructive, corrective offerings from the Field that help me avoid actions that will produce unwanted results in the future.

What you do with the gift of life is your offering to the Field. The Field is obviously intelligently designed, so there must be an intelligent architect. And the Field controls us completely right down to causing us to breathe and eat and digest our food, so it is called God. What we do with the gift of life is our offering to God. If you appreciate this fact, which should be second nature, you will not offer a greedy, angry, vain, licentious life to the Lord. You will offer a pure life as a wonderful gift, with a cheerful smiling face. You may wonder why, considering the downsides of life, that you should present a cheerful smiling face. However, if you are fair-minded, you can find an upside for every downside because life is a perfectly equilibrated duality. The half-empty glass is half-full. A positive attitude is no less realistic than a negative attitude.

The right attitude, *karma yoga*, is not a path. It is a life committed 100% to performance of action as *yoga*. It takes skill to perform an action with the right attitude, which is doing what needs to be done, whether you like it or not. Thus likes and dislikes, how I feel about the situation, do not come into play. Your likes and dislikes often prompt you to perform an action that is not conducive to peace of mind, so a *karma yogi* refrains from performing it, because it is not proper for them. Therefore, for peace of mind, I perform actions in harmony with the natural order (*dharmic* actions) and avoid actions that disturb the order (*adharmic* actions).

KEEP YOUR MIND ON THE MOTIVATION

Karma yoga is keeping one's attention on the motivation behind one's actions and adjusting one's attitude when it is found to strengthen binding likes and dislikes. When the projecting energy (*rajas*) dominates, the mind cannot observe itself. It is caught up in the future, the thought that things need to be different, so the mind acts to correct the situation, usually in negative ways. It does not act to correct itself, because the energy of revelation and clarity (*sattva*) is obscured by projection (*rajas*) and the dulling energy (*tamas*). When *tamas* predominates, the mind is too dull to discriminate; it is prone to denial and avoidance.

A mind at peace accepts that every result is the right result. The more you appreciate the laws, the more you are in harmony with the things around you and can find your place in the scheme of things. Failure to appreciate this fact results in low self-esteem, the feeling that "I am a failure." The solution to low self-esteem is the understanding that one's knowledge of all the variables in the Field that produce results is and always will be limited. Therefore the results of one's actions can never be known, which is why *karma yoga* is common-sense logic!

Karma yoga produces a *sattvic* mind, but it is not that the mind "becomes" *sattvic*; it is that Self-knowledge removes the excess *rajas* and *tamas* which cause the agitation, which prevent you from experiencing your true nature, Existence/Consciousness/Bliss. When the mind is *sattvic*, you automatically think dispassionately about things, and discrimination comes naturally from such a mind. A person who has been on the spiritual path for a long time but whose mind is still *rajasic* does not understand the value of *karma yoga*. As Krishna says, "A little *karma yoga* removes a lot of agitation."

Karma yoga counts most when we don't get what we want, but it is as important when we do get what we want if we take the credit for it. How we relate to results determines how peaceful our mind is. If we are very attached to the idea of getting what we want (strong likes and dislikes), life will soon prove to us that we lose as much as we win, maybe more. At best, we will be happy half the time and unhappy the other half. More likely though, when one is driven by likes and dislikes, the mind is agitated regardless of whether we get what we want, because nothing ever really satisfies the mind for long, other than Self-knowledge. It is the contention of Vedanta that happiness is our natural state, and our true nature exists independently of winning or losing. To actualize this knowledge is freedom.

Two Forms *of* Karma Yoga

1. Secular *Karma Yoga*: *Karma Yoga* With Desire

Secular *karma yoga* works for people with lots of desire who want to accomplish worldly goals, who are not into Self-inquiry and not going for *moksa*. A *karma yogi* applies *karma yoga* to get what they want or avoid what they don't want. But secular *karma yoga* is also mandatory preparation for entry-level inquirers to minimize the pressure of likes and dislikes. The desire for objects/results is still present, and there are usually several qualifications that need development, but there is also a strong drive for Self-inquiry.

2. Sacred *Karma Yoga*: *Karma Yoga* Without Desire

Sacred *karma yoga* without desire is for more advanced inquirers – people who have developed most of the qualifications for Self-inquiry. They have realized that there is nothing to gain by action and are ready for or already engaged in Self-inquiry. At this stage, you have given up the need for anything. You are not after "God's stuff." You are after God. It's not that you no longer have desires, but all desire is in keeping with *dharma* and directed to the Self.

The Renunciation *of* Desire Happens *in* Three Stages

Step 1: Renunciation of Desire

Step one is taking a stand in Awareness and managing thoughts and emotions through the surrender of results to *Isvara* in an attitude of gratitude, consecrating each thought, word and action on a moment-to-moment basis and no longer initiating any gratuitous actions. This does not mean that we do not continue to follow our nature (*svadharma*) and do what is *dharmic* for us, but we do so with *karma yoga* in the spirit of renunciation. We no longer chase anything in the world, and do not require validation for whatever we do. As we have mastered the qualifications for Self-inquiry, we apply Self-knowledge automatically to discriminate *satya*, that which is always present and unchanging, from *mithya*, that which is not always present and always changing.

But although at this stage we know our conditioning does not belong to us, we are not completely free of it either. Unless we understand and practise *guna* management in conjunction with *karma yoga*, even if we are highly qualified inquirers we can get stuck here, because there is still an ego invested in "getting it." What also tends to happen at this stage is the identification with *sattva* as "enlightenment." Many inquirers wrongly believe that if they are not experiencing *sattva*, they are not "enlightened." They forget that all the *gunas* are objects known to the Self, which is unaffected by any of them.

Step 2: *Karma Jnana Sannyas*

Through continual discrimination and application of the teachings to our lives, we assimilate the knowledge that we are actually the Self, limitless Awareness, and not the person. It is the full negation of the idea of doership with the knowledge that we can act, but *Isvara* is the only doer. If Self-knowledge has fully removed the ignorance of your true nature and rendered all binding *vasanas* non-binding, then you know without a doubt that you are the Self and beyond ALL the *gunas*. This is *moksa*, direct Self-knowledge.

Direct knowledge is spontaneous discrimination of the Self, *satya*, from *mithya* without any thought involved. You do not need to take a stand in Awareness, because you are Awareness. At this stage *karma yoga* is no longer a practice as such, it is just knowledge. However, duality does not disappear once you know what it is. *Maya*, macrocosmic ignorance, continues even though Self-knowledge has removed personal/microcosmic ignorance.

Step 3: Self-Actualization, *Nididhyasana*

Unfortunately, even though Self-realization is firm, more often than not there is work to do to render binding *vasanas* non-binding, i.e. purifying the mind of identification with the *jiva* program. Here *karma yoga* becomes a different kind of mind management, *nididhyasana*, the transformation of our remaining binding mental/emotional conditioning into devotion to the Self. *Nididhyasana* is management of the mind's involuntary thoughts as well as our habitual thoughts and feeling patterns that are bedrock duality and can survive *moksa*.

Without self-objectivity and mind management, these patterns can still hijack the mind without a moment's notice and deny it access to the Self in the form of Self-knowledge. There is nothing inherently wrong with involuntary thoughts, but they tend to immediately morph into actions that are liable to create unwanted *karma* in the form of obscuring thoughts and emotions. This period can take many years for most inquirers, and it requires the continued application of *karma jnana sannyas* until the *jiva* identity is fully dismissed.

The Three Types *of* Karmas

Karma yoga is not only the right attitude, it is the right action. Actions can be classified in terms of how well they serve to prepare the mind for inquiry. They are: (1) *sattvic*, those that give maximum spiritual benefit; (2) *rajasic*, those that are neither beneficial nor detrimental; and (3) *tamasic*, those that are harmful and lead one away from the goal.

Tamasic Karmas

These actions build unhelpful *vasanas* that take the doer away from liberation. Violence in thought, word and deed; lying; cheating; stealing; gambling; drinking alcohol; taking drugs; excessive sex solely for pleasure, etc. are examples of the third class of *karmas*. They are considered sins because they produce a dull and agitated mind. They are not recommended for anyone and are definitely prohibited for *karma yogis*.

Rajasic Karmas

The second class is desire-prompted activities that basically contribute to our material well-being. These activities do not directly contribute to preparation of the mind, but are scripturally sanctioned because indirectly they make it possible to pursue liberation. They are not considered sins if they do not compel the individual to violate *dharma* or ignore the legitimate needs of others, in which case they increase selfishness, a detrimental characteristic. In fact the Vedic scriptures prescribe several rituals for getting money, property, certain types of children, etc. They are neither encouraged nor discouraged.

Sattvic Karmas

The first class of actions, *sattvic karmas*, is necessary if *karma yoga* is going to bear fruit. These are giving *karmas*, not grabbing *karmas*. The more you give, the more you grow. *Karma yoga* involves actions that add value to every situation, and offerings that contribute to the well-being of the Dharma Field. The intention of a *karma yogi* is to enshrine *sattvic karmas* at the forefront of her life, to see that *rajasic karmas* are relegated to subordinate status, and to eliminate *tamasic karmas*. Of course it's impossible to eliminate *tamasic* actions altogether. Certain situations demand them. *Sattvic karmas* bring about maturity and spiritual growth. These actions are not based on desires for tangible results like money, fame, status, pleasure, children and so forth. They should be considered compulsory actions, assuming the desire for liberation.

The Five Offerings *of* Karma Yoga

They are called the Five Essential Worships (*pancha-maha-yajna*) and are the essence of *karma yoga* because they directly contribute to spiritual growth.

1. **Worship of God in any form.** *Isvara/Maya*, the Creator of

the *Dharma* Field, is God. *Karma yoga* is worship of God. Most modern spiritual people have abandoned religion because so much suffering has been foisted on humanity in its name. But the religious impulse, the Self loving itself, is as hardwired as the desire for identity. So it is incumbent on a *karma yogi* to choose a symbol of the Self that is attractive and uplifting and worship it regularly. It can be anything because every object is just God in a particular form. It may be a ritual sacrifice or a *puja* in front of an idol or a photo. It can be telling the beads, visiting a temple, doing service or giving money to a church or mosque.

2. **Unconditional reverence for parents, especially difficult ones.** For instance, if you don't feel love when you think of your parents, you should inquire into why you have a problem with them. You should "heal" the relationship in your mind by understanding, for example, that if they could have been different they would have been, and they did their best according to their conditioning. Find a place in your heart to accommodate them and give them credit for the good qualities they instilled in you. They are no longer in your life physically, perhaps, but they are still in your mind. They are part of it, and it is made out of you, the Self. Until you have a loving feeling about that part of your mind, you will not be free to inquire properly. In any case, the essence of enlightenment is love, so you might as well start somewhere. Once you have dissolved the negativity, bring an image of them into your mind and fill the image with love. Keep the love flowing to the image as long as possible.

3. **Worship of scriptures.** As previously stated, it is foolish to think that you will start inquiry one fine day when you are more inclined to contemplation. If you are serious about freedom from limitation, you must set aside a set time every day, preferably in the morning, and contemplate throughout the day. Contemplation is a process that develops the more you focus the mind on the teachings and the mind turns inwards.

4. **Service to humanity.** Worshipful service simply means appropriate response to legitimate small everyday requests for help. When someone wants something from you, see if you can't accommodate them, assuming it is a reasonable desire. If you are helping others, at least you are not wasting your time indulging *tamasic* and *rajasic* habits. Service isn't only doing what others want, although it might include that. It is showing an accommodating openness to others, not shutting them out. Because ego born of a sense of inadequacy and inferiority looks for opportunities to feel special, virtuous and recognized, humble service keeps these tendencies in check. It is based on a recognition of the essential oneness of all. It is also wise because everything we need comes through others. Service-oriented individuals are generally well looked after.

5. **Worship of all sentient beings.** It is our duty as humans to take care of the Field which gives us everything we need to live. An attitude of gratitude is a prerequisite for a happy life. Yes, the Field may not be real, but that does not mean

that we should not care about it. It exists, we exist in it from the *jiva* perspective, and it sustains us while we are in the body. We look after our bodies because we want to enjoy peace of mind. The environment, the Field of Existence, is *Isvara*, is you, the Self. There is no distance between us and nature. We are born in it, live in it and die in it.

Loving action as its steward and contribution to its preservation is a devotional and much-encouraged practice. Worship of nature is continual mindfulness of our environments, beautifying them and contributing to them always, including the body, our most intimate contact with nature. How we relate to everything in our delicately balanced eco-system has a powerful effect on our state of mind. Recycle. Reduce your carbon footprint. Go green.

Chapter 5

Guna Yoga Is Feeling Management

THE THRUST OF Self-inquiry is to remove the ignorance that stands in the way of appreciation of our true and unlimited nature. To succeed, we must understand the forces that make up and condition the mind and the world it lives in, which is what Self-inquiry is about. Studies that investigate cognition below the level of awareness show that rationality is bounded by emotion. We cannot help but perceive the world in biased ways. Because our unconscious frame of reference subliminally creates the context for all experience, it profoundly influences how we relate to what happens in us and to us. Our view of reality is entirely subjective, which means we discount anything outside of our own emotional filters.

Thus we struggle to exercise self-control, and suffer. We usually think of ourselves as sitting in the driver's seat with ultimate control over the decisions we make and the direction our life takes. But alas, this perception has more to do with our desires and how we want to view ourselves than with reality. Without Self-knowledge, we are pawns in a game whose forces we largely cannot comprehend, and we dance to its tune like puppets on a string.

Recently, geneticists, neuroscientists, psychologists, sociologists, economists, anthropologists and others have made great strides in understanding the building blocks of the mind. A core finding of their work is that we are not primarily the products of our conscious thinking. We are primarily the products of thinking that happens below the level of awareness. The unconscious parts of the mind are not primitive vestiges that need to be conquered to make wise decisions. They are not dark caverns of repressed sexual urges. The unconscious parts comprise most of the mind – where most of the decisions and many of the most impressive, as well as destructive, thinking takes place.

These submerged processes are the seedbeds of what causes us to suffer and enjoy, to succeed or fail. Research shows that the human mind can take in eleven million pieces of information at any given moment. The most generous estimate is that we can be consciously aware of only forty of these. Some researchers have gone so far as to suggest that the unconscious mind does virtually all the work and that conscious volition is an illusion. The conscious mind merely constructs a narrative in the attempt to make sense of what the unconscious mind is doing of its own accord. These findings concur with the teachings of Vedanta. If free will is not free at all, how do we manage the mind? There are many options available to us, such as religion, science, philosophy and psychotherapy. But none of them offer a lasting solution to permanent satisfaction. Only Self-knowledge can do that.

Gross and Physical Manifestations

In the following three chapters, the three *gunas* are explained in detail. In terms of mind management, it is very important to understand that all three *gunas* have gross active (or inactive) and subtle psychological manifestations. It is impossible to separate the two, as they are intrinsically linked – nothing in the experiential reality is ever purely material or psychological, because life is an intricate dance of both. All the *gunas* work together, with one usually predominant. Everything we experience starts as a *guna-*

manufactured thought, instantly merges into a *guna* emotion, and then becomes action. All three *gunas* are responsible for making us see things in accordance with our subjective reality, our conditioning, or tendencies. *Sattva*, peace of mind, is the *guna* we want most to cultivate because it is the *guna* of clarity. *Rajas* and *tamas* out of balance with *sattva* is where most of our problems originate. Thus mind management equals *guna* management.

The point of *guna* management is to catch the *rajasic* or *tamasic* thought/emotion before it morphs into a regrettable action with its inevitable blowback *karma*. But until we are trained to think in terms of *guna*-knowledge, we often miss the initial *guna* impulse. It is easier to identify what *guna* is at work when we observe the effects of action or inaction because of the results that ensue, either immediately or later. But by then we have the *karma* to deal with, good or bad. While we definitely want to avoid the bad *karma* and enjoy the good *karma*, both may bring unseen results that are not in our best interests. Who has not regretted what were at the time very pleasurable results of actions, upon receiving the not-so-pleasant results?

On the physical level, *rajas* is easy to identify because it is the dynamic energy of action. There would be no movement possible without it. Everything we do, even a *tamasic* action, has a *rajasic* component driving it, and without it we would not get out of bed in the morning. On the psychological level, *rajas* is the energy of extroversion, desire and projection. *Rajas* out of balance with *sattva* turns the mind outwards towards objects, to the world, and desire/agitation prevents us from appreciating our true nature or assimilating what life is bringing to us. Any impulse that extroverts the mind, whether psychological or purely mechanical, is *rajasic.* Even if it is a pleasant *sattvic* desire, like thinking about a loved one, or a pleasant action, like making love, there is still *rajas* (desire = extroversion) involved.

Rajas can create the painful drive that pushes the mind to seek completion through action or through gain of objects at all costs. It is the energy of excitement, of the "buzz" of passion that we all love so much and believe makes us feel alive and vibrant. *Rajas* does produce these feelings, but unfortunately it is a fire that not only heats, it burns. We are like moths drawn to a flame under its spell and suffer the consequences. In the extreme, a mind controlled by *rajas* is driven by passion, greed and desire (likes and dislikes) to gain or avoid whatever object it is fixated on, to feel the bliss, the burn, the danger. It is a mind oblivious to anything but its own wants, certain that the joy is in gaining the object or experience of its desire or avoiding unwanted experiences.

Tamas seems to be a more inert energy because it is the energy of matter. When we look at a rock or a chair, we are looking at pure *tamas*, no extroversion there, only insentience – ignorance. But from the psychological perspective, *tamas* conditions the mind and suppresses our ability to see ourselves or the world just as much as *rajas* because it clouds the mind. We are more inclined not to act, or if we do, *tamas* blunts our ability to understand and respond appropriately to what is showing up in our lives, because the mind is so dull. A deeply *tamasic* mind is not something anyone enjoys, because it's painful. You are like a narcoleptic, unable to keep your eyes open, with a mind that feels like it has a bus parked on top of it. When the mind is very *tamasic*, it also tends to slide down a very unhealthy path to sloth, addiction and the realm of the senses – dark sensual pleasures of every kind.

Sattva also has both an active and psychological function. A mind that is *sattvic*, meaning wide awake, clear, calm, dispassionate, will see things clearly without projection or denial, and respond appropriately to life, taking appropriate action, doing whatever needs to be done without any stress, no matter what is required. Any action that is done with grace, clarity and focus is *sattvic*. *Sattvic* desires are in harmony with *dharma* and do not imprison the mind, unless the ego has co-opted *sattva* and thinks it is special or superior, both psychologically and in lifestyle. We call this the "golden cage" of *sattva*, and it is prevalent in the spiritual world.

On the material plane, we can immediately feel when our body and environment is *sattvic*, because things are calm and collected, we feel good, at peace and self-confident. Even weather patterns reflect the *gunas*. All three *gunas* are always present to a greater or lesser extent, but *sattva* is clearly identifiable not only by what is present, but by what is not present: agitation (*rajas*) and dullness (*tamas*).

Are Feelings Your Way of Thinking?

Every *guna* generates very predictable thoughts and emotions. What most of us don't realize is that feelings are created by our thoughts. A *guna*-generated thought always precedes a feeling, but it is so fleeting that it's usually covered up immediately by a predictable *guna*-generated feeling. Unfortunately, without knowledge of the *gunas*, we are not in control of our feelings, because we don't understand them or where they come from. Thoughts/feelings recycle automatically and endlessly according to the *gunas* and the law of *karma*.

There is nothing we can do to change this. We can only learn to manage our thoughts/feelings through understanding what the *gunas* are and how to manage their relative proportions with a view to peace of mind as our main goal. Sadly, in the attempt to change our state of mind, many of us repeat doing what didn't work before, thinking that it will produce a different result the next time. This means we get more of the same.

Nobody Makes Themselves Feel Anything

If a negative state of mind plagues you, it may seem as if it is not your own doing. And that is true because nobody makes themselves feel anything. But it is your doing if you are *guna*-educated and understand how *karma* works. In the spiritual world, some people try to wriggle off the hook by tailoring the *guna* teaching to suit their egos with the claim that if you are not responsible for the *gunas*, what you feel doesn't matter. But it is always the ego that says it is not the doer/ego. Bad feelings definitely matter to the ego, as much as it likes to deny culpability. Uttering the statement "I am not the doer" without a complete understanding of the nature of the *guna* field is simply denial. It is not *guna* management or even *guna*-knowledge.

Understanding the *Gunas* Is Managing Them

It is true that we are not in control of the *gunas* and cannot change them. But if we understand how to manage them, we can take the appropriate actions at the appropriate time so that we maximize their positive aspects and minimize their negative aspects for peace of mind. In this way, assuming the Field of Life is receptive (which it generally is when we understand we are not in charge of it), we can mostly get what we want and be mostly happy most of the time, but not all the time. *Guna*-knowledge allows us to disidentify with our egoic needs, desires and fears, and makes possible acceptance of things as they are, even when life is not playing along and giving us what we want but the opposite. The key to freedom is managing our feelings and the repetitive thought patterns that give rise to them, through *guna* management. From this perspective, even if the mind is not peaceful (*sattvic*), it does not interfere with our baseline experience as the Self, *satya*.

A Thought Universe

As previously pointed out, we only ever experience anything in our minds, nowhere else. We live in a thought universe. Everything we see, hear, think, feel and experience is based on a thought. Furthermore, without Consciousness there are no objects to perceive, no thoughts or feelings. Think about it. How do you know what you know or know what you don't know unless you are conscious? Who or what is it that knows what you think and feel? Your thoughts and feelings don't think and feel. They do not know you, so how can they be you? You, Consciousness, with the help of *Maya*, make thinking and feeling possible. Thinking and feeling happen independent of us.

Thoughts and feelings are only a problem if we identify with them and get attached to positive feelings or negative thoughts/feelings that dominate the mind. We need to acknowledge our feelings as the relative truth about ourselves in the moment, not THE truth about the impersonal us, the Self. If I can see that my feelings are objects known to me, I have the power to control them or at least manage them so that they do not control me. Denial of my feelings is as unhealthy as overindulgence in them.

The Importance of Honouring Emotions

If you ignore the ebb and flow of emotions that course through you every second of every day, you ignore an essential part of what makes us human. You ignore the processes that determine what you want, how you perceive the world, your values and what drives you forward as well as what holds you back. Research has found that people who lose their sense of smell suffer greater emotional deterioration than people who lose their vision. That's because smell is a powerful way to read emotions. Lack of emotion leads to self-destructive and dangerous behaviour. As much as overly emotional people, those who lack emotion don't lead well-planned logical lives either in the manner of the coolly rational. They tend to lead foolish lives, because emotion is a component of thinking. Emotions help us measure the value of something and unconsciously guide us as we navigate through life – away from things that are likely to lead to pain and towards things that are likely to lead to fulfilment. A narcissist is someone who lacks empathy and remorse, in addition to an overall disposition that is antagonistic and unfeeling. In extreme cases, people who dissociate from their feelings become sociopaths, untroubled by barbarism, and unable to feel other people's pain.

As we go about our day, millions of stimuli bombard us every second – a confusion of sounds, sights, smells and motions. Amidst all this pyrotechnic sensory chaos, different parts of the brain and body interact to form what cognitive scientists call an "Emotional Positioning System." Like the Global Positioning System (GPS) that might be in your car, the EPS senses your current internal situation and compares it to the vast body of data it has stored in its memory. From there it makes judgment calls about the best course it needs to take to help us navigate our days. But this inner and mostly unconscious EPS system can only ever deliver, at best, an approximation of what is actually being presented to us in the Field at any given moment, hence we often respond in ways that are not in our best interests. We lack any other means of knowledge to do otherwise.

Identification With Feelings Is the Problem

There is nothing inherently wrong with feelings. The problem comes in when we overindulge or identify with our feelings and allow them control over our responses to what is coming at us from the Field. It is almost normal for most people to exaggerate the importance of their feelings or emotions, especially in the spiritual arena, like they confer an exclusive entitlement, the right to indulgence, to self-importance, to self-pity, to manipulate. The world owes me something! How I "feel" is a true statement of who I am. Sad to say, feelings are the least reliable means of knowledge or indicators of truth, because they are always changing. You know this is true with just a little reflection. You feel angry and sad one moment; the next moment you find yourself laughing at something. Or vice versa. I love you today and hate you tomorrow. If feelings are real, they would not change or end. We never know what we are going to feel from one moment to the next.

The Notion of Entitlement

Behind this erroneous presumption that life is not only able to give me what I want, but I am entitled to get what I want. But is it? Or am I? The simple fact that I must only look after myself, but life must look after everything, escapes me. There is a similarity in a way because my world is a small portion of the whole; it represents the whole, for me. To be happy, I must look after the objects in my environment that are important to me, basically people. I must take their needs into account when I want something from them. And I always want something. Everything I get comes from someone or something else. Therefore I am totally dependent on life, my environment, for success.

What Is Success?

Most of us agree that the definition of success comes down to getting what I want and avoiding what I don't want. It's never more complex than that, though most don't see it. From childhood, we all want to succeed. Sadly, success is not a foregone conclusion, because the desire to succeed is not enough to generate situations that conform to our desires and fears, likes and dislikes, preferences and aversions. The problem is that life has its own agenda and is supremely indifferent to our likes and dislikes, which creates a lot of emotion and unhappiness for us. We get angry and despondent when life fails to deliver what we want, and get elated when it does. Somehow we find ourselves bouncing back and forth between these two poles, and inevitably both anger and elation lead to depression, a feeling that life has let me down.

Of course we don't want to blame ourselves for our emotionality, because it has become our identity and we get a lot of mileage out of it. While silently "grinning and bearing" our woes is preferable to blaming, shaming and complaining, both fall short of giving me what I want – happiness, satisfaction, wholeness. When we cannot objectively and honestly look at ourselves and admit that we are no more than an emotionally needy baby, we need rationalizations to blame somebody or something. That something is usually "life." The truth is that all rationalizations are questionable, because they are cop-outs. They hide the basic fact that we don't understand ourselves or the nature of the Field of Existence, and our needs are not important to the whole.

The Needs of the Total Come First

Along with feelings, there is nothing inherently wrong with needing things, but there is something very wrong with the expectation that life "should" give us what we need, the reason being that while I depend on life, it does not depend on me. Since everything depends on it, life must look after everything, including me. If we want to manage our emotions/feelings instead of them managing us, we must learn to appreciate one inescapable fact: the needs of the Total come first. Always. Appreciation of this fact gives us a very different view of life. It also helps us to appreciate another extremely inconvenient truth: life is not here to give you want you want. Life only ever gives us what we need, not what we desire, much to our chagrin.

Desire Is Not Necessarily Your Friend

Most of us do not realize that desire is not necessarily our friend. It may be, if your desire is not contrary to *dharma*; for instance, the desire for freedom. But since this is a lawful universe, when you are too invested in your petty fears and gratuitous desires, you are not interested in the natural laws of life or the needs of the Total. Your idea is "I want what I want the way I want it when I want it!" Rules are merely irritating impediments to getting what you want. As humans, most of us have one extremely tedious and glaring fault: we always have an agenda. We have little appreciation of things as they are, and are simultaneously cursed with an insatiable need to sell something, usually ourselves, in one way or another. We need validation from others to prove that we are unique.

How to Achieve Success

You achieve success by managing your energy, i.e. the *gunas*. Whether you pursue security, pleasure, virtue, fame, power or liberation, you need a dedicated *guna*-managed lifestyle. To achieve an appropriate lifestyle, you need to *guna*-manage your mind. To manage your mind, you need *guna*-knowledge. Blaming yourself for failures and taking credit for successes is a huge problem, because it makes everything that happens about ME, as if I were the only object in existence. Yes, I do exist, and I play a part in life, but anyone with a little objectivity can see that I am only one small factor in a vast web of relationships that extends far beyond my immediate environment. So carrying the burdens of the world makes me a burden to myself.

Guna-Knowledge Is Knowledge of the Big Picture

Guna-knowledge, knowledge of the big picture, is the solution because it lays the responsibility for what happens to me, good and bad, elsewhere. It moves me from the centre of my life to the periphery, where the view is a lot more realistic. It relieves the pressure to perform and allows me to completely relax in otherwise stressful situations. And it is equally good for the world because it greatly improves my needy, dissatisfied personality. It changes me from a liability to an asset in the eyes of others, which bodes well for satisfaction and success for me.

Getting Along With Yourself

Understanding the *gunas* not only optimizes chances of success in the world, but it also optimizes the chances of a successful relationship with yourself. Since you play the most important role in your success, it behoves you to get along happily with yourself. Inner conflict compromises your primary instrument (your mind) and renders it unsuitable for actualizing your goals. Self-obsessed individuals are not generally happy people. Of course you care about yourself, but if you are too self-centred you will short-change the world. What escapes most is that the world, in particular "my" world, is the other half of the life equation. And life, thus my world, will invariably respond in like fashion to the way we treat it. We reap what we sow because this is a lawful universe. So how does *guna*-knowledge solve this problem? It depersonalizes your relationship to yourself and to life in general. And it makes it clear that you are an integral part of this Creation, of life, and it is to your advantage to live intelligently, follow *dharma* and the principle of non-injury.

Personal Uniqueness

Nobody is unique. This statement may seem strange because for most of us personal uniqueness is the essence of our identity. Our total insignificance in a world of more than eight billion creates an obsessive desire to stand out. Behind this need or perhaps because of it is a simple fact: we are not unique at all. Because we come from the same source, we all have the same equipment, the same feelings and emotions, and the same dreams and aspirations as everyone else.

There is only one "story" and we all share it. In fact the more unique I feel, the more problems I encounter, because differences tax communication and efficient action. And it should not be lost on anyone that in the search for success everything we want comes from others. If we share a common identity, communication is simple. But if I think I am special or different from you, I am asking for conflict. Communication will not be easy or simple at all. To get what I want, I need to accommodate myself to life. Instead, this illusory idea that I am special infects me with the vain belief that the world should accommodate itself to me, a very bad and limiting idea indeed!

Specialness Breeds Dissatisfaction

The more special you think you are, the more you dislike yourself and become unlikeable because the more difficult you are to please. Nothing ever satisfies you for long and you get so tired of being "you." If it doesn't bore you silly to listen to yourself whine, rationalize and justify the same old complaints and excuses to shore up your self-esteem, it should. Nearly everyone wishes they were more, a better or different self, precisely because being a doer/enjoyer entity is extremely tedious.

Bad News: Life Does Not Care What I Want!

As frustrating as this fact may be to you, the world is just an impersonal Field of forces, laws and principles, and does not care what you want. It serves you (contrary to what you may think), but it is not set up to pander to individuals. Life and its inbuilt laws of *karma* is the great leveller. The cosmos would become chaos if it had to break its own rules to accommodate uniqueness.

If life were personal, nobody would get out of bed in the morning, because purposeful work would be impossible. Success is possible precisely because life is impersonal. Understand the laws and forces, creatively interact with them and you will achieve more or less predictable results. You can only bend reality to your will if you appreciate the impersonality of everything and manage your mind by managing the *gunas*. You will wake up as a fresh new self every day because you will be growing, not stagnating. Your story will become interesting, and you will become an interesting and interested personality.

The *Gunas* Sneak Up On You

Although feelings are highly unreliable as means of knowledge, they are good indicators of how the *gunas* are playing out in our lives. If you understand the *gunas*, they are easy to spot because knowledge of the *gunas* gives you clear vision. But you need to be quick about it, because the *gunas* sneak up on you. It takes great vigilance to catch the thought that precedes a powerful feeling, because the feeling obscures the thought/like/dislike behind it. Therefore vigilance is the price of freedom. The mind is a thought processor. It is always producing thoughts – most of them non-volitional. There is no way to turn it off. But there is a way to manage it: by owning it as your primary instrument and learning how to choose thoughts and feelings that make you feel good and speak the truth about you. As stated in the last chapter, there is nothing inherently wrong with involuntary thoughts, but they tend to immediately morph into actions that are liable to create unwanted *karma* in the form of obscuring thoughts and emotions.

Duality Produces Positive and Negative Thoughts

The world tells us that if we don't "feel" there is something wrong with us. When I was young, I was exhorted to stop looking under every rock for the truth, to think less and feel more. I never listened, thank goodness! Being a knowledge-seeker was my main motivation in life, and thinking beat feeling. Most people believe that they are only alive and happy when they feel something intensely. It need not necessarily even be a positive feeling, like joy. Some people feel alive when they are scared or in danger, like adrenalin junkies who put their lives at risk for the "ultimate high." Many of us believe that unless we feel intensely positive love or happiness, we have neither in our lives.

Duality being what it is, both positive and negative feelings cycle constantly through the mind. We all want good feelings (or emotions, which are grosser than feelings), such as love, happiness, completeness, etc. No one wants negative feelings. However, both positive and negative feelings/emotions can cause suffering. The inescapable fact that feelings cause so much unhappiness in relationships and life in general is lost on most. It's not that there is anything wrong with feelings or that we can stop feeling. You will never stop feeling as long as you live.

Feelings Are Reflected Love

The truth is that positive feelings, however delicious, are an effect of the transpersonal love that is my true nature. Feelings are not real love. Although the feeling of love reflects the love I am, it is not who I am, just like the image in a mirror is a true reflection of me, but it is not me. However, in essence there is no difference, because personal love, the reflection, and transpersonal love that comes from the Self are one because reality is non-dual. Is there a difference between a ray of sunshine and the sun? No, not really. But there is a difference because although love itself never ends, intense feelings of love always end, which is where the problems arise. What do I do when the feeling of love ends? I feel like I have lost love. Unless the knowledge of completeness assimilates from an intense feeling of love, most of us take the object, the reflection, to be the subject, and suffer. Bring on the broken hearts and sad music.

We Can Transform Negative Feelings

We cannot deny or suppress feelings; we must acknowledge and understand them in the light of Self-knowledge (*guna*-knowledge), not in the light of our likes and dislikes. If I cannot objectify my feelings, I am in trouble, as they will transform into bad feelings. When I identify with my feelings, I relate to the world through them. When feelings are in control of the intellect, discrimination is impossible, and I suffer unless objectivity develops. Our main aim is to transform negative feelings into positive feelings, which we can do with *guna* management, explained further on.

Feelings Are Not Apart from Consciousness

Feelings are never apart from Consciousness, although *Maya*, the power to delude, makes them seem like they are. Feelings are made up of Consciousness, like the spider's web is made up of the spider but is not the spider. The spider is always free if its web, but there is no web without the spider. Just so, Consciousness (Me, the Self) is always free of feelings, even though it would be impossible for us to feel anything if we were not conscious. Feelings are not real, because they are always changing, therefore they belong to *Maya* (the three *gunas* – duality), not to the Self.

Perception and Inference

The five senses, which give rise to our perceptions and the inferences we draw from them, inform all our feelings. The only means of knowledge available to us in the apparent reality is the senses. They fall short when it comes to knowing who we are for two reasons:

1. All sense information is subject to interpretation. I experience everything through the filters of my conditioning. Therefore I experience the world as I am, not as it is.

2. Consciousness is not an object of perception and cannot be known by perception and inference, because it is subtler than thoughts and feelings.

Thus do not trust your feelings about who you are without careful examination! If you do, you might not love yourself or anyone else.

Emotional Intelligence

We hear much about "emotional intelligence" these days. While it is true that "EI" is something we all need to develop, most of us do not have a clue how to do so. And without Self-inquiry into our likes and dislikes, healthy values and living a *dharmic* life, we will not succeed. We do not magically become more emotionally mature or intelligent by thinking about it or as we age, unless we have learned the programs that run our minds and how to render them non-binding. It would be so easy if aging automatically conferred wisdom! Sadly, it does not. Becoming a mature adult is not a function of chronology. It is a function of Self-knowledge. How many older people do you know who truly have wisdom? I bet very few, if any. Without Self-knowledge, you can be 70-year-old astrophysicist with the emotional intelligence of a 15-year-old.

Your Mind Is Either Your Best Friend or Your Worst Enemy

Your mind can be your best friend or your worst enemy. In the extreme, your mind can kill you if negative thoughts/feelings dominate it. Suicides are people who prefer death to their thoughts. It's their thoughts/feelings that kill them, not life or anything else. But when skilfully managed and controlled, the mind will allow us to express and enjoy the beauty that we are in our day-to-day life, no matter what it dishes out to us. When you feel bad because of bad thoughts about yourself, life or others, you can instantly convert your emotional distress, negativity and mental agitation into gratitude and peace by managing the *gunas* and the thoughts/feelings they give rise to.

Summary *of* Points So Far

1. Thoughts produce emotions, and emotions reinforce thinking patterns, which then generate more of the same feelings, ad infinitum.

2. Thoughts are only the relative truth about you as a person, not the ultimate truth about you as Consciousness, because they are not always present and always changing.

Consciousness never changes and is always present. It is the knower of your thoughts and feelings.

3. Duality produces both positive and negative thoughts.

4. Happiness is a preponderance of positive thoughts, and unhappiness is a preponderance of negative thoughts.

5. You have control of your thoughts if your emotions are managed in view of your values, through knowledge of the *gunas* and with *karma yoga*.

6. The *yoga* of the three *gunas* converts negative thoughts to positive thoughts.

7. There are three types of thoughts and personality types: *sattvic, rajasic* and *tamasic*. Each *guna* produces positive and negative emotions, as explained above.

8. How do we manage the *gunas* to get a sunny personality, i.e. one with predominately positive emotions? Happiness lies in mind management.

The Four Steps *to* Effective Mind Management

Solution Step 1:
Understand the Four Types of Thinking

To value a controlled mind is to understand the way the mind thinks. It is to bring it in line with the way the Self would think if it were a person living in the apparent reality. It means that although the mind is capricious, I need not fulfil its fantasies and yield to its caprices. It means that I am the boss, not the mind. I own my primary instrument, and it does not hold me ransom to negative thoughts. There are four basic ways of thinking, three of which are necessary to understand and master if I want to happy relationships:

FOUR WAYS OF THINKING

1. **Impulsive:** Unexamined thoughts born of instincts dominate the mind. I do what I feel without thinking about it, and suffer the consequences.

2. **Mechanical:** Thoughts of which I am conscious but have no power to control, because they are produced by binding *vasanas*.

3. **Deliberate:** Thoughts subjected to discrimination, accepted or dismissed with reference to my value structure.

4. **Spontaneous:** Without evaluation, my thinking automatically conforms to universal values, and my actions are always appropriate and timely. This kind of thinking only applies to those for whom Self-knowledge has destroyed binding *vasanas* and negated doership, and will be prevalent in non-dual relationships.

Solution Step 2: Values and *Karma Yoga*

I have explained the importance of positive values and of *karma yoga* in previous chapters. Without understanding what values motivate us, and applying *karma yoga* to every thought, emotion, word and deed, mind management is not possible. As soon as a strong emotion arises in the mind, I must immediately identify the value behind it and place it on the altar of *karma yoga* before anything else.

Solution Step 3: *Guna Management*
GO FOR THE GUNA

It should be clear by now that the *gunas* arise in the mind according to our conditioning, our mental and emotional patterns. Some of us will be naturally *sattvic*, others predominantly *rajasic* or *tamasic*. Everyone is different because of the endless permutations and combinations of the *gunas*. Our conditioning originates in the macrocosmic causal body, or the unconscious, to use Freudian terminology. The *gunas* do not come from you, so why own them? It is quite enough to recognize and understand them. Understanding is healing.

The *gunas* are global values; thoughts and feelings are local values. You needn't waste a lot of time analyzing the meaning of specific thoughts and feelings if you can identify the *guna* with which a thought or feeling is associated. The law of *karma* dictates the results of your actions. If acting out of *rajas* produces predictably unwanted results in a particular situation, then switch to *sattva guna* the next time the situation occurs. For instance, say you encounter problems whenever you relate to your partner because your sense of insecurity (*tamas*) causes you to assert your dominance (*rajas*) when you interact. Invoke *sattva* by relating to your lover/partner as you would to a friend the next time conflict arises, and see if your relationship doesn't improve.

Perhaps you have a tendency to go on the defensive whenever a conflict arises (or even in small issues where you perceive conflict but there isn't any) and immediately attack. Next time this happens, catch the thought preceding the desire to attack, and say nothing. Observe your mind, even though it will not like it; see the predictable justifications produced by *rajas* and *tamas*, and choose the opposite thought.

Pounce on a bad thought like a hungry vigilant cat on a mouse. It may be true that you have made mistakes, broken the rules of life, hurt others and yourself. We all have at some point. But you will never become the person you think you "should" be by beating yourself up about your failings or blaming others, so why not give it up? Dare to forgive yourself; nobody else can. There is just no way anybody can become perfect, whatever that is. By bringing awareness to our habitual thoughts and understanding how and why they arise, we can align ourselves with values that are in harmony with life. We can make healthier choices in all areas of our lives, and in so doing become happier, healthier people. Success in mind management boils down to uncovering the habitual thinking and emotional patterns that create negative states of mind by tracking the *guna* behind them and transforming thoughts and feelings to those of your choosing. It may sound like hard work, and it is at first. Ingrained, habitual patterns are not easy to change. But it is the price you pay for a happy peaceful life.

AIM FOR PEACE OF MIND, SATTVA

Sattva, the energy of clarity, intelligence and beauty, is the energy we need to aim for peace of mind, clear thinking. To achieve it, we need to bring *rajas* (desire/passion/extroversion) and *tamas* (inertia, dullness, denial, sloth) into balance with it. *Sattva* is like a calm, alert, intelligent, wise old elephant in touch with its world, secure in its ability and intelligence to deal with whatever appears. *Rajas* is like a wild horse we must tame. *Tamas* is like a lazy cud-chewing cow in need of exercise. We need all three of the *gunas*, in balance. All have an upside and a downside, like everything else in this world. Too little *sattva* makes us either too *rajasic* or too *tamasic*. Too much *sattva* can make us spiritually or intellectually vain, take pride in our abilities or hook us on bliss, feeling good. With insufficient *rajas*, we would never get out of bed in the morning or achieve anything. Too much *rajas* extroverts the mind to such a degree that we are like hamsters on a treadmill, driven relentlessly by our desires and fears, going nowhere fast. With too little *tamas*, we would never sleep or have the capacity for endurance. Too much *tamas* and our lives are a mess of sloth, denial, fear, avoidance and drudgery.

We experience *sattva* when *rajas* and *tamas* are not in control of the mind and it is in alignment with its true nature and life's highest values. Such a mind is content, satisfied, *dharmic*, ever aware of life's rules. When we contravene *dharma* (the laws of life) for whatever reason, however trivial, it will produce agitation or denial. The mind will not be peaceful, because *rajas* and *tamas* will condition it. Most of us feel bad (guilty/uncomfortable) when we break *dharma*, which is what we call a "conscience." This mechanism is inbuilt, and unless you are a psychopath or mentally ill, there is no way to avoid it. There is never a time when we do not experience these three energies. The important question is, do we experience them consciously or unconsciously? If we understand what they are and how they work, we can manage them so that we experience almost perpetual emotional, intellectual and spiritual peace of mind.

Solution Step 4: Apply the Opposite Thought

Thought itself is hardwired and involuntary. Did you ever try to be angry, confused, indifferent, joyful or in love when you are not? Without exception, the three energies or powers (*gunas*) that run everything in the Creation cause all feelings. But individual thoughts are not involuntary. So it is eminently possible to deliberately create healthy thoughts and thought patterns. You don't have to go digging deep within your subconscious in a search for them or suffer penury after years in therapy. Just learn to observe your mind when you do or don't get what you want, and you will see them all.

As I have mentioned, duality means that every negative thought has a corresponding positive thought. Sunny, positive and optimistic (*sattvic*) people have a predominance of positive thoughts. So you cancel a negative thought by applying its opposite. Neutralize a stingy mind by giving generously. Neutralize a distrusting mind with a trusting mind. Wipe away a dirty thought with a clean thought, a depressing thought with an uplifting thought. "I am small and incomplete" is a negative thought. "I am whole and complete" is a positive thought.

There Is No Magic or Mystery to a Happy Life

There is no magic or mystery to living life well if you understand who you are or at least understand your conditioning. It is not only for the lucky few. It's for the sane, not the saintly. All we need is Self-knowledge, discrimination and the determination to apply common sense. If you want a peaceful happy life, learn to monitor your thoughts and feelings, and choose them carefully so that they align with the truth of who you are. But I just said above that most thoughts are non-volitional, which is true. They are. And it is because most thoughts and feelings are non-volitional that you must learn to manage them, if you want to be happy.

Dismiss the Voices of Diminishment!

We do this by learning how to think deliberately, not mechanically or impulsively, once we get a grip on the feeling/thinking patterns that condition our minds. Deliberate conscious thought pulls the brake on desire, passion and projection. Deliberate thinking religiously rejects all thoughts that arise from the voices of diminishment (*tamas*), our ever-present inner judge and jury, the part of us that does not love itself, that brings us down, feels less-than, separate, angry, alone, afraid. Deliberate thinking entails conscious choice of the opposite thought, which will automatically produce the opposite feeling. You may have to fake it till you make it; after all, you don't believe the opposite thought about yourself! But this faking is a good one because what you are "faking" is the truth about you.

You Don't Need Permission to Choose Your Thoughts

We do not need permission to choose our thoughts. You can say NO! to *tamasic/rajasic*, destructive, self-deprecating and degrading thinking and emotional patterns. There is no rule against consciously choosing positive thoughts over negative thoughts. So do it. What or who is stopping you? Only your own limiting beliefs, nothing else. A belief is just a thought, nothing more; it is not etched in stone. Commit to ownership of your mind as your primary instrument and align yourself with only the highest, most loving thoughts and feelings, even if you must conjure them up. Refuse all others! Be ruthless about choosing the opposite thought whenever a bad thought arises in the mind.

Summary *of* Effective Mind Management

1. Own your mind as your primary instrument. Understand the way it works.

2. Clarify your highest values by conducting a fearless moral inventory.

3. Practise *karma yoga* religiously.

4. Take responsibility for every experience you have; it comes from your thoughts/feelings, not the world or anyone else. Your thoughts/emotions are not "yours." They come from the three *gunas*. Make sure you understand what they are. Understanding and observation of the *gunas* is the starting point to *guna* management.

5. Identify and monitor the thought/emotional pattern associated with the *guna*. See which thoughts are *sattvic*, which are *tamasic* and which are *rajasic*. See how repetitive these thoughts are, how they cycle through the mind. See the moods they create, how the mind modifies to each *guna*,

positively and negatively. Understand the implications of identification with each kind energy and the thoughts/feelings/actions they cause.

6. Discriminate the habitual emotional thought patterns that compel you to act against your highest values and create pain and suffering. Evaluate your daily actions to discover those that do not support your highest values.

7. Change those thoughts and the actions they produce by conditioning new chosen thoughts into your primary instrument. No matter what *guna* appears on a moment-to-moment basis, go for the *guna*, not the thought or feeling it produces. You cannot necessarily change the thought/feeling, but when you see it coming from the *gunas,* you can "nip it in the bud" and disidentify with it before it consumes the mind. You need to be very vigilant and catch the *guna* before the mind modifies to it. If you discriminate the *guna* from the thought, you need not negate the thought; you need only negate the *guna.* Observe all the objects in your environment. It will soon become obvious that no one is doing anything; it is all a play of the *gunas.*

8. Relax and enjoy, as your primary instrument automatically serves your highest values in your day-to-day life.

Chapter 6

The Energy *of* Revelation: Sattva

ALL THREE GUNAS, *sattva, rajas* and *tamas*, are always present because they give rise to everything in the Creation. But they are also always changing and manifest in the mind in ever-changing proportions. Pure *sattva* is intelligence, knowledge, which is straightforward. We all know we are intelligent (well, maybe not all of us!) and we all know what we know and what we do not know. We also all know we are conscious. Pure *tamas* is total ignorance, also not difficult to grasp, because we all know that matter is inert — it has no knowing function and is neither intelligent nor conscious. *Rajas* is also obvious because it is the energy of action, desire and passion.

What is not simple to understand (and most do not) is that pure *sattva*, prior to the appearance of *tamas* and *rajas*, is the pure mirror of Consciousness, called *prakriti*, or *Maya*. *Sattva* provides the knowing function. It is Consciousness appearing as the Knower, *Isvara*, or God. As the individual, this makes it sound like *sattva* can be experienced on its own. But it is not possible, because for the Creation to manifest, it requires all three *gunas* present. Even though the nature of the mind is *sattva* when the mind is extremely *sattvic, rajas* and *tamas* are also there, but in balance with *sattva*, so they don't cause mental/emotional disturbance. Additionally, even though *sattva* is the subtlest manifestation of *sat*, Consciousness, like the other two *gunas* it is an object known to Consciousness. It is not in and of itself conscious, although by virtue of Consciousness, *sattva* makes Consciousness possible for sentient beings.

It also sounds like there is a progression to the manifestation of the *gunas*. This is true and it is not true, depending on which perspective we take. From Consciousness's point of view, there is no time and no (real) Creation, therefore no *gunas*. From the Creation-and-creature point of view, it seems like *sattva* appears first, then *tamas* and *rajas* – but in truth they all appear together. The *gunas* may just be principles and only apparently real, but nonetheless, in *mithya*, all three are never not present.

For teaching purposes, we must separate the *gunas* to explain what they are and how they function, which is what makes teaching the *gunas* tricky, because they cannot be separated. They only ever work together. On its own, pure *sattva* cannot create, although it is the blueprint for all forms. It cannot think or feel, although it is responsible for thinking and feeling in sentient beings. And *tamas*, the existence aspect of the Creation, cannot think or feel, and has no power to create or cause anything to happen, at all. Something else is needed to bring these two energies together for the Creation to appear. That something else is *rajas*, the power of projection.

Sattva Is the Subtlest Manifestation of Sat

Sattva is the subtlest manifestation of *sat*, the true nature of the mind. *Sattva* is the mode of knowledge and bliss. It is the *guna* springboard both for a happy, healthy life – and for *moksa*, freedom from and for the limited small self. On the physical level, this is the energy of well-being, pleasure, beauty and good health. On the psychological level, it is the energy of revelation, clarity and peace of mind, the result of *rajas* and *tamas* in balance with *sattva*. *Sattva* produces a mind and body in harmony with each other and with the environment, the Field of Existence. Usually, most thoughts and feelings that produce peace of mind are the result of *sattva*. However, if you are furious with someone and think of killing him or her, the mind becomes peaceful, for a while. In this case, a *rajasic* thought produces peace. If the mind is agitated and has a drink or smokes a joint, it settles down and becomes *sattvic*, in which case *tamas* produces peace. In both these cases, the *sattva* is temporary and is soon be replaced by more *rajas* and *tamas* as the fruits of action play out.

We are after the kind of *sattva* that is a permanent "state" of mind, produced only by Self-knowledge.

The Revealing Power

As it is an energy that reveals Consciousness, we refer to *sattva* as the "revealing power." By "reveal" we mean it makes Consciousness accessible as knowledge and experience. If you desire to feel good most of the time, aim for a *sattvic* mind. It is not possible to have 100% *sattva*, firstly because *rajas* and *tamas* supplant *sattva*, as the *gunas* cycle constantly through the mind. Secondly, we are not in control of the *gunas*; the Field of Life is. Luckily for us, however, with a little work, Self-knowledge and lots of determination to end suffering, we can make the changes necessary for a happy, healthy life by creating a predominantly *sattvic* mind.

Sattva is the feeling of peace and satisfaction. When you are satisfied, the mind sits still. Such a mind is valuable for two reasons:

1. It reveals the Self as non-dual and allows you to evaluate objects as they are instead of how rajas and tamas project them.

2. Whether you look at Consciousness/the Self or at objects

(the reflection of the Self), you experience through the subtle body. The quality of energy that dominates the subtle body at any time is of paramount importance – assuming you want a good life – or both a good life and freedom, *moksa*.

Authentic Experience, No-Movement and Peace of Mind

The two benefits mentioned above are connected and not mutually exclusive. If you just want to feel good, you need not seek enlightenment, but you do need to cultivate *sattva*. If your main aim is *moksa*, you will not have peace of mind unless your life reflects the truth as well. Although it is not possible to have a 100% feel-good, flowing life, we can get very close if the mind is predominately *sattvic* because we can be objective about the objects that appear in it (i.e. our thoughts and feelings and the external things that happen to us). If you are clear about what is happening in you, you can work with your stuff creatively and remove obstacles to happiness as they arise.

We can call the experience of *sattva* the experience of "no-movement" because a steady and clear mind reveals the Self as unchanging Consciousness. A beautiful verse in the *Bhagavad Gita* expresses it this way: "The one who sees inaction in action and action in inaction is indeed wise." There is another saying much in vogue in the spiritual world and usually used without understanding: "Nothing ever happened." What this means is that the changes that take place in you and around you are only apparent changes, not actual changes – because as the Self you are unchanging. Only the body-mind goes through changes. When the subtle body is *sattvic*, you can act or not act; you are not compelled to act, nor are you too lazy to act.

Sattva and the Assimilation of Experience

When *rajas* dominates the mind, desire interprets experience. When *tamas* dominates, fear interprets experience. Both obscure the truth. When *sattva* dominates, truth interprets experience.

The Self, Consciousness, shines on each of the three energies in the causal body. Its light, reflected on the subtle body, produces three distinct conditions. If I desire to experience the Self, and the subtle body is the instrument of experience, it makes sense that I would want to have a *sattvic* microcosmic causal body. In fact the substance of the causal body (*chitta*) is Consciousness and reflects Consciousness accurately. However, if *tamasic* and *rajasic* tendencies burden the causal body, they distort the reflection in the subtle body, and inquiry will not bear fruit. If *rajasic* tendencies dominate the causal body, the Self appears as dynamic energy, not radiant light. If the causal body is *tamasic*, I will have no idea of the Self whatsoever. The conclusion here is obvious: if I want to experience the Self as it is, I should cultivate a *sattvic* mind. Experience of the Self is not enlightenment. But it can lead to enlightenment – if the intellect can assimilate the knowledge "I am Consciousness" – that arises when the attention is turned within and the mind is *sattvic*.

Because reality is non-dual Consciousness, the mind is Consciousness. To gain a predominately *sattvic* mind, one capable of discrimination and the easy assimilation of experience, the proportions of *rajas* and *tamas* relative to *sattva* need to be balanced. I need enough *rajas* for motivational purposes and enough *tamas* to ground my ideas in reality. However, the lion's share of the mind should be *sattvic*. A predominately *sattvic* mind will gain success in any field, worldly or spiritual, because it can discriminate properly. Enlightenment – *moksa* – is defined as discrimination (*atma-anatma viveka*). It only takes place in a *sattvic* mind.

How to Cultivate Sattva

The mind is a garden in which Vedanta plants the seed of Self-knowledge, which eventually becomes a great tree. It will not grow in the toxic soil of *samsaric* (dualistic) consciousness. The logic of this chapter leads us to the conclusion that a *sattvic* mind is necessary for liberation – and so does it lead to enlightened lifestyles. How to cultivate it? How to transform *rajasic* and *tamasic vasanas* into *sattva*? *Yoga* practice is a commitment to adjustment of the relative proportions of *rajas* and *tamas* with reference to *sattva* to produce an efficient, powerful and clear-thinking mind. When *yoga* has prepared the mind, discriminating the Self from the objects appearing in it can bear fruit. Apart from *yoga*, we need to take a fearless moral inventory of our values and everything in which we are invested – in other words, our entire spiritual and worldly lifestyle mentioned in previous chapters.

Please note: by "yoga" practice I am not referring to *hatha yoga* or any form of physical *yoga*. The word "yoga" means "to yoke," to join the mind to Self-knowledge.

Connect Actions With Results

We cultivate *sattva* by connecting our actions with the results. This is not always easy, because results have observable and unobservable effects. It is easy to observe the results that take place immediately.

For instance, if you use violent language in communication, you will usually have instant blowback from an injured ego. If you eat spoiled food, you usually feel sick within a short while. If you drink a bottle of wine or smoke a joint, you will usually feel either temporarily stimulated (*rajasic*) or "chilled" (*tamasic*), probably both. You will also feel temporarily happy (*sattvic*). However, the next day regret fills the mind and I have a headache; or I feel dull and depressed (*tamasic*). That you indulge yourself in this way shows that you are in pain. Pain motivates you and pain is the result of your actions. You cannot think clearly when you are in pain.

Unseen Results (Adrshta Phala)

The hardest results to observe are the ones that take place incrementally over years of indulgence – like unhealthy lifestyle habits, such as how we eat or over-/under-exercise. If you truly want to have an enlightened, healthy and happy lifestyle, discrimination is very simple. If something agitates or dulls the mind, you must renounce it. You cannot just keep doing what you are doing and somehow expect your mind to become pure or your life to magically to change. Without a pure mind, the truth will not incarnate in you, and without a pure mind, your life will be a mess. We need to take stock, drop the *adharmic* activities and take up activities that uplift and harmonize the mind. It is not easy, because the ego uses its habits to manage *rajas* and *tamas*. Taking away the habit exposes the ego to an energy that is trying to eliminate it – to which it does not take kindly. It will kick, scream and fight the new intentions tooth and nail.

It's Simple - End Adharmic (Self-Insulting) Habits

It may be simple, but it is not easy. The ego is extremely attached to things that are not good for it and will come up with a million excuses for why it cannot let go. Self-indulgence has become normal. Observe the mind and the conversation that takes place in it when you try to clean up your act. It is predictable, even funny if you can see the humour! If you know very well what is not good for you and you go ahead and do it anyhow, you deserve to suffer, because you are going against *dharma*. As we all know, the definition of insanity is doing the same thing repeatedly in expectation of a different result. This is how the Field teaches us. If you are going to grow, you must face the music and "bite the bullet." As James always says, "Man up and pack it in!" However, we must take responsibility for "our" projections, even though ultimately they do not belong to us. When we fully own our projections, the mind is resolved. Response to life according to *dharma* is then natural and effortless. It does not require nail-biting, mind-bending self-discipline. You are a disciple of the Self because you have broken the back of the binding *vasanas*. They become like burnt ropes with no power to bind.

Sattva Means Self-Knowledge Is the Interpreter

Many practices such as *yoga*, *tantra*, meditation and "sitting in the silence" claim that doing what they prescribe or "doing nothing" will get you "there." Where is "there"? Vedanta says freedom from limitation cannot be found in doing anything or going anywhere, because the doer who wants to transcend is the problem. There is still a doer/meditator attached to or seeking an experience, *sattva*. Experience is an object known to me, the Self, and that includes a *sattvic* mind. But as the individual, I cannot deny experience or try to "transcend" it if I want peace of mind. I must work with it creatively using *guna*-knowledge, not my beliefs and opinions born of mindless desires and unexamined fears. When the vision of non-duality is firm and my mind is pure, I process experience as it happens — in "real" time as the saying goes. Things come up and I respond appropriately, without any *karmic* "drag." I see the big picture and see where I fit into it — I lay my everyday happenings to rest, which leaves space for "old stuff" to come forth and offer itself into the fire of Self-knowledge.

If your subtle body is predominately *rajasic* and *tamasic*, it is virtually impossible to gain Self-knowledge. If you do, it will be a frustrating flash of insight that disappears as fast as it arrives. Even if you are predominantly *sattvic*, you will not necessarily gain Self-knowledge, but you will be able to develop the qualifications, assuming a burning desire for freedom. If we are predominately *sattvic*, we will easily assimilate the teachings of Vedanta. If not, not. There is no escape from the necessity of addressing our experience.

Summary: Typical Symptoms *of* Sattva

The Upside
INTELLIGENCE, CLARITY AND INSPIRATION

Sattva is a beacon of pure intelligence, a mind where all "the lights are on." When the mind's innate intelligence is fully functional, the mind is inspired. Such a mind is not only capable of facing what life brings its way, but it is also capable of clear, concise, calm and dispassionate thinking unclouded by dullness (*tamas*) or strung out by extroversion (*rajas*). It sails through both the small challenges of life as well as the big tests; it is capable of greatness. When the mind is *sattvic*, it is a clear instrument for the Field, and brings forth great works in all fields: art, science, literature, business and medicine. When things effortlessly and successfully turn out, *sattva* is the *guna* responsible "behind the scenes."

ASSIMILATION AND INTERPRETATION OF KNOWLEDGE

Without the correct balance of *rajasic* and *tamasic* tendencies with *sattva*, it is impossible to properly assimilate experience or the teachings on non-duality, and we will interpret experience through projection or denial, *rajas* or *tamas*, usually both. As mentioned, there is no escape from the necessity of addressing our experience. If the unconscious (causal body) is dominated by *rajas*, the Self appears as dynamic energy, not radiant light. If the causal body is dominated by *tamas*, the mind will have no idea of the Self whatsoever. In either case, Self-knowledge will not obtain, and neither will peace of mind. If the mind is predominantly *sattvic*, we might not gain Self-knowledge, but we can develop the qualifications for it, assuming liberation is of paramount importance to us. The conclusion here is obvious: if we want to experience the Self as it is, we must cultivate a *sattvic* mind.

NO-MOVEMENT

Sattva can be called the experience of "no-movement" because a steady and clear mind reveals the Self as unchanging Consciousness. We can see inaction in action and action in inaction, which translated means that we know that the changes taking place in and around us are only apparent changes, not actual changes. As the Self, we are unchanging; only the body-mind goes through changes. When the subtle body is *sattvic*, we are free to act or not. We are not compelled to act (*rajasic*), because we are not pushed around by the *gunas* or our *vasanas*. We are also not too lazy (*tamasic*) to act.

PEACE AND HAPPINESS

A *sattvic* mind is at peace with itself, the world and everyone in it, regardless of what is going on around it, characterized by love, intelligence, knowledge, peace, pleasure, bliss, etc.

SELF-REFERENCED, SELF-SATISFIED AND SELF-VALIDATING

Sattvic minds are self-referenced, self-validating and self-satisfied, know they are whole and complete, and lack nothing. They do not need others to confirm their self-worth, because their self-esteem is real (always present and unshakeable) and not dependent on the opinions of others. A *sattvic* person is not trying to become a perfect or better person, because both good and not-so-good people suffer a sense of limitation and crave freedom. He or she is trying to realize (or already has realized) his or her primary identity, the ever-free Self, the non-experiencing witness of the person – and lives accordingly.

KIND AND LOVING

A *sattvic* mind accepts others unconditionally; it is compassionately honest and kind. It does not find fault with others and does not judge or blame. It knows its own essence to be love and sees love in everything around it. Because love is unchanging Consciousness (*anantum*), love cannot really grow, because it is always present and always full. Nevertheless, it grows in a *sattvic* mind as practise removes *rajas* and *tamas*. As *sattva* develops, the mind feels more loving towards itself and life. The more this mind gives love, the more love grows. When the mind loves, *rajas* and *tamas* have no reason for being. Everything always works out for a loving mind – life responds in kind because love is its own reward.

BEING LOVED

As much as development of the skill to love is necessary for peace of mind, so is development of the openness to being loved. A *sattvic* mind accepts love in whatever form, and sees it as a reflection of itself giving back to itself; it never withholds, blocks, denies or measures love.

PAYING ATTENTION

With a *sattvic* mind, I pay attention to life and especially to the people and situations in my environment. I am not invested in my thoughts and feelings above those of others and I pay attention to what others really need, and give it unconditionally and without complaint. We do not love what we not pay attention to or ignore.

BEING OF SERVICE

A *sattvic* mind is uncomplainingly of service to its environment and does not act for reward, acknowledgment or thanks. Its service is service to its own Divine Self, not the mindless servitude of *tamas* that allows others to use or manipulate for their own ends. If others do not respond in kind, it does not matter, because a *sattvic* mind loves itself enough to avoid abuse and is not looking for reward. This is not because it sees the abuser as wrong, but because allowing this kind of behaviour serves neither the abuser nor itself. Abusers are not wrong, as they are also the Self. They are wrong to violate the principle of non-injury. To allow an abuser to continue abuse causes injury to the abused and the abuser. A *sattvic* mind will never enable other minds to injure themselves in any way. There is never a good reason to take abuse from anyone.

GRATITUDE

Gratitude is such a beautiful emotion, the most beautiful in fact. It is the same as the feeling of love. The ability to be grateful is a gift the Field gives us because Consciousness is unchanged by the presence or absence of gratitude. However, the Field of Existence changes – and as we are part of the Field, the ability to be grateful deeply changes us. It brings to our attention the abundance of life. When the abundance of life becomes our focus, abundance grows. The more gratitude we have, the more we have for which to be grateful. And it is the best attitude to have towards everything. Privilege without gratitude is entitlement, which robs us of authenticity, self-worth and a sense of belonging. Gratitude is always a far more reasonable approach to life than presumption, and it is what separates privilege from entitlement, and thereby eliminates shame. Gratitude counts when things are not going your way, not only when circumstances are conducive to gratitude.

A *sattvic* mind lives in gratitude because it sees life as a great gift from the Field. It consecrates all its actions with an attitude of love and gratitude to the Field of Existence. It does not need to dig up a feeling of gratitude or remind itself "to be grateful." Gratitude is always present when *sattva* is present (and not when it is *rajasic* and *tamasic*), even if it is not feeling well or life is not delivering what it wants. This is because a *sattvic* mind knows that life is not about indulgence of the likes and dislikes of the wanting person, but it is about appreciation of the Self, the one who does not want anything other than what it is.

KARMA YOGA

A *sattvic* mind acts with the *karma yoga* attitude without fail, as a matter of course because it understands that *karma yoga* is knowledge in practise. A *sattvic* mind knows that the Field of Existence belongs to the Field, the giver and controller of all results. It will do the appropriate actions to gain the desired result, but it will be unattached to getting the result it wants. It knows that whatever result it gets is what it needs.

GENEROSITY AND CHARITY

A *sattvic* mind does not feel lack, and shares what it has freely as the need arises. It does not hold on, hoard or fear that its needs are not met, and gives with a glad heart because faith in the Field's abundance is unshakeable. A *sattvic* mind knows that life is a gift that requires reciprocation. It is its duty to give what it can to those in need, be this money, food, time or attention.

SILENCE AND BEAUTY

A *sattvic* mind loves silence and beauty, but it sees beauty and hears silence everywhere, even when things are neither silent nor beautiful – because it is the source of silence and the beauty that makes beauty beautiful.

PURITY

A *sattvic* mind is pure, not self-righteous nor necessarily "holy." It is whole because it is in balance with *rajas* and *tamas*. Although a pure mind is good and kind and often manifests palpable, observable goodness and kindness, purity is not necessarily obvious. There is no formula for what constitutes purity other than peace of mind. A pure mind is not always discernible from the "outside"; *sattvic* minds come from all walks of life, in many shapes, flavours and sizes. They may not even be overtly spiritual or "nice."

SECURITY AND SELF-CONFIDENCE

When *sattva* is operating without obstruction from *rajas* and *tamas*, the mind radiates self-confidence, discrimination, calm, balance and security. Self-confident people are attractive to themselves and others because self-confidence is almost irresistible. Without it, to accomplish anything in the world is difficult. A self-confident person can influence unconfident minds, for better or worse. It creates the mystique that people in power emanate. Genuinely *sattvic* minds never abuse self-confidence or try to prove it. They have no need for outside validation.

THE VALUE OF VALUES

If I have a *sattvic* mind, I will have an unshakeable value for values in harmony with my true nature (*svadharma*) and those that serve the Field of Existence. I will not deviate from these values. I will always fund my life from them because the underlying value is feeling comfortable with myself. If I understand this and appreciate the fact that there is an upside and a downside to every action, I can inquire directly into the Self because the joy that comes from the fulfilment of any value, personal or universal, comes from it.

Sattvic Values I Uphold
NON-INJURY

Primarily, a *sattvic* mind values non-injury in thought, word and deed, but not because it believes that it must conform to a particular ideal or become a perfect person. A *sattvic* mind values non-injury, the number-one value, because it values peace of mind. Therefore it follows its own as well as universal *dharma* without fail. I have a value for non-injury because I do not want to be hurt. It is the same for all living beings. Non-injury is a nuanced value difficult to apply, owing to the apparent nature of the world in which we live. Three categories of injury prevail: actions, words and thoughts. The most obvious expression of an injurious action is physical violence. However, our sensitivity to violence of any kind needs to extend to include careful consideration of the effects of our words on others and the effects of harmful thoughts on our own minds. You may think that your bad feelings are justified by the *adharmic* behaviour of others, but they do not punish the offender or make the situation right; they only serve to hurt your own mind.

ACCOMMODATION, LIKES AND DISLIKES

With a *sattvic* mind, I have a willingness to forgo my likes and dislikes. I want what I have always, even if my likes and dislikes are unmet. I trust the Field to give me the results I need, and accordingly to my environment, and respond appropriately to life, in trust that everything is always perfect the way it is. To develop this important quality, I should learn to appreciate variety, cultivate an attitude of diversity and constantly monitor my mind for a sense of dissatisfaction. If dissatisfaction arises, I reduce my expectations. It is helpful to see myself and everyone else as helpless fools or inert objects. I have good relationships with inert objects because I expect nothing of such things. I suffer fools gladly because I know they cannot be otherwise.

The key to accommodation is that I respond to and identify with the person, not to their actions, because I understand that the person is the Self temporarily bewitched by *Maya*. I do my best to remember that the Field is behind angry outbursts, fits of jealousy or a domineering action. I appreciate the fact that the people involved have no control, and that I have even less. With this kind of understanding, it is easy to be accommodative – and to maintain *sattva*. To accept any type of person or situation cheerfully and calmly (not with resigned indifference, please note) is to be accommodating. It is clear that, owing to the law of *karma*, things cannot be different from the way they are.

A person's behaviour is a consequence of conditioning and is not subject to willpower. When *sattva* dominates the mind, it is clear to me that people incarnate to work out their *karma*, not to please me. Situations are the result of all the factors in the Dharma Field and are beyond the control of individuals, and it is foolish to like or dislike them. All successful relationships depend on one's ability to accommodate to others. Similarly, I cannot be different from what I am, and my situation is the result of my *karma*, so I cheerfully accommodate my apparent self; I do not desire it to be different or struggle to change its circumstances.

HONESTY

Alignment of thought, word and deed is straightforward. Saying one thing and doing another or doing something and saying something else is not conducive to peace of mind and inquiry.

Straightforwardness not only includes truthful speech but carefulness and kindness in speech, thought and actions. Non-alignment fragments the mind, and subjects us to a restless mind disturbed by conflict. Honesty without compassion constitutes a kind of violence, a subtle hostility under the banner of virtue. It also results in unwanted blowback and injury.

RESPECT FOR SELF AND OTHERS

A *sattvic* mind has an unerring appreciation for the feelings of others as well as its own. It knows that while feelings are transitory and reflect only a relative, subjective truth – they are not The Truth. All the same, for emotional coherence and self-respect, *sattva* acknowledges the feelings that present in the mind factually and without self-indulgence. To demand respect from others invites many disturbances in the mind, because the one who asks for respect is not in control of the result. If I take time to analyze the factors involved, I will clearly see that the demand respect from others cannot bring comfort or satisfaction, even if I am a highly accomplished person.

APPRECIATION OF TIME

Because the objects on which we depend for happiness are obviously subject to time, to make *samsara* work for the sake of peace, *sattvic* minds respect time even though they know it isn't real. If I am wilfully ignorant of this obvious fact, it prevents inquiry, because it keeps me tied to objects, and my life will be a mess.

HUMILITY

Humility is the firm knowledge that no one is greater or lesser than anyone else. It is the knowing that everything and everyone is connected in the "Sacred Hoop" of life as the Native Americans beautifully describe the Self; self-aggrandizement is never an option if there is only the Self. This produces a lack of egoism or feeling "better" than anyone else.

LACK OF PRIDE, PRETENSION OR AFFECTATION

Pride arises from real accomplishments or abilities, but pretension is self-glorification without a cause. I want to give a certain impression, so I pretend to be something I am not. With a *sattvic* mind, however, I know that all tendencies, talents, skills, gifts and abilities sprouted from the Field by no will of their own. I can utilize them, but cannot claim authorship of them, because all achievements depend on opportunities provided by life itself, even if I worked "hard" to master them. In my early thirties, I "discovered" I could sculpt anything I could see. As I previously had no interest in or known talent for sculpture, it really was a mystery to me (and those around me) how this talent suddenly appeared. How could I possibly lay claim to it? Even if I had studied for years to develop this skill, how could the ego have given it to me if the ego is not real? If I want to maintain peace of mind, I appreciate whatever talents and skills I have and make use of them (or not) without fanfare. Even if unnoticed or unappreciated by others, "my" talents speak for themselves and do not concern me. A flower in a vacant lot in a slum blooms unnoticed for no other reason than its nature is to bloom. Pride has ceased to be important when *sattva* reveals it is a false value that does not work.

NO OWNERSHIP

A *sattvic* mind, never deluded by the belief in ownership, knows it did not create anything and everything belongs to the Field. It therefore has an absence of overbearing, clinging attachment to loved ones or objects.

SAMENESS OF MIND IN ALL CIRCUMSTANCES

No matter what is going on inside or the outside world of a *sattvic* mind, an overarching sameness of mind informs all its responses.

CHASTITY

A *sattvic* mind has a respectful attitude towards the opposite sex, which does not denote a lack of physical intimacy. Sexual activity is entered with love, not lust.

UNIVERSAL NON-DUAL DEVOTION TO GOD

Devotion is natural to a *sattvic* mind in whatever way it perceives the Creator and is naturally devoted to the Field of Existence because it sees it as the Self manifest in form. It does not need elaborate rituals to demonstrate devotion – although it often practises ceremonial prayers (*puja*), like lighting incense or a candle, seeing the flame as a symbol of the eternal flame of Consciousness, the Self. For secular humanists, devotion often takes the form of a walk in nature, sitting in silence or meditation.

SOLITUDE

If my mind is *sattvic* and centred on the Self, I will love solitude, and the craving for company or "the other" does not arise.

DELIBERATION AND RESTRAINT OF THE SENSES

Sattva always acts with discrimination, deliberation and restraint of the senses.

RESOLUTION AND COMPLETION

Sattva does its utmost to finish what it starts, and gives of its best while doing so. To correct the inclination to initiate projects impulsively, I value caution and deliberately think things through, and carefully consider the upside and the downside before I jump in with both feet. Once committed, I work patiently to complete the task at hand.

CONSTANT PRACTISE OF SELF-KNOWLEDGE

Self-knowledge translates fully into all areas of my life.

SERVICE TO THE TEACHER

Service is a state of mind that does not require physical action, only the willingness to act. A qualified teacher is a stand-in for the Self and serves by providing an object of meditation for the student. If the teacher is established in the Self as the Self and has worked out all his or her personal issues, the opportunity to serve such a teacher is the greatest blessing.

CLEANLINESS

The value of external cleanliness and orderliness is obvious, as far as it makes life pleasant and brings about attentiveness of mind. What is less obvious is cleanliness in thought, word and deed: all *sattvic* qualities.

STEADINESS AND RELIABILITY

Sattvic people have constancy and perseverance, but this does not mean that they must be consistent. The only way they are always consistent is that they always follow *dharma* and non-injury to self and others in thought, word and deed.

LACK OF "EMOTIONALITY" AND DISPASSION

Sattvic minds have no emotional hooks. They are not reactive to emotional triggers (whether positive or negative), because they are dispassionate. They are not cold or unfeeling, although they may sometimes appear to be aloof and uncaring, but this is not the case. They are unattached to results and not influenced by what others think of them, good or bad. They honour their feelings and those of others, and they feel deeply, but are not overemotional or sentimental. *Sattvic* minds are aware of all thoughts and feelings that appear and know that most feelings are not reliable as a means of knowledge. They enjoy objects for what they are and are fully aware of all their inherent defects. *Sattva* is indifferent to results, not attached to them. Dispassion also extends to its likes and dislikes and to the sense organs.

RENUNCIATION AND AUSTERITY

Sattva values a simple, uncomplicated life without gratuitous desires for objects or experiences. Not cursed with the constant need for more, better, different, it happily renounces experience. Renunciation is undertaken in the spirit of fullness, not as a means to achieve a spiritual advantage or points.

DHARMIC DESIRES AND APPROPRIATE ACTION

Although desires still arise in a predominantly *sattvic* mind, they are not gratuitous desires and are in harmony with *dharma*. As a *sattvic* mind has *sattvic* values, consequently the conscious and unconscious thoughts that arise in the mind are all of service to the person. It will always know the *dharmic* action to take in every situation. Such a mind owns all projections instantly, cleans up whatever *karma* arises and does not create new *karma* or leave anything unfinished or unresolved. It does not expect anyone to pick up the slack or shortfall for its own activities and takes responsibility for itself, in trust that the Field of Existence takes care of all needs.

SELF-ENTERTAINED

A *sattvic* mind does not need to be entertained and finds entertainment naturally and without effort.

NO EXPECTATIONS OR PROJECTIONS

Sattva does not project expectations of any kind onto others; if projection does happen, it instantly recognizes it, owns it and dissolves it in Self-knowledge.

The Downside of *Sattva*

As we have said, all three *gunas* have a downside, and all are always present in greater or lesser degrees. All three *gunas* are necessary to maintain balance. Imbalance means a *guna's* negative qualities predominate in the mind – and the other two *gunas* are less dominant. *Sattva* has a negative side, and *rajas* and *tamas* have positive sides. When the negative aspects of *sattva* manifest, *rajas* and *tamas* contaminate the mind and obscure *sattva*. *Rajas* and *tamas* act as limiting adjuncts, apparently contaminate *sattva* and cause impure emotions. For instance, when the negative side of *sattva* manifests, I often think I am superior to others and project (*rajas*) my ideas of how I believe they "should" behave.

SPIRITUAL EGOS

There are no experiential qualifications for enlightenment, only the right *guna* balance. Non-dual, mind-blowing epiphanies such as *samadhis, satoris* and *nirvanas* can be as much a hindrance as a help. If the mind is predominately *sattvic*, it assimilates information carefully and quickly, and lays experiences to rest. If you have a consistent issue in your life, be it love, food, recognition or power, it means you have an assimilation problem and your mind will be unfit for inquiry. Unprocessed experience can stay with you your whole life long.

The more pure your mind becomes, the greater is the danger that you will develop a spiritual ego. The ego is that part of the subtle body that owns actions and the results. It associates with the sublime feeling of *sattva* and says, "I am pure. I am holy. I am spiritual." The ego can co-opt Self-knowledge, tend to identify with it and claim it. We call this "enlightenment sickness." Unfortunately, the doer can survive *moksa*, as most of us still have "*jiva* stuff," the remnants of psychological and emotional issues to resolve, even "after" Self-realization, hence Self-actualization, which is when the doer, all *adharmic* desire and all fear has been permanently rendered non-binding, can take a good deal longer to obtain.

TRYING TO PERFECT THE PERSON

A *sattvic* mind/ego can become extremely vain and obnoxious in an obsequiously loving way. The intention to practise discrimination is not to improve you or make you pure. The fact is you are already accomplished Consciousness and as pure as the driven snow. A pure mind, a pure heart is not the goal. It is only a means to an end, and provides the field in which Vedanta can establish the vision of non-duality. The vision of non-duality destroys the ego's sense of ownership and establishes Self-knowledge as the doer. There is no purifier like Self-knowledge.

Trying to perfect the person is always a problem, because the world does not necessarily conform to ideals of perfection. Existence is Consciousness, and Consciousness is value-neutral – but a mind under the spell of the *gunas* is not value-neutral. *Sattva* causes the individual to interpret reality in terms of "higher" or "spiritual" values, like goodness, truth or beauty, for example. However, the Field's Creation is not all sweetness and light. It contains everything in equal measure from pure goodness to unrepentant evil, from sublime beauty to wretched ugliness.

ATTACHMENT TO KNOWLEDGE, PLEASURE AND HAPPINESS

Although *sattva* is a necessary stepping stone to Self-realization, it binds through attachment to knowledge, pleasure and happiness. When the mind is *sattvic*, you feel good. When you feel good, there is a strong tendency to identify with the feeling. There is only one "I" which does not feel good or bad. When the "I" is apparently ignorant of its nature, it thinks it is an enjoyer. The pleasure that this "I" feels is always associated with an object, and objects are experienced in the mind, so when *rajas* or *tamas* take over, the pleasure disappears. By identifying with happiness, you are asking for unhappiness. Because *sattva* is responsible for knowledge, and because knowledge is necessary for survival, attachment to what you know (or do not know) is common. As we know, Consciousness is not a knower. It illumines the knower, knowledge and the objects of knowledge – and it illumines the absence of knowledge. Therefore attachment to *sattva*, not *sattva* itself, stands in the way of Self-knowledge.

THE GOLDEN CAGE OF SATTVA – SATTVA GENERATES SUBLIME EMOTIONS

Self-realization, *sattva*, generates sublime emotions, i.e. *bhakti*, or devotion, which makes us attractive to others and to ourselves, a common trap for spiritual people. If I believe I am enlightened, I feel good, which is definitely preferable to the time when my happiness depended on the intermittent, unpredictable and impermanent happiness of the *jiva*. I enhance my self-esteem by the "I am Consciousness" practice. The downside is that this can inflate the ego, which imagines it is superior to everyone, even the *guru!*

Experiential bliss and the belief that you are quite special is what we call stuck in the "golden cage of *sattva*." Many spiritual seekers' teachers wrongly identify with the feeling of *sattva* and believe that without it they (and nobody else) qualifies as being "spiritual" or "enlightened." This kind of mind is very quick to judge other minds that do not conform to whatever ideal held to be true (*tamas*) or project their fantasy of how a spiritual person "should" look or act (*rajas*). Because *sat*, Consciousness (of which *sattva* is the subtlest manifestation), is actually the true nature of the mind, it is not a quality of which we can really gain more. When the downside of *sattva* manifests, and *rajas* and *tamas* obscure *sattva*, it seems like we can become "more *sattvic*." In fact it is with the removal of *rajas* and *tamas* that the predominance of *sattva* is reinstated. *Sattva*, like all things in the apparent reality, is an object known to Consciousness – a state of mind that is purely experiential and therefore does not last. It certainly will not free the person from dependence on objects or end the subtle existential suffering that comes with it.

ANANTUM AND ANANDA

The problem of getting addicted to bliss arises with the misapprehension of what *moksa* really is, as well as the different meanings of the word "bliss." There are two kinds of bliss: *ananda*, or experiential bliss; and *anantum*, which is the bliss of the Self. The bliss of the Self – that which is always present, unlimited and unchanging – is not an experience, because it is your true nature, *anantum*. Consciousness is present whether *ananda* is present or not. The bliss of Self-knowledge (*anantum*), however, can be experienced as a feeling, such as the bliss of deep sleep, which is inferred when you wake up; or as *parabhakti*, when love is known to be you, your true nature, meaning Consciousness, the Self.

SPIRITUAL IDENTITY, ATTACHMENT TO PURITY, SPIRITUAL ARROGANCE

This kind of mind builds a "spiritual" identity that makes it feel less small and afraid – because the drive behind being "spiritual" is fear, *rajas* and *tamas*. Being "spiritual" becomes a lifestyle, a subterfuge, a self-deception or façade for an ego that feels inadequate, less-than, powerless (all *tamas*). *Sattva* out of balance produces spiritual arrogance (*rajas*), thinking one is special because one is more "pure" or virtuous than others. It produces a false sense of importance and often causes the belief that one is duty-bound (or has special powers) to teach or to "save" less fortunate "others." The façade here is the need for recognition and power (*rajas*) under the guise of "teacher/saviour" (*tamas*). The number of so-called spiritual teachers that have used this trick to gain power over others is "as old as time."

If Self-knowledge removes ignorance from the mind, using the logic of our own experience as revealed by Vedanta we discover that our true nature as Consciousness is whole and complete, non-dual, partless, unchanging and limitless. Purity and impurity are still experienced in the mind when we know we are Consciousness, but the aim of Self-inquiry is to produce a *sattvic* mind, as that is what makes life for the *jiva* free of suffering. However, a *sattvic* mind is still an object known to you, Consciousness – so identification with *sattva* still produces suffering, because it causes the *jiva* to project purity and holiness as an identity.

Renouncing the World

Many spiritual seekers embark on Self-inquiry to cope with their unresolved psychological issues or as a balm to salve emotional wounds. Often they have the vanity to think they are pure and holy because of a transcendental spiritual experience or they believe they have more knowledge because epiphanies or revelations have occurred to them. This is another common trap in the spiritual world. Many deluded spiritual seekers believe they are superior because they have walked away from their "worldly" lives, but their "renunciation" is escapism; they swap worldly materialism for spiritual materialism. A typical sign of the downside of *sattva* is the idea that the world is a "bad" place, and negation of the objects to maintain peace of mind requires renunciation of the world and everything in it. What is unconscious in this attitude is the idea that there is something wrong with the person, which is then projected onto the world (*rajas* and *tamas* working together). The truth that there is nothing wrong with the world or the person, because neither is real, therefore there is no need to renounce anything.

This attitude is usually an attempt to "dodge the bullet" of the consequences of one's unresolved psychological issues or *karma* in the world. The underlying problem is always unresolved unconscious conditioning, which causes a blockage in the mind. It arises from fear of the hurt, anger or pain that underpins the buried blockages. As with everything in the apparent reality, this can only be dissolved through *nididhyasana* – deep and fearless reflection, assimilation and resolution of one's emotional identity through Self-knowledge. Until it is resolved, there will be an attempt to impose *satya* onto *mithya*, which never works. Knowing the difference between *satya* (what is real – Consciousness) and *mithya* (what is only apparently real – all objects) spells freedom for and from the person. This involves the ability to discriminate between Consciousness and the objects that arise in Consciousness on a moment-to-moment to basis. When unconscious psychological content has not been resolved, the mind is stuck and the ego tries to "whitewash" what it does not want to see through assumption of the position that, as none of it is real, it does not touch the person, which is true – but for permanent peace to obtain in the mind, all the content of the mind must be resolved completely in Self-knowledge – or freedom is not that free.

ABUSE OF POWER

Sattva produces self-confidence, which is a powerful aphrodisiac for minds looking for love, recognition, validation or self-esteem through influence or control of others. Self-confident people are the most charming and influential people on the planet; this gives them the power to manipulate and get what they want. This is born out in many leaders from time immemorial, whether political, spiritual or business titans, who have used this power for good or bad. This kind of "self-confidence" usually masks a small and weak ego desperate for recognition. We can trot out dear Donald Trump here again because he is such a great example of everything that is bad about *rajas* and *tamas!* It is not hard to find other examples – from Genghis Khan to Stalin and Hitler; their number is great and their infamous deeds are legion.

SATTVA AND ENLIGHTENMENT SICKNESS

Some people with very *sattvic* minds exposed to Vedanta get fanatical about getting it "right" in the belief that they need to "study" Vedanta. They often get lost in the dream of enlightenment, and believe they are not lost. What they do not see or ask themselves is who it is that thinks they are enlightened and improves by "perfecting" the knowledge. When James recently told a student he had taught for years things that he did not like to hear about the *jiva*, he quit communicating with him, although he remained intensely involved "studying" Vedanta and Sanskrit, believes he is already enlightened, which of course he is – and is not. The ego is identified with the knowledge and has not resolved all its conditioning, i.e. rendered the binding *vasanas* non-binding and negated the doer. I coached a young man who had strong teaching ambitions, and although his dominant *guna* was *rajas*, he had a *sattvic* mind and understood the logic of Vedanta perfectly, so we gave him a chance to teach. He was a very good teacher, but he made me promise that if he ever showed any sign of enlightenment sickness, I was to point it out ruthlessly. When some signs of ego identification with the knowledge did show up and I pointed it out, he ended his relationship with us. This has happened with numerous people taught by James or me over the years; another young man James taught for years and attained *moksa* through him suffered the same fate, and still clings to his "rightness" to this day. The ego identifies with *sattva* and thinks it is enlightened. More purification is necessary, as *rajas* and *tamas* still cloud the mind.

THE GURU AMBITION

The best way to recognize if you have enlightenment sickness is a strong ambition to be the "*guru*" or a tendency to *guru* people who don't ask for teaching. Knowing you are Consciousness is an improvement on the identification with the person, but it is just the first stage of *moksa*. If you think it is the final stage, you will have problems, because of the seduction by identification with *sattva* before Self-actualization has taken place. One of the most common traps in the spiritual supermarket that most seekers fall prey to is the need for others to think that they are "spiritual." Most of the modern Neo-Advaita *gurus* fall into this category. They prematurely claim enlightenment and rush out to "enlighten" the world. "I am enlightened" does not mean "*only* I am enlightened" or "I am more enlightened than others." There is only one Consciousness, so how can anyone other than the ego claim to be superior or "special"?

Sattva and Hubris Masked as Humility

There is an untold number of *gurus* who promote the idea that enlightenment is something you must work to gain (and of course only very few ever do achieve it) and their enlightenment is "special." Everybody else ranks somewhere below them. The *jiva's* vanity and duality is hard to miss, yet it is amazing how many fail to see this. Another perverse downside of *sattva* manifests as the kind of enlightenment sickness that claims it is "nobody." This kind of ego becomes "anti-*guru*" which is not afraid to expose the ignorance of others. This kind of enlightenment sickness is a kind of passive aggression, and in place of the claim to enlightenment claims humility as a front for an inflated ego. Typically, this kind of mind says, "I know nothing. I am just a normal person." Of course the implied meaning of the statement is that only an enlightened person could say that he was not enlightened!

If people ask James or me if we are enlightened, our reply is: "I am not enlightened, but I am not unenlightened either." This means that enlightenment is not the issue; it is not an event or something we have gained. Consciousness is the nature of the Self, and as the Self is eternal, it was never not Consciousness. Enlightenment has nothing to do with it. It is just an idea, an object that appears in Consciousness. So one needs to be mindful of who claims what — and why. The pitfalls of *sattva* are many and very subtle.

Sattva and Taking a Stand in Consciousness

Taking a stand in Consciousness sometimes turns out to be a little tricky, because the split mind watching itself has a slippery tendency to claim to be Consciousness. "Stand-taking" is done with the mind and can lead to a kind of self-hypnosis that makes the *jiva* think it is the Self without the full understanding of what it means to be the Self. Of course, based on logic alone (Is there an essential difference between a ray of the sun and the sun itself?), the *jiva* can claim its identity as the Self, but only when its knowledge of *satya* (what is real) and *mithya* (what is apparently real) is firm. It is one thing to say "I am the Self" as the Self, and quite another to say it as the *jiva* or ego. The Self's experience of itself is qualitatively different from the *jiva's* experience of the Self as an object or as objects.

One Cannot Hold Onto a Sattvic Mind

Because of the nature of the *gunas*, which make up and govern the creation of everything, the nature of the Field of Existence constantly changes. A peaceful (*sattvic*) mind is not something we can hold onto indefinitely. You need to gain the knowledge that you are always fine, no matter what is going on in the mind, even though you aim for peace of mind always. To make sure our life conforms to *dharma* in every way is of great importance if peace of mind is the main aim. A highly *rajasic* or *tamasic* life is not conducive to peace of mind, and will make Self-inquiry impossible or at best very difficult.

Living a *dharmic* life gives you an experienceable peaceful mind capable of inquiry. However, what *moksa* gives you is the bliss of Self-knowledge, which is very different from experiential bliss. When *moksa* has obtained in the mind, I may and usually do feel experiential bliss regularly, but I do not depend on it, because I know I *am* the bliss. In fact I could be sick, in pain and half-dead, broke, jobless or stuck in a situation I do not enjoy but cannot change, and feel blissful regardless of what is going on in the mind or around it. That is not to say that experiential bliss disappears when Self-knowledge is firm. It just does not matter whether the experience of bliss is present or not, because the bliss of Self-knowledge is always present and known to be my true nature, which keeps the mind steady, dispassionate and confident. At this stage, both ignorance and knowledge have become objects known to me, Consciousness. Self-knowledge has removed ignorance and becomes the default position in the mind. I do not have to think about the knowledge anymore; it is known to *be* me.

ADDICTION TO BEAUTY

Sattva out of balance often manifests as an addiction to beauty. *Rajas* contaminates *sattva,* and the mind develops a kind of hubris about its identification with external beauty, whether of the body or the environment. This kind of mind turns its nose up at anything that does not reach the mark of what it determines to be a proper reflection of itself and eschews anything or anyone that is not "beautiful." It projects its own lack of self-esteem onto the appearance of objects.

ATTACHMENT TO "GOODNESS"

Like attachment to purity, the mind attached to being "good" believes it must perfect itself and be "loving" towards all beings and all life. Because it lacks self-esteem and is not secure or aware of its innate nature as love and goodness, it tries in vain to feel good about itself by "being good" to others. These are the rescuers and "do-gooders" and fanatical vegan types who think they are quite superior to others for being so ethical, virtuous, kind, moral, humane and self-righteous.

Sattva, Spiritual Vasanas and Magical Thinking

Many spiritual seekers with strong spiritual *vasanas* are stuck in the belief that a *sattvic* mind is the end goal and not a means to an end. They resort to "magical" thinking or any number of practices and rituals in the belief that they can do something to gain or maintain a mythical "expanded" Consciousness. "Channelling" is a good example of this kind of deluded thinking. Another good example is the belief that something like so-called "Christ Consciousness," which is an "awakened" or "transcendental" state of mind, is achievable — by the minority. Without Self-knowledge, this will result in inevitable failure and disappointment. Consciousness is the most ordinary thing in existence, because it is all there is. It is not expandable, because everything expands or contracts in it; it is not directly experienceable, and enlightenment is not an experience, it is knowledge — so you cannot do anything to gain it, because you *are* it. No action taken by a limited entity can produce an unlimited result other than Self-inquiry, which is a "doing," but unlike all other doings leads to Self-knowledge, which is unlimited.

Sattva, Space Cadet Syndrome and Drugs

When *sattva* is out of balance, it may also produce the "space cadet" syndrome, a mind out of touch with its environment, ungrounded — a mind that is "zoned-out" – "gone with the fairies" as the saying goes. Many deluded seekers also make claims about the power of hallucinogenic substances to produce "spiritual" insights or a calm state of mind. What these people do not see/deny (*tamas*) is the negative effects and the distortions (the gap between the real and the apparently real widening) that occurs after long-term abuse of these substances.

The simple fact is that whatever outside means one resorts to for help to gain what one already has will in the end become an obstacle. There is no shortcut to (and no chemical solution or substitute for) Self-inquiry. If one is looking for peace of mind, it is a well-known fact that all drugs, whether used sparingly or repeatedly make the mind *tamasic* (dull). They seem to produce *sattva* (peace) if your mind is very *rajasic* (agitated or extroverted), but in reality, all mind-altering substances produce *tamas* masked as *sattva*.

The *tamas* slows down the mind and one experiences relief and temporary clarity, but it is not *sattva*. The best drugs can do for you is to give you some idea that reality is not how it appears to be to "normal" sense perception. This is often why drugs, just like any far-out so-called "spiritual" experience, become a trap, because one starts to believe that one must do something to achieve this "altered state" and then goes chasing after the experience (*rajas*). Alternatively, one believes one can only achieve this state with an outside means.

It is true that everyone reacts to drugs differently and if used recreationally and infrequently, it is no big deal – although Vedanta definitely does not encourage this behaviour. It is very dangerous, because of its tendency to build binding *vasanas*. Self-inquiry requires extreme honesty in all areas of life. Many drug-users hide behind the supposed "spiritual" insights to justify the use of drugs, when the real reasons they use drugs is to escape from subjective problems. This type of person is not interested in freedom and not interested in cleaning out the sewer of the subconscious mind. India is full of phoney *sadhus* who shout: *"Bom Shiva Shankara!"* and hoist their *chillums,* and it all looks very romantic and spiritual. However, they are just pleasure-seeking dropouts too lazy to do honest spiritual work (*rajas* and *tamas*). It is like the *tantric* people who want to have sex and cook up a spiritual reason for it.

Sattva and Insomnia

There is nothing as beneficial to the mind and conducive to peace as the bliss of sleep. There are many reasons for lack of sleep – apart from ill health or physical problems, there are two basic reasons:

1. When the mind is very *sattvic*, it is so blissful and inspired that it is very hard to find enough *tamas* for the mind to lock onto to sleep well.

2. When the mind is too extroverted (*rajasic*), it is too agitated to find enough *tamas* to sleep.

When too much *sattva* causes lack of sleep, it can be harder to modulate the mind to *tamas* than when the mind is too *rajasic*. The only solution is to surrender to the Field, find the *tamas*-thought and lock onto it, and let all other thoughts slide away. It takes practise, but it does eventually work.

How to Encourage and Manage Sattva
Rajas

If the mind is too *rajasic*, deliberately and consciously quiet the mind. If you walk too fast, work too fast, think too fast, SLOW

DOWN! If you rush around like a demon, and multitask, driven by the pressure of doership, JUST STOP! If you talk too fast or too much, SHUT UP! Listen to yourself and others without judgement and JUST OBSERVE! See how self-defeating it is to live this way – and destructive to you and those around you.

Take yourself away from the fray, from noisy, action-filled places and people. Find a silent place to sit on your own, preferably (but not necessarily) in nature. Go inwards and meditate if you can, focus on your breathing, read something inspiring and uplifting or just sit in silence, watch your thoughts without censure. Do some gentle exercise like *hatha yoga* or *tai chi*; go for a slow walk in nature if possible, but anywhere will do. The Self is everywhere – find the beauty that is not always obvious.

Light a candle and see it as the eternal light of the one Self – as you. Listen to beautiful *sattvic* music. Eat foods that calm and nourish. If you are wired and tired and can neither sleep nor relax, try eating something *tamasic* as a last resort. Avoid caffeine, alcohol, drugs and all stimulants. Watch a boring movie or a *sattvic* nature documentary. For those of us whose dominant *guna* is *rajas*, the challenge is always to maximize the positive aspects of *rajas* by bringing it into balance with *sattva*. We can never get rid of it, so we need to utilize it to our best advantage.

TAMAS

If your mind is too *tamasic* and *sattva* eludes it, making it incapable of thinking – force yourself to do something physical, like exercise, go for a walk, take a cool or cold shower, go for a swim, eat or drink something *rajasic* – any activity that gets the mind out from under the heavy cloud of dullness. For some, caffeine helps, but it has a price to pay, as it forms very strong *vasanas* and leads to more *tamas*, as do all stimulants. Excess *tamas* does not create the immediate *karma* that excess *rajas* does, but it destroys peace of mind, and eventually our lives just as surely. It just takes longer. With *rajas*, blowback and repentance come fast and furious. With *tamas*, blowback is usually slower, and we get to repent at leisure. But repent we do.

Tamas is often the result of excess *rajas*, but for some it is their dominant *guna*. In this case, the aim is not to remove *tamas* (because you cannot) but to bring it into balance with *sattva*. Some people are in love with "their" *tamas* and use it as an excuse to be lazy, to live in a mess or for their lives to be a mess. If this works for you, well and good. Being lazy is just what over-zealous *rajasic* types often need — however, if this tendency rules our lives, it is as binding a *vasana* as any other. It will keep us from enlightened lifestyles and from *moksa*.

Chapter 7

Rajas: *The* Projecting, Active Energy

As STATED PREVIOUSLY, all the *gunas* are always present and work together. On its own, pure *sattva* cannot create, although it is the blueprint for all forms. It cannot think or feel, although it is responsible for thinking and feeling in sentient beings. And *tamas*, the existence aspect of the Creation, cannot think or feel and has no power to create or cause anything to happen, at all. Something else is needed to bring these two energies together for the Creation to appear. That something else is *rajas*, the power of projection. *Rajas* is a complex energy and difficult to understand, harness and manage. To do so, we need to understand *sattva* and *tamas* and how the three energies work together.

Rajas (*vikshepa shakti*) is a power in Consciousness that projects the Creation into manifestation by transforming the substance, *tamas*, in accordance with its blueprint, *sattva*. Without *rajas*, the Creation would not exist in physical form. *Brahman*, or *Brahma*, the Self in the form of the Creator, represents *rajas*. Matter is value-neutral and created solely for the individual's experience so that as individuals we can work out our *karma*. If the individual came from pure *sattva*, it would be all-knowing like *Isvara*. If it came from pure *tamas*, it would be completely ignorant like a rock. All matter, whether subtle and sentient or gross and insentient, comes from all three *gunas*.

Rajas Is a Mixture of Ignorance and Knowledge

Rajas is a mixture of knowledge (*sattva*) and ignorance (*tamas*) called *avidya*, personal ignorance of our true nature. Therefore all individuals are a mixture of spirit and matter, which is why they are perpetually confused. And no one makes themselves this way, please note. It comes with the territory of being human, which is why we need Self-knowledge to remove ignorance. When *rajas* enters the equation, pure *sattva* mixed with *rajas* and *tamas* "becomes" the causal body – the repository of the individual's conditioning and what "causes" things to happen. Limitless Consciousness then appears as a limited entity under the spell of ignorance, *avidya*. It identifies with the subtle body (reflecting medium) and believes it is separate from itself, Consciousness.

The Self under the spell of ignorance, the individual, looks outwards into the ever-changing matrix of life instead of inwards at the ever-present, silent, unchanging Self. It feels insecure and is full of desire, so it performs actions to get results and chases objects to complete itself, and suffers. When the extroverted mind gets what it wants, anxiety is removed (for a while) and we feel good. So we chase more objects to get more results. It can be said that the individual is Consciousness plus *rajas*. *Rajas* is what brings the individual into manifestation, what "stirs the pot" and makes things interesting. Unsurprisingly, *rajas* is also the root cause of most of the individual's problems, because although the individual knows it exists and knows that it is conscious, it does not know it is limitless, whole and complete Consciousness. *Rajas* extroverts the mind, and because of this, the individual believes it is limited and incomplete. Duality is taken as a fact – and therein lies the problem.

The Upside and the Downside

Fortunately for us, like all the *gunas*, *rajas* has upsides as well as downsides. Without *rajas*, we cannot act to achieve anything and feel dull, stupid and lifeless because *tamas* clouds and dominates the mind. As mentioned, *rajas* and *tamas* are inseparable – in fact it could be said that they are really the two sides of one energy: *rajas-tamas*. And it bears repetition here that *rajas* and *tamas* are only a problem when they are out of balance with *sattva*. When they are in balance with *sattva*, their positive energies produce a peaceful, clear, steady, functional, quiet and efficient mind. We need all three energies to function optimally in the world, so not only is it futile to attempt to eradicate *rajas* and *tamas*, because all the *gunas* belong to *Isvara*, it would be to our detriment if we could do so.

Rajas Is the Mode of Doership

Rajas is the mode of doership. It is a dangerous energy because if you operate out of this *guna* for a while, activity itself becomes a goal. It makes us attached to the idea that we "should" be doing something all the time, and we feel guilty or agitated if we are not busy. Our identity becomes entangled with doing and achieving the results we want. It is the energy behind a driven, obsessive work ethic – working for work's sake. Sometimes the compulsive desire to act is so strong we perform unnecessary, even self-insulting, gratuitous actions, simply because deliberate action or inaction is impossible. We just cannot sit still for more than a few minutes, and start to fidget the moment action is constrained for whatever reason.

The rabbit in the children's story *Winnie-the-Pooh* is a good example. He is so rushed, in such a hurry and busy all the time that he doesn't know if he is coming or going. He can never appreciate anything, and as soon as he gets anywhere, he feels he must be somewhere else. He can never be still. The sign on his burrow, "GoN OUT BIZY BACK SooN," is a good way to describe a *rajasic* person! Animation films make a large profit on characters who typify this stereotype, from the rather aged *Road Runner* to the crazy squirrel in *Ice Age*, to mention just two. It seems that movie producers see the value in exploitation of this powerful energy. Highly *rajasic* types also tend to hate silence. They will have the TV, radio or some noise or music blaring in the background – anything to drown out the silence or to drown out the noise in their own minds.

Identification With Doing

Rajas in balance with *sattva* produces an efficient but relaxed doer – which is desirable to function well in the world. The problem comes with identification, not only with the doer, but with doing. The most common justification for the state of constant activity is identification with the active, purposeful doer, the one "who gets things done," the efficient one, the survivor. Highly *rajasic* individuals pride themselves on their "doings" and believe that their activities are responsible for their identity and survival – and therefore they believe they are responsible for results. They quickly take the credit when things work out and just as quickly project blame when they do not.

The fact that nobody is in control of results is lost on them. So is the emptiness of a work-related identity, not to mention the fact that if they were not surviving, they would be unable to perform any activity. Highly *rajasic* individuals are like the proverbial hamster on a treadmill, who believe they are achieving their goals, but in reality going nowhere fast and often achieve very little. This is not to say that action is "bad" as far as liberation is concerned. We do need to take appropriate action to achieve our goals and, if we don't, success in any endeavour will not happen. But excess *rajas* militates against success, as far as success depends on the quality, appropriateness and timeliness of your actions – not to mention a clear, *sattvic* mind. When the mind is extremely *rajasic*, its actions are (more often than not) inappropriate and untimely. And it is frenetic, frantic, anxiety-ridden about results.

When our mind is agitated, we are impatient and do not act deliberately and skilfully. Action becomes unconscious. Excess *rajas* makes us careless. We forget things, drop things, have silly accidents, like cutting our fingers or burning ourselves in the kitchen because we do everything too quickly. We put things in places without being aware of what we are doing and blame others when we cannot find them. *Rajas* is behind most serious accidents of every kind; driving too fast or recklessly are good examples. The death toll on our roads is always caused by either excess *rajas* – impatience and aggression – or *tamas*, its opposite energy, dullness and inattention – usually both working together. *Rajas* is also behind much violence, domestic and otherwise, as well as greed-based crime and corruption.

Doership and a Busy Mind

We have often heard the saying "An idle mind is the Devil's workshop." This may be true. But as true is "A busy mind is the Devil's workshop" unless the "busyness" is balanced by *sattva* or the mind is busy inquiring, assuming your ultimate goal is liberation. When driven to busyness, we suffer because we cannot relax and often have trouble sleeping. Insomnia is an epidemic in the U.S. because of *rajas*. In the sixties, being "uptight," or wound up, meant "stressed and unhappy." It is a good term, as it epitomizes victims of "doership." Doership is not about doing. From womb to tomb we are active. It is not up to us, because we cannot not "do" – even not doing is a doing. Doership is an identity issue, not an action issue. You think you are a doer because you have never examined the constituents of inaction involved in the doing of anything. Even without Self-inquiry, if we make a simple inquiry into how doing anything actually takes place, we soon realize that it is impossible to do anything without untold factors not in our control being part of the equation, even something simple like making a cup of tea.

Doing happens, no doubt, but you are not doing it, either as the individual or as the Self. The *gunas* are the doer. If you are *rajasic*, you evaluate yourself in terms of what you have accomplished or failed to accomplish or want to accomplish. This leads to a psychological problem: an inflated or deflated identity. You have an exaggerated sense of your self-importance when you get what you want, and feelings of failure, depression and loss of self-esteem when you do not.

Deluded Doers in Conflict With *Isvara*

Highly *rajasic* types find themselves in constant conflict with the world because they think their wants are more important than the wants of *Isvara* – in the form of the wants of others. Usually *rajasic* people think they are very clever because they accomplish so much. What they do not see is how much energy they waste spinning their wheels, nor the cost that frenetic activity has on them and everyone around them. Stress levels go sky-high, relationships and health suffer, we wear ourselves out – yet when *rajas* reigns, we are like a horse with blinkers on. We blindly and stubbornly do the same things over and over, expecting different results which never materialize. From a spiritual point of view, highly *rajasic* people are often not "the sharpest knives in the drawer" to use a common (and not very kind) phrase. They are so busy acting out their desires, and the mind is so extroverted, that they fail to evaluate the results of their actions dispassionately – if at all, which means that they make the same mistakes repeatedly. They tend to be stubborn and defensive, and vigorously cling to their doings and defend their wants, no matter what.

Doership and Language

We can also identify doership by observation of the way we talk, as well as our language. If you hear yourself saying you are "supposed to," "have to" or "must" do something, doership is alive and well. The truth is we are never compelled (or obligated) to do anything. We are free to see that we are not the doer – and we are free to say NO. Furthermore, we can consider life from the point of view of who we really are, as the Self. If we do, it will be clear that life is a dream that comes and goes, but you do not come and go, because you are the ground of being on which the coming and going (actions) take place.

Doership and the Flow

The feeling of "flow" is a situation where you are getting what you want. When *Isvara* does not deliver the desired result, stuckness, *tamas*, ensues. The feeling that life is flowing is obviously desirable for everyone, but it is particularly desirable for predominately *rajasic* individuals. *Rajas* is the mode of action, as it inclines one to activity. It is also the mode of passion. A *rajasic* person is goal-oriented and wants results badly because his or her happiness rides on results. If the doer is in control of *rajas*, it is not necessarily a problem, provided action is taken with the *karma yoga* attitude. However, because *Isvara* is in control of results and does not necessarily give you what you want when you want it the way you want it, *rajasic* people are by definition highly emotional and not inclined to *karma yoga*. Typically, they are high and happy when they get what they want, and angry and depressed when they do not.

If you know you are Consciousness, you are not concerned with being "in" or "out" of the flow of life, because your likes and dislikes are negated. There is no sense of doership – you know you *are* the flow. If, however, you don't know you are Consciousness and are identified with the doer-experiencer-enjoyer entity, then you would obviously want your life to flow according to your likes and dislikes. However, if we truly want our lives to flow, we benefit greatly from the knowledge of the *gunas* and how they play out in our lives and the world.

Rajas and the Assimilation of Experience

As previously stated, if *rajasic* tendencies dominate the causal body, the Self appears as dynamic energy, not radiant light. If Self-knowledge should appear, it will be as a flash and soon be gone. If the causal body is *tamasic*, I will have no idea of the Self whatsoever. If the subtle body is predominantly *sattvic*, it does not necessarily translate to liberation, but as the mind will be clear and peaceful, I cope with life without agitation or dullness if enough qualifications are present. I can experience the Self as it is. *Rajas* has a huge impact on the assimilation of experience. Whether our goals are worldly or spiritual, and whether we realize them or not, a *rajasic* intellect is not concerned with the truth of experience, only with how a particular experience relates to the fulfilment of the ego's desires. The fulfilment of desire is a *rajasic* mind's chief concern – and it will do whatever it takes to achieve its goal, not, as it believes, because it really wants the object of desire.

It is driven to gain the object/experience because desire is painful and the mind is desperate to get rid of it. Desire gnaws ceaselessly at the mind like a hungry rat. Excess *rajas* is always a source of frustration, because everything gained is inevitably lost. An object gained causes attachment, and an object lost produces grief, neither of which is conducive to happiness. *Rajas* cannot accept the impermanence of life as a fact and be satisfied with what is. It propels the ego to seek fulfilment continually in new experiences – new objects, places, people, etc. Even though the individual knows better, *rajas* can cause such lack of discrimination that we will consistently repeat actions that produce suffering. It often generates so many actions in such a short time that the intellect can never determine which action was responsible for a given result, and thus prevents it from learning from its experiences.

Rajas Always Produces *Tamas*

When a pleasurable experience ends, *rajas* produces disappointment (*tamas*), because it wants the pleasure to continue, even though the intellect knows that pleasure is fleeting. If an experience is mediocre, it wants it to be better. If it is bad, it should end instantly and not happen again. If experience repeats itself again and again, as it does due to unresolved conditioning, *rajas* causes boredom and produces a strong desire for variety. "More, better, different" is its holy *mantra*. It produces an endlessly active time-constrained life of loose ends – and dissatisfaction. No matter how much is accomplished, the "to-do" list never shrinks. It is a closet, garage, basement and attic overflowing with a confusing assortment of neglected and unused objects. It is a late tax return, a forgotten appointment, an unreturned call, a frantic search for one's keys. Our *rajasic*, aggressive and extroverted forays into *samsara* inevitably make us exhausted, fragmented, divided, separate, confused – *tamasic!* The price of excess *rajas* is always excess *tamas*; they work together as inevitably as night follows day.

James says, "When I was young, my father, who was wise in many ways, used to say, 'You can't win.' At the time, I did not understand what he meant, but a life well-spent thanks to the teachings of Vedanta made it clear. Life is a zero-sum game, an eternal war within one's self in which neither side prevails for long. For example, when *tamas* appears in a person whose predominant *guna* is *rajas*, a painful experience is inevitable. You have many things on your 'to-do' list, but your mind is so dull that every action becomes painful. You are wired but tired. It is not fun. Conversely, when you need to indulge your *tamas* and sleep, your mind is too busy, so you suffer."

Unresolved Experience

Assimilation of experience only takes place when the mind is alert and present. Any experience that is unresolved adds another layer to all previously unresolved experiences. Therefore when *rajas* dominates the subtle body, the innate wisdom of the Self, much less common than sense-knowledge, is not available to help the intellect accurately determine what is happening and resolve doubts. Trying to make sense of experience through the senses is always limited, and invariably faulty due to our conditioning, or *vasanas*. When our experience is resolved through Self-knowledge, however, it leaves our attention present and alert, so that the mind can meet the next experience without prejudice or projection.

Because life is an unending procession of experiences, especially in this pressurized age, it is important to lay each experience to rest as quickly as possible, preferably as it happens. This is what is meant by "cleaning up" our *karma* moment to moment, keeping it on a short leash right in front of us like a little dog. When we are so *rajasic* and our mind is totally wrapped up in dealing with an endless succession of trivial and gratuitous desires, we are too busy to look at our "issues," so they become compounded and more entrenched. Our "stuff" remains running in the background and gets projected out, and influences how we experience life, which causes much suffering. It follows us like a dark shadow, and contaminates everything.

Unresolved experience subliminally drains attention. When I have difficulty focusing on what I need to do and avoid what I should or should not do, it is a sign that the mind is excessively *rajasic*. What is lost to us when our mind is extroverted is not only that "slow and steady" wins the race, but the growth-enhancing benefits of assimilation of unwanted or unpleasant experiences. A *rajasic* mind instinctively rejects unwanted experiences and always attempts to escape them by whatever means. But alas, it cannot escape. They pile up and ferment in the unconscious. As unresolved experience accumulates, we suffer existential constipation, overwhelm and stress; we are unable to keep up with life's demands. Growth rarely comes through the easy attainment of desires.

Summary *of* Typical Symptoms *of* Rajas

The Downside
No Objectivity and Lack of Discrimination

When *rajas* dominates the mind, it cannot be objective or observe itself, because it is caught up in the future, the thought that things need to be different, so the mind acts to correct the situation, usually in negative ways. It does not act to correct itself, because it cannot see that it is the problem. The mind, run by its likes and dislikes, is "under their command"! An extroverted mind lacks discrimination because it is at the disposal of its desires, like an automaton – or a puppet on a string.

Defensive, Stubborn and in Conflict With the World

A *rajasic* mind is in constant conflict with the world (*Isvara*) because of its strong likes and dislikes. *Rajasic* people think their wants are more important than the wants of *Isvara*, the Field of Existence appearing as the needs of others. *Rajas* stubbornly digs its heels in and repeats actions that do not work. It blindly pursues what it wants regardless of evidence of its faulty methods, and becomes highly defensive and aggressive when this is pointed out or when challenged.

Insensitive, Selfish, Self-Absorbed

Because *rajasic* people think their wants always come first, they are typically very inconsiderate and often insensitive to the needs of others. They will be the person who pushes to the front of the queue, who climbs over everyone at work, who hogs the limelight in any situation, who talks over you, who cuts you off on the road, who always thinks of themselves first. We all know the type!

PROJECTION, DENIAL, REACTIVITY AND ATTACK

Projection, along with its attendant denial, inevitably causes reactivity and attack. These are three signatures *rajasic* qualities. An extroverted mind is incapable of looking at itself, so it will almost without fail project its feelings, positive or negative, outwards – and deny it is doing so. Projection of our negative feelings onto others makes us unhappy, mistrustful, surly, sulky, combative, argumentative, "spiky" and highly reactive. Everything sets us off; we attack, blame, argue and defend to the bitter end. We engage in senseless quarrels over stupid things, and insist on being "right" even when it is obvious we are not. Projection of our positive feelings just as often backfires on us, because we are not in touch with reality. Projection produces a non-functional state of mind incapable of peace and happiness, because *rajas* makes us see things the way we are instead of the way they really are. Projection of our subjective reality onto *Isvara* is dangerous, because *Isvara* does not care about our own creations or interpretation of reality. If we cannot accurately assess what is going on in our world, we will pay the price and suffer.

EMOTIONALITY AND BLAME

Unbalanced *rajas* makes us highly emotional because no object is under our control. We are wildly happy (for a short while) when we do get what we want. But because *rajas* does not easily submit to *karma yoga*, nor takes appropriate action, we often do not get what we want, which makes us depressed, dissatisfied and angry. Inevitably this will make us blame someone or something. We will not see that we are projecting our stuff onto others or the "world." We go "unconscious" (*tamas*). Emotionality and blame create an extremely painful state of mind at odds with its environment, work, relationships, objects, the world; it is an intellect in servitude to emotion instead of clear thinking and the futile drive to find more, better, different.

EXCITEMENT, PASSION AND ADDICTION

Passion and excitement are highly valued by *samsaris*. It is taken as the sign of a good life – that you are happy, that your life is working and you are successful. Passionate people are very charismatic and others feel drawn to them. As much as we can all enjoy and appreciate the feelings produced by *rajas* that make us feel excited and passionate, passion for anything comes at a price, if it is not balanced with *sattva*. Ideally, what we need to be passionate about is the truth, peace of mind and Self-knowledge, but even then passion needs to be tempered with steadfastness and humility. A steady, burning desire for truth may seem like passion, but it is not the same, because this kind of desire is clear-sighted and humble, it lasts and does not burn. Passion is passion and passion is blind, it has no patience, endurance or humility.

It not only burns, it is a fire that is easily extinguished. And being human makes us susceptible to passionate feelings about things that do not benefit us, experiences that bind us to objects and keep the mind projected outwards. Passion is a dangerous wild horse we ride at our peril, because it can throw us off in an instant – and it produces the insatiable need for more, and often leads to addictions of all kinds, from substances and situations to people and experiences. People who are addicted to dangerous activities and sports are hooked on adrenalin, the fuel that is the hormonal equivalent of *rajas*. It makes them feel "in the now," alive, present and focused. It's a *samsaric* way of feeling the bliss of the Self. Out-of-control passion for anything often destroys as surely as does its opposite, passion for nothing, *tamas*. Balance is the key, as with all the *gunas*.

The Inability to Assimilate Experience Creates Bad Karma

Rajas makes us incapable of seeing that how we experience life is determined solely by faulty sensory information coming from our conditioning. We cannot evaluate anything accurately or assimilate the meaning of our experiences, so we do not learn from them. We become prejudiced and judgmental, and our experiences confirm our negativity and prejudices. We constantly repeat our mistakes. Even our knowledge of the empirical world will be through the filters of our unresolved conditioning. We continually add to our bad (*papa*) *karma* with our thoughts and actions, and the fructifying *karma* from our unassimilated experience causes mental and physical overload. Our lives do not flow, we feel stuck, frustrated, uptight and overwhelmed.

The Doer Identity

Rajasic people evaluate themselves in terms of what they accomplish, want to accomplish – or fail to accomplish, which leads to an inflated or deflated identity. However, *rajasic* people think they are very clever because they think they accomplish so much, but fail to understand how much energy they waste and the cost that frenetic activity has on them and everyone around them. When *rajas* is out of balance with *sattva*, the extroverted mind is always busy with desire-based action. It is completely identified with doership and with survival through doership. The *rajasic* doer has an endless to-do list, to which it keeps adding. It believes that it makes a difference to its life and life in general through doing and will wear itself out with endless action. We have made it clear that doing never ends for the person while it is alive. *Maya*, the power in Consciousness to delude, makes the Self seem to be a doer. Desire for and pursuit of knowledge (*sattva*) is understanding the difference between action and knowledge, and the rediscovery of the actionless Self. Pursuit of action involves a sense of doership, so the two pursuits are opposite in nature. Freedom from limitation requires renunciation of one's sense of doership through *karma yoga,* not renunciation of doing itself.

Rajas Claims Credit and Owns Experience

Rajas claims the credit for success and owns experience when it is in its favour, but projects blame when not.

The Red Flag of Dissatisfaction and Boredom

Dissatisfaction of any kind is a marquee that advertises the presence of *rajas*. It is one of the surest signs of the presence of *rajas* and could be said to define it. Dissatisfaction is behind most desire and the need for new experiences or objects. When controlled by *rajas*, boredom often plagues us. We want variety, specialness, thrills, entertainment – to make life "interesting." Just take a quick look at the huge industry the entertainment business is — the "weapons of mass distraction" as I call it! And it is never enough. No matter how fast new things are churned out, it's not fast enough. Instant gratification takes far too long. Nothing satisfies the mind for longer than a moment. We need new everything all the time because maybe, just maybe the new thing will have something that we need or something better — and we cannot risk missing out, no way! Dissatisfaction is the curse of a *samsaric* mind; it never finds rest, peace or contentment, never wants what it has, never has enough, and is always sure what it wants is somewhere else.

DISAPPOINTMENT

Holding hands with dissatisfaction is disappointment, a signature sign of *rajas*. When *rajas* drives the mind, it makes us incapable of *karma yoga*, and we inevitably face disappointment, because even if we get what we want, we are never happy for long. And because of the nature of objects, we often fail to get what we want, so we compound the relentless drive to complete ourselves through the pursuit of objects, which never works. Disappointment etches the faces of some people as they age. Unfulfilled expectations so often create a tight, bitter visage. It is indeed a sad way to live.

RAJASIC SPEECH AND LANGUAGE

You can identify *rajas* by observation of how you talk — and by how you (don't) listen when others do manage to get a word in. Instead of listening, you wait to talk. A *rajasic* mind speaks too fast, is not interested in what others say, talks over others, is usually oblivious to the effect of its words on them, unconcerned or unaware of the implied meaning of its words. It finds fault, is critical or cynical, a "sharp tongue" that uses words to undermine, hurt or inflict doubt and pain. To bring a *rajasic* mind under control, we need to listen to what we are thinking and saying, put aside our thoughts, shut up and listen to what others say to us instead. We can train ourselves to calm the mind and pay attention to others and the effect of our words on them. *Rajas* blinds us to the needs of those around us and to what life requires of us, and we pay the price when we do not pay attention.

DESIRE

Rajas is the mode of passion. It triggers desire/fear-based thoughts, actions and words. Desire is a positive fear, and fear is a negative desire. You only desire something if you fear you do not already have it, and you can only fear something if you believe the gain or loss of it will harm you or make you less than you are. Fear and desire are inseparable. There is nothing inherently "unnatural" or wrong with desire of any object – be it sex, money, a house, anything – if the desire is not opposed to *dharma*. We never stop desiring, because to be alive is to desire. Krishna says to Arjuna in the *Bhagavad Gita*, "I am the desire that is not opposed to *dharma*." You need to have a strong desire for *moksa*, for instance, or you will not be qualified for it. The Buddhists believe that desire is the cause of all suffering – which is true. However, the solution is not the futile attempt to rid oneself of all desire – even if that were possible, which it is not. The solution is to understand what is behind desire. Who or what is the desirer, and why does it so desperately desire what it desires? If you can see that you are the knower of the desirer, and therefore you are not what you desire, all gratuitous or *adharmic* desire ends. That is the only way to be free of desire (*rajas*).

When the mind is extroverted and desperate to get what it

wants, it really wants the pain of desire to end. When the desired object or state of mind is achieved, the pain of desire disappears and the mind feels relieved, happy and content – for a while, as it has attributed feeling good to the obtainment of the desired object. What has actually happened is that as *rajas* abates, the barrier to *sattva* temporarily dissolves, which floods the mind with the joy of the Self. As no object satisfies the mind for long, the whip of desire soon drives it to chase the next object. Usually sooner rather than later the inevitable result is depression, despondency and hopelessness (*tamas*), the experience of all minds that try to find fulfilment through objects.

When it comes to gratuitous sensual desires such as sex, for instance, we must use dispassion and discrimination, because indulgence does lead to and builds *vasanas*. It is always a question of motivation. Do you want the desired object because you feel empty, bored, greedy, dissatisfied? If so, it will not give you what you are looking for, which is fullness – nor put an end to the suffering that desire causes. No matter what the desire, what is behind it is always a desire for the Self masked as a desire for an object or a result, which is also an object. The question to always ask is, who desires this and why? The problem with desire is that all actions create *vasanas*, which are the seeds for other actions, thus the chain of action-desire-action entraps us.

The "enlightened person" knows that because their true nature is whole and complete, they are the fullness that needs nothing. There is no need for more, better or different. They can enjoy the presence or absence of objects; it makes no difference. They can indulge any desire or not; either way the mind is happy before, during and after it either does or does not get what it desires. The mind will not seek pleasure – which is inherently dissatisfying, because if one seeks pleasure, one does not know that pleasure, *parama sukka*, is one's true nature. In fact it is the seeking itself, the desire for the object, that causes the agitation, dissatisfaction and suffering in the mind.

Once Self-knowledge has obtained in the mind and it is peaceful, calm and clear (*sattvic*), this is the only time we enjoy objects for what they are because we no longer need them to feel full. Objects do offer a limited kind of bliss – so when we no longer need them to deliver more than they are capable of – we enjoy them without fear for what they offer: temporary bliss. Therefore we are always satisfied and see all objects (or lack of them) as the Self. We enjoy life, and give thanks for our many blessings, as transient as they are.

GREED

One of the seven deadly sins, greed, in any of its many manifestations is a sure sign of *rajas'* dominance of the mind. Unchecked it is usually an unconscious desire for wholeness projected onto objects – whether material or psychological, like power or fame; or physical, like sex or food. It is not the object per se that greed desires; greed is typical of an ego run by fear in search of safety through recognition, being feared or admired.

FALSE PRIDE, VANITY, ARROGANCE

Rajas often manifests as an exaggerated sense of our importance – or lack of it. False pride is on the list of seven deadly sins for a good reason, usually caused by an underdeveloped, arrogant and insecure ego that hides behind a false and inflated opinion of itself to mask fear, low self-esteem, feeling inadequate or lesser than others. A person who lives by the opinions of others squanders his or her valuable mental resources, will not be qualified for inquiry and will not have a good life. Because many of us secretly fear that we are not good enough, we are unable to develop the confidence needed to be happy with our lives, so look to external factors (or to others) for validation. To gain validation, we are often tempted to exaggerate our qualifications and accomplishments so that others will think we are special and glorify us. We may try to attack and defend our positions to make people fear us as a way to gain self-importance or hide our lack of self-confidence. Alternatively, we use arrogance, a product of low self-esteem, to protect ourselves from others and the world.

If we are completely certain about our talents and abilities, we take them for granted, and have no need of validation or support. *Rajas* does not take time to analyze the factors involved, so does not see clearly that demand for respect from others cannot bring comfort or satisfaction, even if I am a highly accomplished person. *Rajas* makes me believe I am the author of my actions, the producer and owner of my gifts and skills. It creates a mind that cannot investigate what it actually did create. If it did, I would see that I created nothing. I appeared here one fine day encased in a fleshy meat tube by no effort of my own. I did not create my sense of individuality either: it came along with the body and the world in which the body exists, a world that I definitely did not create. Tendencies, skills and abilities sprouted from within me by no will of my own. I can utilize them to great effect and derive pleasure from doing so as the person, but I cannot claim authorship of them. Whatever achievements I claim depended on opportunities provided by life itself.

THE NEED FOR VALIDATION AND APPROVAL

Demand for respect from others invites many disturbances because the one who asks for respect is not in control of the result. People give respect for reasons only known to them. When their minds change, the validation is withdrawn and hurt arises. Any form of hurt is due to pride, an inflated ego, one that is excessively attached to what it thinks it knows, believes, possesses or how it looks. For example, vanity in the form of body-conscious individuals who spend an inordinate amount of time grooming or calling attention to their bodies with expensive clothing, outlandish hairdos, tattoos and piercings often do so to attract attention they are incapable of giving themselves. Such egos, inflated by pride and vanity, invariably end up deflated. Often they waste time and energy trying to "save face" or they plot revenge. In addition, it is not always easy to determine another person's true feelings.

To understand the psychology of pride, we must see the projection that *rajas* creates and remain alert when it raises its ugly head. We must examine the psychology behind it dispassionately without a sense of guilt or self-condemnation (*tamas*). Why do I care what people think? Because I feel inadequate. Is it true that I am inadequate? Will the attention of others remove my sense of inadequacy? Even when acknowledged by people, the sense of satisfaction pride engenders does not last, and I am forced to seek approval once more. When does it end? Is it reasonable to claim qualities or things when clearly I did not create them? Is this whole *samskara* real? For whom is this need for validation? It is for my ego. Is my ego real? It is not even apparently real, because it disappears when I investigate it. Why do I invest so much energy in something that is not even real? I cannot just drop my prideful ego except by meeting it head-on. I see how pointless my expectations are, and after some time this *samskara* loses its power to disturb my mind. The habit of seeking approval eventually winds down, and I become an uncomplicated person.

LIES, PRETENSION, AFFECTATION

Pride can be based on real accomplishments or abilities, but pretension is self-glorification without a cause. I want to give the impression that I am something I am not. If I dress up to the nines but am drowning in debt, I am pretentious. If I can't answer the doorbell without first tidying the living room for fear that someone might think I am a messy person or I cannot appear in public in a mismatched outfit without my lipstick and every hair in place, I am a poseur. If I had done no meaningful spiritual work but don orange robes, shave my head, carry a staff and wander around spiritual centres with a beatific smile pasted on my face to convince others of my mystic attainments, I am not a *mahatma*, I am a phoney.

All unhealthy *samskaras* stem from the same basic reason, the understanding of which should never be far from my mind: I do not feel good about myself. I cannot accept myself. I want to be different. I am so extroverted (*rajasic*) that I cannot see my own psychology and take responsibility for it, so I rely on others to do what I should be doing for myself, i.e. make me feel good. I need to impress people so they will validate me.

This is a particularly difficult problem because I don't even have the satisfaction of knowing that what I say about myself is true. I am therefore committed to falsehood and find myself in direct conflict with truth. This attitude is particularly unsatisfactory because there is no way to compel others to respond favourably to my lies. Because I badly need others to respond, and because at any time my lie may be exposed, the result is high levels of stress. To make it work I need to be very alert, keep all my friends apart and have a very long memory. There is a belief that *karma yoga* (leaving the result to *Isvara*) works in this situation, but it does not, because *karma yoga* assumes that one's values are in order. It does not *get* your values in order. *Karma yoga* does not work if we use it to mask a psychological problem or manage an *adharmic* situation.

MENTAL AND PHYSICAL PAIN

Pain has many forms. *Rajas* is painful for the mind and manifests physical, emotional or psychological symptoms. Our most fundamental pain is the pain of compulsive action, because it strips us of our most precious asset — the freedom to choose and act in a way that produces peace of mind. "Stone walls do not a prison make, nor iron bars a cage." All human activity is centred on an attempt to remove the sense of limitation brought about by ignorance-inspired desires and fears. *Rajas* also indirectly causes physical pain and illness because stress levels are through the roof; the *rajasic* individual pushes the body without mercy with too much work, exercise or play — or it is so busy doing that it neglects the body's needs with bad nutrition and lack of exercise.

AMBITION

Aggressive and relentless ambition, with its attendant dogged determination to win at all costs, is typical of highly *rajasic* minds. It is not that ambition in and of itself is necessarily *adharmic* — it is blind ambition that will brook no opposition to get what it wants that comes at a very high cost to us and everyone associated with us. It is called "blind" ambition because its vision is very limited. Such ruthless ambition most often means we have lost touch with the value of non-injury to ourselves and others, and will do whatever it takes to achieve our goal.

COMPETITIVENESS

Highly *rajasic* people need to win. They are highly competitive in sport, business and life in general. They need to be No. 1 and typically are referred to as "A"-type personalities. They do not make good team players, are not inclined to share, lack empathy and will often do whatever it takes to promote their needs and to succeed.

ANGER

Highly *rajasic* people are often very angry, to the extent that anger becomes an identity. At its worst, angry people employ anger as a strategy to attack and counterattack, and never apologize so as to make people fear them and do their bidding. The cause of this kind of *rajasic* anger is that the Field of Existence is not giving us what we want. Unconscious obstructed desire turns to anger or its opposite, depression. It is not healthy to stuff our anger somewhere where we (or no one else) sees it, because it never stays put. Denied anger is truly dangerous, both physically and psychologically. Science has proved that the "molecules of emotion" wreak havoc with the body, and anger tops the list, not to mention what it does to your relationships with other conscious beings. We must manage anger – and if we don't, it destroys us. Anger is not socially acceptable, because it is a violation of *dharma*, which underpins the mutual expectation of individuals, which is why we often try to pretend that we are not angry. We don't want to deal with angry people, and people don't want to deal with our anger. It makes us "look bad." Anger is a violation of life's most fundamental *dharma*, non-injury. You may define violence in physical terms, but anger is injurious both to others and to yourself. Non-injury as defined by Vedanta is in terms of "thought, word and deed." The best stress management tool and the only way to deal with anger in a healthy way is through *karma yoga*.

Need for Control

A *rajasic* mind typically needs to always feel in control, whether of its environment, people or situations. *Rajasic* people and environments impose rigid rules of conduct, and sometimes resort to threat and menace if the rules are contravened. *Rajasic* people tend to be anal about their home and workplaces, wear themselves out trying to keep everything as they like it – or conversely they live in a mess because they are so frantically busy they have no time to keep up with what needs taking care of, either in their personal or work lives.

Need for Perfection

The need for perfection is also control, and typical of *rajas*, and originates from an inadequate ego (*tamas*, low self-esteem) that appraises itself on results. Such an ego needs to prove its worth in everything it does and has no knowledge of *karma yoga*; it is so driven that nothing short of perfection will satisfy it. But what escapes it is that perfection is not possible in this world – it is unachievable, so it is never satisfied, even if it does achieve its goals. There is always something better to achieve next time. It wears itself out trying to achieve goals, which often causes problems with the body like high blood pressure, blown-out adrenals, heart issues, physical and mental exhaustion, weight loss or gain – all because of high stress levels. What this *rajasic* mind is really trying to achieve is love, self-acceptance, peace – but it is so under the whip of *rajas* and extroverted that self-reflection is impossible. Perfection is an egoic stronghold, a consequence of the belief and deep fear that you are flawed, limited and inadequate.

WILLPOWER

Because we have limited free will, in that we can chose one thing over another, *rajas* makes it seems like we can manipulate situations and people to get what we want through sheer willpower and determination. While willpower is a useful and positive energy when used appropriately, such as commitment to study of the scripture, cleaning up our bad habits or negative thinking, etc., it often results in frustration, anger and blame, because *Isvara* simply does not care about our personal ambitions, whether we are try to manhandle our own psyche or anyone else's.

AGITATION

A red flag for *rajas* is any thought or feeling that causes agitation. Agitation can be obvious, and manifests as passion for anything; frantic; overstimulated; overactive; driven; jittery; can't sit still; insatiable; anxiety over results; fear-ridden; nervous; restless; hurried and worried; fragmented. Or it can manifest as your garden-variety mental disturbance from all the little pinpricks of life – the cuts from a thousand lashes of life and ignorance that destroy peace of mind.

ENVY, JEALOUSY, COMPARISON

Rajas (working with *tamas*) manifests as some of the most common, unreasonable and pernicious forms of impurities, such as jealousy, envy and comparison, also the result of low self-esteem (*tamas*). These negative emotions accompany possessiveness, expectation and criticism, to name a few. When *rajas* controls the emotions, which in turn run the intellect, the mind is capable of anything from mild to extreme acts of violence — such as domestic violence, child abuse and crimes of "passion." It unconsciously compares itself to others for better or worse, and projects its ideals as to how the mind thinks things "should" be (*rajas*). Envy and comparison usually manifest usually in the following steps:

1. I want what you have;

2. I want to be like you;

3. I want to prevent you from getting what you want;

4. I want to destroy you.

Jealousy and envy exist because the world is vast, filled with millions of entities which provide myriad opportunities (real or imagined) for self-demeaning, comparative judgments. Jealousy (like envy) is disguised anger that usually leads to depression (*tamas*) produced by a sense of lack brought on by comparison to someone I think is superior in some way to me. It is unreal for this reason: I am never jealous or envious of the whole person, only some aspect. He or she is more intelligent, beautiful, wealthy or popular than me. The fact that I would like to be like this person shows that there is some sympathy for him or her. We cannot separate the qualities that invoke jealousy from the person, because the complete person (who is really the Self) can never be completely an object of envy, therefore there is no real place for my bad feelings to attach themselves. Finally, it is also clear that there are certain things in the person I envy or am jealous of that I do not want. Additionally, if I am honest, I will find that I too am not perfect and am the possessor of certain unenviable qualities. To admit this makes it difficult to judge others. If the shoe fits, wear it.

Jealousy and envy are unwarranted reactions to the apparent nature of reality. They are completely without merit. In other words, they are *rajasic* projections that mask an insufficient appreciation of my own nature and the abundance of good qualities that spring from it. A Self-realized person is never jealous or envious, because he or she is mindful of his or her fullness and sees everyone else as full too. Although the Bible's statement that God is "a jealous God" means that when you know God you cannot love anything else, many people believe that God is a "superbeing" sitting somewhere else, who is endowed with certain human qualities, one of which is jealousy. But God is not a person subject to any form of limitation. It is the Creator and possessor of everything and, like an enlightened person, knows it is fullness itself. So jealousy and other *rajasic* emotions, positive and negative, do not apply to God.

When I feel jealousy or envy, I should apply the opposite thought and nip it in the bud lest it devolves into *schadenfreude*, delight in the misery of others, a truly despicable (and *tamasic*) emotion. I should think: "I am happy for the good fortune of this person. I admire his or her good qualities. I am happy that he or she is happy, and I neutralize any negative feeling opposed to peace of mind by applying the opposite thought." At first it may seem untruthful to think this way (after all, I really don't feel it!), but a deliberate daily practice will cleanse the mind, bring *rajas* into balance with *sattva* and prepare it for Self-knowledge.

UNCONSCIOUS ACTIONS

Typical signs of *rajas*-based activity are carelessness and haste; always in a hurry; impatience; speaking too quickly; doing things too quickly; driving or walking too quickly; dropping things; bumping into things; breaking things; accidents and injury to oneself or others; difficulty focusing; lack of concentration or ability to pay attention.

CAN'T STAND SILENCE

A *rajasic* mind has a strong dislike of silence, and will go out of its way to make sure there is always some sound to drown out both the silence and the noise of its own painful thoughts.

INSOMNIA

Insufficient or poor sleep plagues many people. In some parts of the world, especially in the U.S. and other First-World countries, insomnia has become an epidemic. The causes of insomnia are many and usually complicated. It could be a physiological reason, like the lack of certain nutrients; lack of exercise, sunshine or an unhealthy diet; it could be a medical reason, like adrenal or thyroid gland malfunction; heart, kidney or musculoskeletal and kidney problems, among others; it could be situational: how you live and work, where and when you sleep; it could be neurological or the result of mental health problems. Or any combination of these factors. Most often, the reason for lack of sleep is psychological – usually the result of too much *rajas* – stress, anxiety, worry, anxiety over results, the perpetual doer syndrome.

The Upside of *Rajas*
FOCUSED AND MOTIVATED

When an equal proportion of *rajas* and *sattva* manifest, we are focused, motivated and do actions that harmonize with *dharma*. Without *rajas*, we would not have the drive or willpower to do anything. Either we would be zoned out with too much *sattva* or so *tamasic* that we cannot even get out of bed. As stated above, not all desire and passion is a bad thing. We need a strong desire or *vasana* for truth, for instance, to pursue Self-inquiry.

EFFICIENT

Sattvic rajas is responsible for quiet, measured, unhurried efficiency, organization, productivity, competence, professionalism – any action that requires skill without the neurotic obsessive and frantic result-based behaviour typical of unbalanced *rajas*.

SELF-DISCIPLINED

Sattvic rajas is characterized by self-discipline, but not the white-knuckled determination to beat the mind into submission to achieve whatever goal it has set for itself. *Sattvic rajas* applies self-discipline to become a "disciple unto the Self." The goal in any endeavour is not to succeed at all costs but peace of mind. A *sattvic rajasic* mind is capable of sustained, productive effort to gain specific goals which result is satisfaction. When the mind is truly on board with what produces peace of mind, whether it is diet, exercise, work or anything else, it effortlessly and easily sticks to intelligent life choices, not because it wants to be better or "right," but only because it enjoys peace of mind.

EXCELLENCE AND KARMA YOGA

Sattvic rajas produces a mind committed to excellence, but not perfectionism. The quest for excellence always involves doing your best, taking into consideration all the factors involved. Most importantly, it involves being satisfied with the results because the actions are taken with the *karma yoga* spirit. It is accepted that one's best is not always the same from day to day, because the factors that control the body-mind and its environment are always changing, so one does the best one can under the circumstances, always with dispassion and accommodation.

POSITIVE PRIDE

Positive pride is the opposite of false pride and entails genuine contentment and self-esteem from performing anything we do well with integrity, grit and courage. A simple, factual self-respectfulness is a good quality based on real accomplishments or abilities.

USING ANGER AS A POSITIVE ENERGY

In the right situations, anger can be *sattvic* if used constructively and with wisdom. It can actually help you achieve what you want without injury to anyone. But making a habit of using anger in this way is not advisable, owing to the long-term effects on health, but sometimes it is necessary to set up healthy boundaries with others.

Solutions for Negative *Rajas*
FIRST IDENTIFY, THEN DISIDENTIFY
First Step

If the mind is too *rajasic*, the first step is to recognize this and take stock of the state the mind is in – without identifying with it. Observe how "unconscious" you and other people are (and behave) when under the whip of *rajas*. Negative tendencies are often easier to see in others than in ourselves. Seeing produces objectivity and leads to understanding, which produces peace of mind. One must be quick and alert to catch this *guna* before it turns into highly reactive emotion and runs off with the mind! We must be determined and dedicated to master *rajas,* because it is like a wild horse. Untamed, *rajas* will bring great harm and injury to yourself and everyone associated with you.

Second Step

The next step is to take appropriate action that calms the mind down – like a slow walk in nature; meditation; *tai chi; yoga;* lighting a candle and seeing it as the eternal flame of Consciousness; saying prayers; a devotional practice such as a *puja* – anything that brings peace of mind. Anything that slows the mind down will work. Prepare a *sattvic* meal and pay attention and observe every move you make. Set the table, sit down and mindfully bring attention to the abundance of life, give thanks for it taking care of all your needs. Eat the meal slowly, taste the food. If you share the meal with others, resist small talk. Bring attention to how busy the mind is. If nothing works, eat something *tamasic.* Watch a slow, thoughtful and inspiring movie, a documentary or read a good book, but not on your phone!

Become Media-Free!

Avoid violent or aggressive movies or books and all negative sensationalist media. Become vigilant about what you expose the mind to — how too much TV and other media depletes and agitates the mind. Become aware of the lighting in your home, as fluorescent and "blue" light is not only harmful to eyesight, it is mentally disruptive and harmful, especially the blue light from mobile phones, computers and tablets. Curtail the usage of these items a few hours before bedtime, especially if you want to sleep well. Go on a media fast. Most media reporting focuses on the negative because that is what sells — it makes a living by preying on fear. It inflates and collates news reports in such a way that it inures the mind to the idea that the world is a bad and terrible place. This is never true.

Avoid Highly *Rajasic* People

If you find yourself surrounded by highly *rajasic* people, places or situations, remove yourself as much as possible. If you cannot remove yourself, put your attention on the one who knows the frantic activity, Consciousness. *Rajas* (as with all the *gunas*) is highly contagious. Even if the mind is *sattvic*, exposure to highly *rajasic* people is extremely painful because the mind has to work to not modify to *rajas*. If the mind is already *rajasic*, exposure to more *rajas* will just create more *rajas*. The positive and negative aspects of all the *gunas* build on themselves if not managed.

Find Something Noble for the Mind

Find something noble for the mind to do and think about or it will eat you up. This can be anything, like a creative hobby; reading scripture and reading books about the lives of inspiring people;

take a course in something like writing; learn a new language; do research into areas of interest. Become a knowledge-seeker in all areas of life. *Isvara* gives us all special knowledge and skills, but it is up to us to develop and use them for our enjoyment and to make a valuable contribution to life.

The Sweet Pleasure of Doing Nothing

Applied consciously, *tamas* can be effectively cultivated as an antidote to excess *rajas*. It can also work to slow down the perpetual doer to enjoy "doing nothing." Laziness can be a virtue if it helps to manage excess *rajas*. Italians have a good term that captures this: *"dolce far niente,"* the sweet joy of doing nothing. Although this will take some practise for a highly *rajasic* mind, applying this thinking to the typical work-oriented frantic, results-based (*rajasic*) mind can be of great benefit in the production of *sattva*.

Chapter 8

Tamas: *The* Concealing Energy

THE ENERGY of concealment, *tamas*, is called *avaranna shakti*. An *avaranna* is a cloud – therefore it produces a cloudy, dull mind. *Tamas* is the energy-giving substance to gross matter, the "existence" aspect of the Creation. It is responsible for physicality. Without *tamas*, there would be no actual matter in existence. It is also called the mode of inertia, *dravya shakti*, and it produces delusion, *moha*. It is not capable of doing, feeling or knowing anything. It absorbs light, so it is not capable of reflecting Consciousness as is obvious in inanimate objects. We can project Consciousness onto insentient objects, but no amount of wishful thinking will make them sentient. Total *tamas* equals total ignorance. The more *tamasic* the mind, the more ignorant. Lord Shiva, the Self in the form of the God of destruction, represents *tamas*.

When *tamas* predominates, the mind is too dull to discriminate. It is prone to denial and avoidance as signature states of mind, but the list of *tamasic* qualities is very long. On the psychological level, it is the energy that produces all negativity – such as laziness; depression; messy homes; drama-filled lives and relationships; lack of self-worth; lack of self-confidence; stuckness; gullibility; fanaticism; cruelty; avoidance; self-indulgence; hedonism; addiction to substances, to pleasure or feeling good; gluttony; lust; uncertainty; forgetfulness; neglect; procrastination; emotionality and sentimentality; romanticism and fantasy; manipulation; mistrust; indifference; self-abasement; neediness; envy; financial and emotional debt; poor mental or physical health; feeling a failure; physical, mental or existential fatigue; bitterness; pessimism; dejection; complaining and whining; gloominess; unhappiness; victimhood; martyrdom; self-pity; guilt; blame; shame; doubt; confusion; second-guessing; dithering; formulaic thinking; resentment; comparison; hoarding; possessiveness; helplessness; criminal or dishonest tendencies; despair; grief-ridden; suicidal; bored and boring; dread; no objectivity; *schadenfreude*; bad memory; hopelessness and fear – the list goes on. On top of this, *rajas* and *tamas* always work together without fail. Where you find projection (*rajas*), you will find denial (*tamas*). See more on how these terrible twins work together at the end of this chapter.

Tamas and the Assimilation of Experience

Tamas distorts perception and inhibits assimilation of experience, because it produces delusion, which gives rise to fantasies and fabrications, which in turn cause distrust of oneself, others and "the world" or life in general. When the subtle body is predominately *tamasic*, the Self, masquerading as the ego, feels totally stuck. The feeling of "stuckness" is not the fault in our stars or Mercury retrograde as the spiritual crowd is inclined to believe. It is a failure to see and appreciate what we need to in any situation, what life requires of us, and a lack of will to take the appropriate steps to accomplish what is required even if we do. *Tamasic* people are messy, forgetful, prone to accidents and losing things. They are perpetually confused and lazy, and prefer to enjoy without doing (which is not such a bad thing, if you know what it means not to be the doer). Many *tamasic* spiritual people try to use the truth to avoid dealing with their issues or to legitimize being enjoyers/doers by saying that, because their conditioning comes from the Field, there is nothing they can do about it. While this is true, this attitude is a common trap for seekers and even for Self-realized people (one the ego likes), because the truth is that the Field helps those who help themselves.

Often the problem is not lack of Self-knowledge. It is just that the "Self-realized" person is *tamasic* and avoids doing what it takes to change their behaviour – which means to clean up their act, look objectively at their *vasanas* and get their actions and lifestyle to conform with *dharma*. Many people try to rationalize the *karma yoga* approach in situations like work, relationships, etc. that are unworkable and require change. Our lives must serve the truth, not the other way around. Truth is impersonal – we cannot make it fit our idea of what we want it to be. Neither Consciousness nor the Field cares one way or the other, because neither Consciousness nor the Field has a problem with duality. It is up to the *jiva* to choose peace of mind and balance the *gunas* by taking appropriate action.

A Rudderless Ship: *Tamas* Masquerading as *Sattva*

Tamas inhibits the assimilation of experience as efficiently as *rajas*, but for different reasons. Under its influence, the subtle body, though seemingly quiet and calm (you can fool yourself into thinking you are *sattvic* when the mind is *tamasic*), is dull. Efficient evaluation of experience requires mental clarity. Perception is distorted when a stagnant veil covers the subtle body and assimilation is compromised. When the intellect is dull, it has difficulty connecting the results of its actions with the thoughts that motivate them, which causes uncertainty with respect to what it must and must not do. It cannot respond appropriately to the Field and pays the price. The bad news is that when the subtle body is predominately dull, you are negotiating the ocean of *samsara* in a rudderless ship, adrift at sea. "Where should I go? What should I do? What's going on? I don't know. I can't decide. I don't want to know," are some typically *tamasic* thoughts and responses. The undigested experiential backlog brought on by a *tamasic* mind causes the ego to dither and procrastinate. Alternatively, if you have a highly *rajasic* lifestyle and feel constantly exhausted, *rajas* inevitably causes *tamas*. Although *rajas* is the antidote to excess *tamas*, *tamas* is always the price to pay for excess *rajas*.

Poor Lifestyle Choices

The worldwide obesity and illness epidemic spawned by the Western diet and lifestyle is a sad testament to the power of *tamas*. If you are overweight, out of shape, in bad health, perpetually low on energy, self-medicating with food, alcohol, drugs or sleep, *tamas* is the *guna* to clean up. If you find yourself sitting endlessly in front of the TV with a greasy or carb-loaded takeout meal, glass of wine or can of beer, you are in the grip of *tamas*.

Tamasic people usually have a raft of personal and lifestyle problems because they avoid cleaning up their mess and keep adding to it with the constantly accruing blowback *karma*. Because they continually indulge themselves, they do not accumulate good *karma*. In fact they collect bad *karma* or simply spend whatever good *karma* stands in their account until it is gone. They are perpetually in debt, financially and energetically. Life is a huge weight, a millstone around the neck that drags them down. They neither grow nor stay the same. They devolve. If we want to live a happy, healthy life, there is no avoiding cleaning up our lifestyle, as without a simple, healthy approach to how we live and treat the body, the mind will not be healthy either (much more on healthy lifestyle choices follows in the second book of this series, *Lifestyle Solutions*).

Inertia and the Abyss

Tamas is inertia, and although it takes more time to destroy your life than *rajas*, destroy it will. To overcome it, you must act. *Rajas* is about obtaining things, and *tamas* is about keeping them. Even maintenance requires energy. If you don't take care of the details, they will eventually take care of you, but not in a way you will enjoy. If we don't pay our parking tickets, our car will be impounded and sold. If we don't take care of our finances, we land up in the poorhouse or as someone else's problem. If you don't brush your teeth, they rot. If you don't love and serve your wife, she runs off with someone who does. If you don't eat healthily or exercise, your body will give up on you. If you don't use your mind, it will atrophy. Everything in *samsara* is sliding into the abyss all the "time" even as we speak. However, when you are *tamasic*, you are too lazy to protect what you have – or to care. Nothing in your life lasts, so there is nothing to build on. You end up living hand to mouth. It wears you out. You become fatigued; a sense of failure and despair will overcome you. Depression sets in and your self-esteem plummets.

Summary: Typical Symptoms *of* Tamas

The Downside
DULLNESS

Whenever *tamas* is predominant because of illness, insomnia or poor lifestyle choices such as bad eating habits, the after-effects of drugs, the overconsumption of alcohol or the *karma* from the overexertion of too much *rajas*, the mind will be dull, unable to think clearly or discriminate. It is morose, depressed, wallows, feels sorry for itself, unhappy, "down in the dumps." Excess *tamas* "sits" on the mind like a dead weight, which creates pressure that can be extremely uncomfortable and painful. We have all had this feeling at some point in our lives; some of us live with it constantly.

Denial

The tendency to deny culpability or responsibility, refusal to see situations and people for what they are and refusal to take appropriate action, are typical symptoms of *tamas*.

Low Self-Esteem and Fantasizing

A dull mind tends to fantasize and fabricate. The suppression of unresolved psychological issues behind fantasy is caused by *tamas* accompanied by low self-esteem, along with lack of confidence, feeling less-than or worthless, in constant comparison with others perceived to be more powerful, attractive or secure.

Lack of Direction

A *tamasic* mind lacks direction, feels lost and confused, and inevitably the result is compounded low self-esteem. It is so lazy, lacks either confidence or drive or is so stuck in negativity that it cannot commit to developing the skills and/or knowledge it requires to change its situation for the better, no matter how unhappy. It sticks with bad marriages, bad jobs, bad life situations and seethes with (usually unspoken) resentment.

DEPRESSION AND INSOMNIA

Depression has many causes. It seems that half the world is on antidepressants to cope with life. Illness, whether mental or physical, is *tamas* playing out (although *rajas* helps to bring the body-mind to illness) and may or may not be the result of lifestyle issues. It often is, however. An unhealthy diet and lack of exercise, along with low self-esteem from any number of causes, is very often the underlying cause of depression. Depression can also cause insomnia because the mind is overrun with negative thoughts, although depression usually causes an irresistible urge to sleep.

NEGLECT AND CRUELTY

When *tamas* is particularly heavy, even small daily duties like brushing teeth, combing hair or taking out the garbage seem like gargantuan undertakings. Neglect is *tamasic* and is responsible in large part for the rampant emotional dysfunction seen in materialistic societies. Parents become so caught up in their own lives or mental/emotional dysfunction that children are neglected. Unloved children quickly develop low self-esteem and are unable to fulfil their roles in society in a positive healthy way, which perpetuates a never-ending cycle of misery for everyone concerned. It is not only children who are neglected by *tamasic* minds; spouses, family, friends, the environment, everything gets neglected. Neglect is cruelty.

SCHADENFREUDE

A *tamasic* mind can often relish another person's suffering, because it makes it feel less small, less lacking and less unlovable.

PROCRASTINATION

Tamas says, "Why do today what you can put off until tomorrow?" It sticks its head in the sand, like the proverbial ostrich. Because a highly *tamasic* mind is stuck and suffers interminable lack of self-confidence and self-doubt, it can never make up its mind about anything; it puts off making decisions for as long as possible, which creates an ever-growing anxiety about life and a feeling of doom as things pile up and never get dealt with, which in turn results in ever-diminishing self-esteem.

GIVE ME A FORMULA, NOT FREEDOM

Tamasic people do not want to think. Thinking is hard work. They want to follow formulas because they cannot see the value of knowledge. *Tamasic* people seethe with bottled up resentment and grievances that are always someone else's fault. Many highly religious people also fit the *tamasic* cohort as does the typical public servant and military type, among many others. The more rigid the dogma or rules the better, if it does not require them to think for themselves. "Just tell me what to do and absolve me of any responsibility for my life," is a typical *tamasic* mindset. A *tamasic* mind runs unthinkingly on conditioned patterns. Unlike *rajas*, it hates the new. Because creative thinking takes so much energy, the *tamasic* mind does not value inquiry. Therefore it cannot gain control of events (or the *gunas*) and is thus forced to continually revisit negative situations. Consequently *tamas* is responsible for the feelings of helplessness that cause deep and lasting depression.

When unwanted *karma* happens, it teams up with *rajas* to lay the blame elsewhere.

DISHONESTY AND CUTTING CORNERS

Criminals tend to be *tamasic* in their thinking, although they may very well be *rajasic* physically. They would rather figure out ways to beat the system than to work for a living. "Easy money" is their holy *mantra*. While most of us may not be criminals, there are many ways that *tamas* makes us cut corners in our lives, from lying and blaming to cheating on our taxes or anything else; *tamas* exacts a hefty price on our peace of mind. *Tamasic* people are very often dishonest and evasive, not only because they are lazy but often because they are guilt-ridden and ashamed.

SHAME AND GUILT

Shame exists to keep us objectified, even to ourselves. And of course we all internalize it. Shame is the water we learn to swim in as children, in which some of us drown. It seems to be more of a problem in the West, where we have the luxury of neurosis. People who are focused on survival do not have that luxury. For those of us whose main concern is not survival, we cannot talk about privilege without encountering shame. The important thing to understand about shame is that it is not the same as guilt. Shame is highly destructive in every way, while guilt can be constructive if we act on it appropriately. Guilt is only ever useful as an indicator that *dharma* (the natural laws of life) has been broken and appropriate actions must be carried out to remedy the situation.

However, the ego also uses guilt as a way of "punishing" the mind for breaking *dharma* when it has no intention of taking stock or rectifying bad behaviour. We will feel bad for a while, get over it – and do it again. Unless guilt is understood and dealt with appropriately, it almost never works to prevent breaking *dharma* in repetitive cycles. A highly dull *tamasic* ego that uses guilt as a manipulation strategy gets others to do what it wants them to do, apologizes profusely and says things like, "I feel so bad!" but never means it, and repeats the pattern of abuse. Guilt is often the underlying cause of depression caused by suppressed anger we believe we do not have the right to express, which causes more suppression and more depression in a vicious cycle.

While shame and guilt invariably manifest together, there is a big difference between them. Shame is a focus on the small egoic self. Guilt is a focus on behaviour.

Guilt says, "I did something bad."

Shame says, "I *am* bad."

Guilt says, "Sorry, I made a mistake."

Shame says, "Sorry, I *am* a mistake."

Shame is directly and highly correlated with self-punishing behaviour such as unhealthy relationships; addiction; violence; depression; aggression; bullying; suicide; eating disorders; and social isolation. You name it, if it's self-punishing, shame is probably behind it or part of it. Guilt is inversely correlated to all those things.

Where does shame come from and why does it affect almost everyone? Psychologists tell us that between the ages of three and five we develop the moralistic part of the psyche, the "superego," which is a conglomeration of the positive and negative values we have absorbed from the people in our lives responsible for raising us, and the environment we grew up in. The superego is meant to keep the childish ego in check. Even if we were never indoctrinated by religion, shame somehow finds its way into the psyche of most people because it's universally part of the human (dualistic) condition. The only people who never experience shame at all are people who have no capacity for empathic connection with others – sociopaths and psychopaths.

Guilt can serve a purpose sometimes, but shame is self-negation at its worst. There are many reasons why we feel ashamed, all of them destructive to peace of mind, which originate in and build on the lie that we are "flawed" and unworthy, the scourge of duality. It causes an ugly, dark and thoroughly negative psychological condition, which attaches itself like a parasite to everything good about life or about who we think we are.

Unknown to us, shame becomes the filter through which we experience life. It whispers ceaselessly in our ear with the "voices of diminishment" and sucks us dry of confidence, of trust in ourselves and life, of goodness, of joy, and gorges itself like a leech on our mental lifeblood. We can boil the voice of shame down to two basic voices: (1) "You are not good enough," and if that does not work, (2) "Who do you think you are?" Shame so often goes undetected because it is very good at masking itself, either through self-aggrandizement or its complement, self-debasement. It imprisons the mind in the vice-like grip of highly destructive patterns of self-hatred which play out negatively in every aspect of life and alienate us from those we love who could be there for us. We push them away because we feel so unworthy.

Many of us are so paralyzed by the fear of shame and the shame of fear that we engineer smallness, insignificance, in our lives. We do not take chances or put ourselves out there for fear of criticism or failure or worse, ridicule. It is not worth it to us to step into our power and play big, because we don't know if we can literally withstand the criticism and judgments that are bound to come our way when we stick our necks out. Our voices become mute and rage boils inside us. When we try for so long to stuff ourselves into the smallest possible idea of who we are, it makes the psyche like a pressure cooker. It is impossible to be brave in such cases, because true bravery involves a willingness to face shame and be vulnerable. We can always measure how brave we are by how vulnerable we are willing to be. The myth that vulnerability is weakness is insidious in our culture, and it is profoundly dangerous, especially but not exclusively to men. I know many amazing women who deliberately hide their light under a bushel for fear of being seen.

If we face our shame, we will see that we always have two choices: (1) we can accept our vulnerability and face shame with discrimination born of Self-knowledge, which of course requires the ability to take an honest look at our mental/emotional patterns and baggage; it also requires the courage to see "our" baggage from the vantage point of self-acceptance, not blame. Or (2) we can run from it, and it owns us. But there is no escape from shame that way. Shame is like our shadow and cannot be outrun. It is the swampland of the soul and it kills, if not the body, our mental health. It corrodes everything it touches, and eviscerates self-esteem and kills any possibility of joy, of creativity, of healthy loving relationships, let alone a peaceful mind or happy life. It destroys our belief in change, that we can be more, that we *are* more.

The first step to healing shame is to acknowledge its presence and have the guts to bring it out from the shadows directly into the light of day, in all its warped ugliness. Though shame is always a lie about who we are, no matter what caused it, when it is the root cause of a deeply buried mental/emotional pattern, it is very difficult to eradicate by transformation into Self-love. But it can be done when we have the courage to face it through discrimination, the understanding that all thoughts, however toxic, come from the collective unconscious, or causal body, and not "from" us. Nobody makes themselves think negative *tamasic* thoughts – they just appear in the mind from buried mental patterns. Shame is an ugly hidden secret that never stays hidden.

Outwardly shame may be masked by humour, aloofness or other subterfuges that hide a mind that judges, beset by dark, mean-spirited thoughts, looks for the flaw in "others," filled with self-loathing. And it creates a mind suspicious that others judge it, and fears criticism. Shame also masks a mind that seeks criticism because it believes it deserves punishment, while it defends its fear of "being discovered" as unworthy, useless, of no value to anyone. Shame will prevent the experience of healthy relationships, and in fact will make us seek out bad ones and push away any chance of accepting love from the people who do care for us or could care for us. Shame and guilt never fail to hurry towards their complement, punishment. Only there does satisfaction lie.

Whenever we are prepared to stand up in our greatness, shame is the gremlin, the ever-present voice that whispers in our ear: "You will fail, you are useless, you are bad, you are _____" (fill in the blank). And when we are in pain, it is so much easier to cause pain to others than to feel our own, so we work out our shit on others, which is why the world is so full of broken relationships, of haters, judgment and criticism, hurt people who hurt others. But we only ever hurt ourselves. We are stuck in a vicious cycle of shame and shaming. So many people's identities have been shaped by shame, by smallness, and it is very sad indeed.

When that strong shame/guilt pattern arises, if we get hooked by the dark, turbulent thoughts and emotional patterns inherent in being the small, limited, messed up person, even in seemingly small day-to-day issues, we will never be free of the shame/guilt pattern. Yet the mind will try to defend this position even though the ever-changing and limited idea of whom we are trying to keep alive is nothing more than a thought, a toxic mental program. If we want to be free of it, we must be prepared to do battle with this formidable foe.

The first step towards freedom from this program is to see it for what it is, and its origin, that it does not come from "me" or my past, however flawed or imperfect. Everyone is a product of their *karma* and conditioning, until and unless Self-knowledge obtains. There is no blame; we all do our best or worst with the Self-knowledge we have (or don't have). To take responsibility for our actions does not require blame. It's another opportunity to assume the ability to respond appropriately to what the Field of Life has presented to us. If reparations can be made, we must make them. If not, we must forgive ourselves and everyone involved. Self-forgiveness brings out the only antidote to shame: self-empathy. Self-forgiveness is not about justification. It's about the courage to love your (small) self, warts and all. On that level, we are all flawed; that's life. But we are so much more than the small self.

Shame needs three things to grow exponentially: secrecy, silence and judgment. If you douse it with empathy, shame cannot survive. Most of us don't have much empathy for ourselves and construct all sorts of coping mechanisms in place of self-acceptance and love. We practise self-empathy when we say NO! to the voices of diminishment, with the *karma yoga* attitude. *Karma yoga* is an attitude of gratitude to life, and consecration of all our actions to the Field in the knowledge that the results are not in our control, and taking what comes as a gift. *Karma yoga* is existential burnout insurance and the only way to objectify the ego. Just do it. There is no law against it, because the voices of diminishment never speak the truth about who we are. We must be vigilant and keep practising *karma yoga*, no matter how long it takes, one thought at a time. Never give up.

What price freedom? When the guilt/shame pattern rears its ugly head, douse the fire of shame with the healing waters of self-empathy and practise *karma yoga* immediately by giving all the thoughts and feelings to the Field or to God. Don't identify with them. Practise the opposite thought and take a stand in wholeness, even if you must fake it till you make it. It's not really faking, because the truth about you is much more than you are willing to accept. Take small steps but keep at it. It can take a while to beat a lifetime of negative thinking patterns into submission. The first law of *dharma* is non-injury in thought, word and deed, and that applies first to us. Aim for peace of mind by managing with Self-knowledge the thoughts and emotions that constantly and repetitively appear unbidden in the mind. Do not listen to the neurotic voice of the ego.

We need to treat shame as we would deadly toxic radioactive waste. The only difference is that while radioactive waste is almost impossible to eradicate, shame is not. When we understand how this energy works and we pounce on it every time it raises its ugly little head with Self-knowledge, we will kill it.

BLIND LOYALTY

Tamasic people are stubbornly loyal, to a fault. No matter how much their allegiance to whatever idea or person is proved faulty, they will turn a blind eye and reinforce their pledge of loyalty. Again, Trump is a great example! So is Osho, who even today, long after he and his "path" are completely discredited, is stubbornly worshipped by many of his "devotees." The number of these flawed and often phoney *gurus* throughout the ages is legion, yet many still cling to their misguided beliefs. With all the evidence to the contrary, this type of follower is still enthralled by the *tamasic* way of life or ideas defective teachers espouse.

PESSIMISM

The list of *tamasic* qualities seems never-ending and varies according to different people and situations, but pessimism (along with denial and low self-esteem) is invariably on the list when the mind is highly *tamasic*. *Tamas* makes it extremely difficult to see the up-side of any situation, and in fact it seeks the downside and often revels in it. It will deny, avoid or walk away from any positivity or solution to its problems, and morosely sulk and masochistically feel good about feeling bad, as nonsensical as that is. It is a toxic state of mind, both to the bearer and to those in contact with it. If you have the misfortune of having to cope with someone like this, it is best avoided if possible.

FANATICAL BELIEFS, FUNDAMENTALISM

Tamas tends to absolutism, fundamentalism, gullibility, conformity. There are three types of fanatics. The first type, whether religious, spiritual or secular, is the relatively benign and gullible person who believes what they believe contrary to all evidence that may contradict or challenge their beliefs. The second type is called *asura*, meaning an ignorant person with their face turned away from the sun, a danger to themselves but not necessarily a danger to others. An example would be the more fanatical non-violent religious or political person. The third kind is called *rakshasa*, a demon. When *tamas* totally dominates the mind, ignorance and cruelty become extreme, and this kind of person becomes a danger to themselves and everyone else, for example Hitler, Stalin, bin Laden, a member of ISIS or the Ku Klux Klan, to name but a few, in other words, psychopaths and some sociopaths. They are active *dharma*-violators. They enjoy and gain pleasure from the pain of other people.

GRIEF, TRAGEDY OR LOSS

Grief is a very difficult emotion for humans to dissolve. For instance, it is very hard to be dispassionate about losing a loved one – after all, Self-knowledge is not a "magic pill" for the ego. Even with Self-knowledge it takes time to process devastating emotions like grief, and it is very important that we allow ourselves to do so. While our emotions are not real and not the truth about who we are, they are the relative truth of what the *jiva* is going through. If we deny them, we create more problems for ourselves. However, if we have experienced trauma, tragedy or loss, it is possible to develop the tendency to identify with "our" pain – addicted to melancholy, sadness and mourning – the so-called "pain body." We become sombre; distrustful of life and love; cheerless; despairing and grief-stricken; lugubrious; always in expectation of the worst or "the next shoe to drop"; a constant sense of bereavement or impending loss; morbid; excessively emotional and blaming; a victim of victimhood. A victim identity is a dangerous trap, as it can ensnare us in this hapless groove for years. The identity that grief creates becomes a substitute for the perceived loss of whatever or whomever we have lost or to which we are attached. This mind clings to this identity like a drowning person to a life raft, and typically joins victim groups or becomes a crusader for others with similar losses.

SUICIDAL THOUGHTS

These thoughts can be symptomatic of very deeply suppressed and unaddressed psychological issues. They are highly negative thoughts produced by the suffering experienced through the identification with the body-mind and the unpredictable nature of *samsara*. It is possible that the mind is in so much pain (*rajas*) that it seeks to end it by ending the life of the body-mind. In a way, suicide is a strange attempt at survival, because beneath these thoughts is love for oneself – and the desire to experience this love by ending pain.

These thoughts can sometimes also arise in a mind not particularly traumatized – even committed to Self-inquiry – before Self-knowledge has obtained. These thoughts do not belong to the person, although it certainly feels like they do. Like any thought, they can be negated by seeing them as not-Self, but this is very hard to do without an independent means of knowledge to subject the mind to which is capable of producing Self-knowledge. Suicidal thoughts can also be the result of terminal boredom with life – or fear of really living, all a result of *tamas* clouding and dulling the mind.

NEGATIVITY VASANA

When the mind has had to overcome extremely damaging and destructive programming because of difficult life *karma*, very often its default position is negativity, *tamas*. It goes mostly unnoticed, as a *tamasic* mind tends to normalize the abnormal. To rise above the heavy blanket of *tamas* that covers it usually requires a Herculean effort, which often is unsustainable. Occasionally there may occur a spontaneous bursting-through-the-clouds of some joy, but it never lasts long and often leaves the mind feeling worse than before because of the seemingly ephemeral nature of happiness. The only permanent solution is Self-knowledge.

Boredom and Predictable Language

Like highly *rajasic* people, highly *tamasic* people are terminally bored with life and with themselves – and they are dreadfully boring to others. Even a few minutes in the company of a highly *tamasic* mind can make one feel negative and depressed. Mired in a stew of negativity keeps *tamasic* minds bogged down in the mud of dullness, depression and limitation. Their language is very predictable, and their predominant thoughts are, "I can't, it won't work; I will fail; nobody loves me; I am worthless; nothing good will come of it," etc. I call it the "Eeyore syndrome," from the chronically depressed donkey in *Winnie-the-Pooh*, who always expects the worst and usually gets it.

No Objectivity, Dread, Self-Pity, Victimhood and Martyrdom

Because *tamas* covers the mind in a cloud of dullness, highly *tamasic* minds have lost the ability to see themselves objectively. They have no faith in themselves and are often overcome with feelings of dread and impending doom. For the most part they are drowning in self-pity (poor me) and have created a martyr identity of their negativity to which they are highly attached because they get a lot of mileage out of it. It gives the mind a reason life is not what they believed it "should" be, why they failed or believe they are failures.

Envy and Jealousy

Envy and jealousy can be either *rajasic* or *tamasic*. When it is *tamasic*, we delight in the misery of others, because underneath the jealousy we want to be like them but believe we are less-than, so we want them to fail because we want to destroy them. We deny and hide these toxic feelings from ourselves and others. When jealousy is *rajasic*, we think we own other people or things, and are desperately afraid we will lose them.

Manipulation

The martyr/victim identity is an excuse and a very clever ego manipulation strategy to control others to get them to do our bidding Underneath the *tamasic* and seemingly benign, weak, frail and vulnerable exterior of the martyr/victim mind is a malignant frightened ego that knows exactly how to get what it wants and uses weakness as a tool to get it.

Neediness and Lack of Confidence

Lack of confidence and neediness is a common sign of excess *tamas*, as are all unresolved love issues that require a "special" other who will complete us but never does, sending us on the futile quest for completion that never comes. It stems from not getting the emotional support and or/love from our parents, the "needy lonely child" syndrome in all of us, desperate for attention and love.

SELF-ABASEMENT

Typical of *tamas* is self-abasement, putting ourself down to get attention or because of low self-esteem, as is normalizing the abnormal and taking abuse from others in whatever form. Excessive *tamas* undersells itself, easily falls into the underdog position and settles for less as a matter of course, but seethes with resentment.

INDIFFERENCE, INATTENTIVENESS AND DISINTEREST

Disinterest; indifference; could not care less how I look, dress or act, nor about the state of my home, car or workstation; "sick and tired"; lack of attention; these are all typical symptoms of *tamas* out of balance with *sattva*. If you want to see poster children for *tamas* and lower your expectations for the human race, spend some time in international airports, especially in America.

IN LOVE WITH DOUBT, LACK OF SELF-TRUST

Tamasic people are often immobilized by doubt. A healthy doubting function is good in all matters of this world, up to a point. Equally important is not to fall in love with our doubts. A love affair with doubt produces dithering, and ditherers are never happy, because they cannot trust themselves or anything else. You need to be able to resolve your doubts.

MISGUIDED OBLIGATION

Another symptom of misguided desire-based action is an excessively refined sense of obligation, either to what you think you owe others or things you think they owe you. While it is important to discharge your duties in a timely and appropriate fashion, if you find yourself saying that others should do this or that or you "must" or are "supposed to" do things that are not in any way required for the basic maintenance of life, *tamas* is in charge. This symptom is extremely common in so-called "developed" societies, where luxuries have become necessities. "Obligation" is just a fancy socially acceptable word used by the insecure to dress up desire. It can also be a subterfuge for a fear-filled ego, desperate for validation.

EXISTENTIAL, MENTAL AND PHYSICAL FATIGUE

Tamas is a dead-heavy weight in the mind to the point that it is constantly tired, unable to function properly or cope with even the smallest things in life. It feels overwhelmed, frightened, lost and confused. The body is often neglected, has very poor energy and health is impaired, often to the point of serious illness.

LOSS OF MEMORY

Tamas makes the mind so dull that it cannot clearly process or evaluate the information coming into it from the environment. It misses things, misinterprets communication, forgets things and thus gets easily offended, dejected and gloomy.

LAZINESS, SELF-INDULGENCE AND SELF-ABSORPTION

Sloth is one of the seven deadly sins. Laziness is typical of excess *tamas*, as is entitlement; unawareness of the needs of others; self-absorption; selfishness; irresponsible behaviour; and expecting others to pick up the shortfall of one's own *karma*.

GULLIBLE

Highly *tamasic* minds are run by unconscious emotions. They believe in the infallibility of "intuition" and tend to be naïve and gullible.

ADDICTED TO FEELINGS AND FEELING GOOD

People in whom *tamas* is predominant want to "feel" everything. Feeling is easy. They love to indulge their feelings by whatever means, be it in their drama-filled-and-fuelled relationships; sentimentality over people, situations, experiences and objects; and drippy movies or romance novels. Their way of communicating and interacting with the world is through emotion, not the intellect. *Tamasic* intellects are run by their "inner" feelings or instincts, intuition and moods, and as a result these people cannot see how irrational and incoherent their lives often are. They look down on thinking and believe that feeling is superior, and will tell you that you need to "think less and feel more" or that "your problem is you think too much."

SHORT-TERM PLEASURE

Highly *tamasic* people are inclined to sensuality and the pursuit of short-term pleasure, hedonistic enjoyers addicted to feeling good, even though the methods they employ to achieve it are almost always very unhealthy. Very often it is not what they do but what they avoid doing that causes problems psychologically and physically. *Tamasic* people love sleep because it allows them to shirk unpleasant tasks. Eating large quantities of sensuous foods is a favourite activity for *tamasic* people. Sex is a big draw, although unfortunately it tends to involve a bit of effort. The narcotic post-coital effect is pure *tamas*. "Yum! Feels great," soon becomes, "Ugh, feels awful, why did I do that?!" The short-lived success in the eighties and nineties of the famous sex *guru* Osho was due to the power of *tamas*. Sex addicts, alcoholics, drug addicts and gluttons are *tamasic*. How much effort does it take to get stoned or drunk? When you drink or get stoned, your problems seem to disappear, temporarily: "Out of sight, out of mind." But sadly, never for long. Our *vasanas* are Hydra monsters, growing as many heads as we try to cut off through avoidance, excessive indulgence or any other means.

When we talk about *tamasic* minds, we are not talking about a healthy appreciation of taking it easy and not stressing over results, which is advisable and the result of *tamas* in balance with *sattva*, nor the healthy appreciation of enjoyable sensual experiences, good food and sex included, quite the contrary. A life devoid of pleasure is not much fun – and also exacts a price. The "sweet joy of doing nothing" as the Italians coin it has a lot going for it, especially for highly *rajasic* types. We are talking about unbalanced *tamas* that makes it impossible for the mind to discriminate properly and becomes our way of dealing with life, an engrained stimulus-response of excess, dullness and negativity.

Physical and psychological pleasures are inseparable – and while both are wonderful while they last, all pleasure has a serious downside. To seek pleasure is an inbuilt drive in the human psyche, especially when we have taken care of our basic security needs, which is a primary human drive. Apart from the obvious fact that the relentless pursuit of pleasure is a trap, its fulfilment never satisfies the mind for long, but builds and strengthens binding *vasanas*. The Christian saying "the wages of sin is death" may sound extreme, especially because the Christian view of sin is guilt-oriented, but it is not far from the truth. To sin really means "to miss the mark" – to fall short of the truth. We all want to feel good, and pleasure feels good. It is natural to enjoy pleasurable experiences, and we deny ourselves pleasure at a cost to human happiness. But what we really want is to feel good all the time by knowing the fullness that is our true nature – and lasting joy is not to be found in objects or experience.

To become a prisoner of the fruitless search for increasingly more pleasure by whatever means leads many to very sad and tragic ends – others to unmitigated misery through the loss of mental or physical health, loss of quality of life and loved ones, loss of peace of mind. If we can observe our mind in the grip of deeply binding pleasure *vasanas,* even though it is obvious that the addiction to pleasure (whether it is to sugar and carbohydrates, alcohol, sex, drugs or anything else) causes much more suffering than the reward can possibly offer, nonetheless, the mind will cling tenaciously to it. In our futile search for lasting pleasure, we deny the price we pay, despite all evidence to the contrary. The seduction of pleasure's entitlement and fulfilment regales us from every corner, the unconscious desire for fullness militated mercilessly against us by ruthless advertisers that want to sell us *nirvana* in every form.

SELF-MEDICATING WITH FOOD, SEX OR DRUGS

This is typical of *tamas* at its worst. The mind is a helpless victim of its own desperate attempt to fulfil itself by whatever means, but fails miserably. Mental or physical ill health results, even death. This pattern will continue until the mind has had enough suffering, gains some objectivity and turns inwards. One does not have to look hard to find people who are clearly suffering intensely because of bad lifestyle choices driven by the search for pleasure, which is really the search for the bliss of the Self. For instance, in American society it is now taken as normal for people to be grossly overweight or obese. Unless one eats only real food, it is almost impossible to avoid sugar, as it is ubiquitous. Drug addictions of every kind (whether recreational or medical) are almost socially acceptable. Opioid and painkiller addictions are rampant.

GLUTTONY

Gluttony is another of the seven deadly sins and applies to anyone who cannot control their desires, whatever they are – food, sex, luxury, drugs or money. They are addicted to pleasure and never have enough of anything, always feel dissatisfied and are by definition insatiable – and miserable.

LUST

We have mentioned sex above, but as it is another of the seven deadly sins, lust and insatiable desire for sex is worth a mention on its own. Out of balance, this drive is the cause of so much suffering, debasement and evil. Sex is so intimately connected to a desire for union with the Self, and has enormous power over the mind because of the pleasure it delivers – albeit fleeting. Because it is impossible to hold onto and it ends so quickly, a mind heavily under the influence of *tamas* can become addicted to sex – and of course never has enough of it. The addiction to sex leaves the mind deeply dissatisfied, degraded and empty, yet the compulsive search for more pleasure gives rise to all manner of depravity – fantasies played out or imagined.

LIVING "IN POTENTIA," HOARDING AND AVOIDANCE

The tendency of a highly *tamasic* people is to hold onto the past as a reason to justify action or inaction as an avoidance strategy to deny fears, make excuses for dishonesty or the inability to make decisions, rationalizing. Such minds tend to hold onto everything, whether it is people, feelings, the past or "stuff." Their houses are a mess, full to over-flowing with things they cannot let go of and do not need. They avoid confrontation, so they have unresolved emotional and psychological issues, cling to and feed grievances and bad thoughts about themselves or others – which they try to hide or use to manipulate. They often put off doing what they need to do, and so have blowback *karma* that piles up, which compounds feelings of guilt, lack of confidence and self-esteem. Instead of facing the *karma* they have with people and situations, they try to run away from it.

BLAMING, EXPECTING OTHERS TO TAKE CARE OF US

Tamasic minds see everyone else as the cause of their problems: parents, siblings, ex-partners, employers, you name it. The fault never lies with them; they are incapable of objectively looking at themselves, are full of blame and unreasonable expectations of others to take care of their problems. The pay-off is that they be-lieve they can shirk responsibility for themselves in this way. This kind of mind usually feels martyred, victimized, hard done by life and everyone around it. It does not want what it has, wants things to be different from the way they are.

TAMAS MASQUERADING AS SATTVA

Tamasic minds, being prone to self-delusion, often like to believe that their sloppy, slobby lifestyles and dull minds are a sign of *sattva*.

The Upside of *Tamas*
ENDURANCE

Tamas is the very substance of matter, a heavy and steady energy. Balanced with *sattva* it is a grounding, stabilizing force. It produces endurance, forbearance, patience. Without it, we would not have the staying power to complete anything and we would not be "earthed," or grounded, nor would we be able to sleep. A *sattvic tamasic* mind is solid, earthy, realistic, steadfast and reliable.

ACCOMMODATION AND PATIENCE

Tolerance, patience, accommodation and careful methodical actions are indications of *sattvic tamas*.

USING DOUBT IN A HEALTHY WAY

Doubt is an essential faculty of the mind, and we need to use it with discrimination because things are rarely what they seem. *Sattvic tamas* uses doubt as a tool to navigate life and determine what it encounters. But it does not get stuck in doubt or make a meal of it.

ABILITY TO ENJOY LIFE

Nervous *rajasic* minds can never enjoy anything and require drugs, sex or entertainment to "have fun." *Sattvic tamas*, on the other hand, is "laid-back, chilled." When *sattvic tamas* is present, we can enjoy ourselves anywhere, whether there is anything "exciting" going on or not. We do not need to be entertained, party, drink or take drugs, but can join in with whatever is going on around us without overdoing anything – or not join in at all. Either way we are satisfied, happy.

ACCEPTING AND TOLERANT

A mind grounded in *sattvic tamas* likes its own company and is tolerant and accepting of other people. It exudes a friendly, open-minded and affable nature. It does not care much what other people are up to, because it has great tolerance for and understanding of the vicissitudes of human nature. It also knows that it is pointless to try to change anyone, because unless they have Self-knowledge, they will remain true to their conditioning.

REALISTIC AND CONSERVES ENERGY

Sattvic tamas is realistic about what energy it needs to employ to do anything and plans carefully, and takes its circumstances and nature into account. It does not expect things of itself that it cannot give and never promises what it cannot deliver. Its expectations in any given situation are consistent with its Field of Existence.

KARMA YOGA, STEADFASTNESS AND RELIABILITY

You can depend on *sattvic tamasic* types; they will not let you down without very good reason. They give their word and keep it, steadfastly doing what needs doing or they have promised, within reason. A consistent effort to achieve a stated goal is required to achieve goals, and *sattvic* minds can stick with the program and apply *karma yoga* always. Certain actions that flow from a commitment to a goal should be steadily performed. *Rajasic* types are very resolved at the beginning of any endeavour, but quickly lose interest when confronted with the enormity of the task and quickly seize some pretext to opt out of the required *dharmas*, whereas *sattvic tamasic* types stick with it. Steadiness, sometimes called devotion, implies an acute appreciation of the power of *rajas* and *tamas* to distract and cause laziness.

GOOD SLEEP

Tamas is essential for good sleep, and without it sleep is not possible.

Sleep is a thought in the mind, but it is a very particular kind of thought which occurs naturally when the mind and body are in balance with *rajas* and *sattva*, which produces *tamas* at the appropriate time so that the mind can shut down and rest. We can develop *sattvic tamas* with appropriate actions to keep *rajas* and *sattva* in balance. More on sleep in the next chapter on the negative side of *rajas*.

Solutions for Excess *Tamas*

RAJASIC ACTIVITY

If excess *tamas* clouds the mind and makes it incapable of functioning when it needs to, the answer is to do something *rajasic*, like exercise, a brisk walk on a cold day or a cold shower/swim on a hot day. Drink a cup of strong coffee or eat something *rajasic*. We must apply caution to not overdo anything, as the downside of too much *rajas* is, once again, too much *tamas*.

TAKE DISPASSIONATE STOCK OF YOUR LIFE

Take dispassionate stock of your health, what you eat, how you exercise, where you work, who you are in relationship with or associated with, how you handle spending and making money, sex, etc. Make a list of what you value most and least. Track yourself on the negative values you wish to change and the positive values you want to instil. Don't get militant; remember that fanaticism of any kind never works in the long run. Change what you can (without shirking your duty) and accept what you can't change with the *karma yoga* attitude. Stop making excuses for self-insulting habits, and commit to peace of mind. Become a disciple unto your own good Self.

STOP WASTING MENTAL ENERGY

Stop watching too much TV, wasting mental energy on social media, stupid movies, books or other media that deplete and depress the mind. Avoid all sensationalist reporting and doomsday thinking. Find something noble for the mind to do – read or write scripture or read inspirational books about people who have made a difference to the world with their contributions. Learn a new language. Become a knowledge-seeker in all areas of life – research and compile your own records about things that interest and excite the mind. Become dispassionately informed about what is going on in the big picture of life – especially the great things that are happening on the planet. Focus on the positive.

BECOME CREATIVE

Start a hobby or do something creative. You don't have to be an artist to be creative. Creativity is a natural function of the mind, feeds other mental/emotional faculties and is deeply satisfying for everyone, so develop it. Even if just the way you arrange spices in your kitchen, the toiletries in your bathroom or furniture in your home, appreciate your own style and taste. What matters is that you feel good about it, not that creativity has to live up to some ideal to qualify as "artistic." Take drawing or painting lessons – and press "pause" every time you hear yourself think or say "I can't" or "I don't have the talent" – and change it to "I can" and "so what?" What do you have to lose? Identify the language of *tamas*, because it is so predictable, so repetitive and so utterly boring.

FIND A NOBLE CAUSE

Find something noble for the mind to do. It does not matter what it is — as long as it uplifts the mind and brings genuine contentment and a feeling of contribution. If we don't find something noble for the mind to do, *tamas* will eat us up. Boredom and low self-esteem are the inevitable result; they drag the mind into self-destructive and self-insulting thoughts and actions, despondency and depression.

AVOID NEGATIVE PEOPLE LIKE THE PLAGUE

As much as possible, avoid negative people like the plague they are, to themselves and everyone around them. *Tamas* is highly contagious, and if you spend time with *tamasic* people, before long it will creep into your mind and make you dull, tired and depressed. Negative people are like psychic vampires who suck the blood of *sattva*.

TAKE STOCK OF YOUR DIET
Clean Up!

Fear runs highly *tamasic* people, so they hang onto everything. The answer is to get ruthless and clean out those unwanted things that clutter and bog down your life — whether they are physical objects, psychological issues or unresolved *karma* with people. There is no way around this if one wants to feel good about oneself and follow *dharma*. Everything one holds onto or puts off facing becomes worse and keeps us stuck in fear — but all fears are just paper dragons once faced head-on.

Sleep

If the mind cannot shut down due to excess *rajas* or *sattva*, there are practical steps to take to maximize one's sleep environment and lifestyle to cultivate *tamas*. If you are sleeping too much, the underlying problem is psychological, and you are either depressed and/or in denial about being angry/sad, etc. The only solution is Self-inquiry.

How the *Gunas* Influence Each Other

As I have made clear, it is fundamentally impossible to isolate the *gunas*, because they always work together, at least to some degree. I mention below just a few of the more obvious examples of how *rajas* and *tamas* work together.

Rajas-Tamas and Evil

Evil is a difficult thing to come to terms with and understand. If the Self is another word for love and love is all there is, how is it possible that evil exists? When *Maya* appears, *Isvara* in the form of the Creator appears and the Creation manifests. As we know, the Creation consists of and originates from all three *gunas*, the impersonal forces that shape the way duality (*samsara*) plays out. From the perspective of the person identified as a person, how we see the world and what happens to us – and it –will be interpreted by how the mind is conditioned by the *gunas*, i.e. the *vasanas*, which are also generated and coloured by the *gunas*.

"Evil" is *rajas* and *tamas* working together at their worst. It will always be present in the Creation because the apparent reality is a duality and one thing cannot exist unless its opposite also exists. If we had to remove evil, good would also not be possible, because the show would end. For the *gunas* to work to bring about a Creation and to keep it going, they must have the potential to express from one end of the spectrum to the other – thus we have good and evil (apparently).

Isvara's Creation is playing out as it must – we cannot see the big picture, because as a person we are not omniscient. *Karma* is impossible to understand from the person's perspective, because the person can only look at what takes place in the apparent reality from within the framework of the apparent reality – and that is subject to the influence of their subjective reality. Without Self-knowledge, this perspective will always be limited, as it is seen through the filter of duality, ignorance. The only solution is to see everything from the point of view of Consciousness.

Evil, *adharmic* acts (extreme *rajas* and *tamas*) and all their many manifestations are abominations, and one cannot but de-nounce them if *dharma* and peace of mind are what one values most. Nevertheless, to become emotional about this topic is to for-get the most important fact: it is not Consciousness in operation as the Creator, *Isvara*, that causes evil. Consciousness is not a big person with desires and fears, because Consciousness is limitless and as such has every conceivable power, including the power for so-called good and evil, ignorance. If ignorance is excluded from Consciousness, Consciousness becomes limited by its inability to limit itself, which, when we investigate, we know is not possible. The evil that one sees is a result of the incomprehension of the true nature of reality as a non-duality. If we know who we are, we hold non-injury as our highest value because we see everything as the Self. We know this is true because *sattvic* minds who understand their nature as Consciousness do no evil. Moreover, even those who don't know who they are, but understand the nature of the

Field of Existence, don't do evil either, because they follow *dharma* for their own peace of mind.

This is why Christ said, "Father, forgive them for they know not what they do." *Maya* (apparently) makes Consciousness think it is an individual and does not know that it is actually whole and complete Consciousness. When Consciousness is under the spell of *Maya*, it does actions that cause suffering to it and to others. At the same time, there is more good in the world (*sattva*) than there is evil because *dharma* is built into the Creation. Evil is just more obvious. *Maya* also makes Consciousness realize its nature as Consciousness, follow *dharma* and do many wonderful things. More people help and heal than perpetrate evil deeds. However, evil gets the most limelight, thanks in no small part to the internet and the media's addiction to bad news. That is what sells.

When we say the world is perfect as it is, we mean that it cannot be anything other than what it is. If the world could be different, assuming *Maya* "thought" that it was not serving Consciousness, it would make the world a different place. However, it never does. Therefore it must be true that there is a good reason for suffering, and indeed there is. Although *rajas* and *tamas* make Consciousness appear as dull and ignorant individuals, it also makes them kind, sensitive and "awake" (*sattvic*), which provides indirect knowledge of their nature as Consciousness, thus motivates their quest for direct knowledge.

Rajas-Tamas and Psychopathic Tendencies

Dharma is upheld by the majority of people on the planet, all appearances to the contrary notwithstanding. Even hardened criminals usually have an honour code they follow. *Dharma* is only totally absent in psychopaths or sociopaths, which results in what Vedanta calls *rakshasas*, devils: people who actively seek to harm others. The cause of psychopathy is different from the cause of sociopathy in that psychopathy is largely the result of "nature" (genetics), a physiological defect that results in the underdevelopment of the part of the brain responsible for impulse control and emotions. Sociopathy, on the other hand, is more likely the product of childhood trauma and physical and/or emotional abuse. Because sociopathy appears to be learned rather than innate, sociopaths are capable of empathy in certain limited circumstances but not in others, and with a few individuals but not others. Either way, they are both the result of the *gunas* and not personal.

It is pointless to ask why these aberrant mutations in the human race happen, because *Isvara* is not a person and does not allow or disallow anything. Nor can we say that *Isvara* is responsible for these conditions by not setting limits for good or bad. Everything is possible in *Maya*, which is why *Isvara* has built *dharma* into the matrix or life would be utter chaos. A good example is a place like Syria, where one can see the effects of the total breakdown of *dharma*. It's like the whole country has gone psychotic.

Statistics and the Big Picture

Statistics of whatever kind are a record of the "big picture." Regardless of seemingly endless statistical evidence to the contrary, the *Dharma* Field can only function as a *Dharma* Field if the majority upholds *dharma* – otherwise it functions as an *Adharma* Field. Of course the field is just Consciousness and is value-neutral – neither *dharmic* nor *adharmic* – but it is the way the *gunas* play out in the field that creates one or the other extreme and everything in between. It is a very small percentage of *adharma*, practised by the minority, which creates evil in all its forms, from the worst brutality to social, economic and spiritual abuses to petty crime. Psychopaths and sociopaths fall outside the spectrum, as they have no ability to evaluate their actions according to *dharma*. For some reason, that function does not operate in the mind – and of course it is not their doing. All tendencies arise from the causal body, and nobody is deliberately "evil" even if it appears to be the case.

The Subject of *Karma*

The way *karma* plays out is very often inexplicable. For example, who can explain the victims of psychopaths (including the psychopath, who is a victim of their own mind) and any other way *adharma* is experienced or inflicted on innocents? Again, *Isvara* does not dole out punishment via the infliction of psychopaths or evil deeds on us; the mechanism at work is impersonal, always. The psychopaths and perpetrators of evil suffer too, even though it appears they are incapable of remorse. Of course, when *adharma* and bad *karma* touch innocent people, especially if it comes too close to home, we are appalled and immediately personalize it; it is hard not too when it cuts so deep or presents such a dark and dangerous threat. What to do but apply the knowledge of the *gunas* in all situations and work on keeping the mind pure? We can only say, "There but for the grace of God go I."

Rajas-Tamas and Free-Floating Anxiety

All individuals are born in fear, *tamas*. The ego is a fear-thought born of the belief in separation. The king of all *vasanas* is what we call primordial beginningless ignorance, another name for *tamas*, or *Maya*. The more user-friendly term is "free-floating anxiety," which, if Self-knowledge is not firm, causes a non-specific unnamed existential fear, or dread. It is the fear that causes knots in the solar plexus, sometimes called the fear of "being and becoming." The Christians call it "original sin." It is always present, yet hidden in the causal body, and looks for objects to attach to (*rajas*). It is related to "others"; it is the ultimate experience of duality, or "otherness." Not everyone experiences it directly, although many do. In most *samsaris* it works out in petty mundane and indirect ways all day long, year after year, death by a thousand cuts. One can see it in the faces of most worldly people as they age – the accretions of disappointment, disillusion and the existential exhaustion of doership.

You will notice that it is called "beginningless" ignorance. The implied meaning of this phrase is that it is not endless, because Self-knowledge ends personal ignorance (*avidya*) for good and removes all existential suffering. For most people, it disappears and reappears with monotonous regularity. Because it is not permanent, we can determine that the fear is not real. It is a by-product of very deeply rooted *samskaras* (conglomeration of tendencies) that originate from macrocosmic, or universal, *rajas* (projection); it is part of the *Dharma* Field. If identified with being a person, it affects us all to some degree. Usually the *vasanas* will exhaust themselves after a while, but this one, this unnamed fear, is constantly "on" for most people. It is manageable if one does not identify with it, but to be free of the person, we must purify this fear through Self-knowledge, as it causes great mental agitation, which makes peace of mind impossible.

The Need to Be Right at All Costs

The need to be right at all costs arises because I don't feel good about myself, trust myself or feel secure in myself. I have low self-esteem (*tamas*), so have created a false protective identity around being right (*rajas*), which I depend on and will fight to defend. In the extreme, this becomes a totalizing identity – an identity that dominates all others (*rajas*) – and I am unconscious of it (*tamas*). The mind is so extroverted and unconscious (*rajas-tamas*) that it is totally identified with its point of view, belief system or ideology and will do almost anything to maintain it – in extreme cases even to the point of death for itself or anyone whom it sees as opposition. Religious wars are a good example, with the most recent brand of extremist terrorists (ISIS), who brandish their angry self-righteous views, kill themselves and murder innocent people – all in the name of the Greater Glory of God. All wars are the ultimate pursuit of a point of view.

On a lesser scale, a person who can never admit they are wrong, back down, can never apologize and must have the last say, is similarly identified with the body-mind. When their point of view or belief system is threatened or challenged, they feel as if their life is in danger. This kind of mental affliction meets all perceived threats with a rush of highly reactive energy, usually anger (*rajas*). Such identification is often the unconscious fear of death (*tamas*). This kind of mind will argue its point of view relentlessly. Not everyone has this unconscious tendency to this degree all the time; most people exhibit the tendency to some degree at times when the mind unconsciously identifies with its point of view.

Need for Control, Obsessive-Compulsive

Another symptom of the fear of death is the fear of loss of control

– surrender to *Isvara* (*tamas*), usually seen in people who are "control freaks" – anal-retentive about control of their external environment – home, work or pleasure. If things do not go their way, control freaks get upset, insecure and agitated (*rajas*). They have a compulsive need to do things their way and expect those around them to conform, and often extend their control to not only the behaviour but the appearance of others. They are extremely attached to and identified with appearances, especially their own. The fear of death also manifests in obsessive-compulsive behaviour of any kind.

Loss of Ego-Self, Fear of Death

Fear of death is one of the most common fears that humans must face and make peace with – and the biggest. Like all fears, it is completely gratuitous. However, unlike most fears, this is not because the fear of death has no basis in truth, but the opposite – it is completely unavoidable. No one gets out of life alive – as much as some New Age spiritual beliefs invest in the fallacy of "ascension." For the majority, this fear is constantly present in the mind, an ominous threat, always ready to pounce – but when it does, usually manifests in unconscious ways. People with strong religious or philosophical beliefs fare better with this fear. Belief that life continues in some way, if not for the body then for the soul, in a "better place" or the "world to come," some place other than the world it finds itself in, is usually seen as a place of sublime peace where one has everything one never had here on earth. Religious people sublimate the fear of death to their beliefs. However, only Self-knowledge can eliminate this fear permanently with the logic of our eternal existence as unborn and undying Consciousness.

A common symptom of the need for control and the unconscious fear of death is insomnia – resistance to *tamas*. We also see this fear when our minds cannot surrender to the loss of the ego-self in meditation. The ego is so afraid of letting go of the "small I" and allow itself to be subsumed by the "big I" – pure *sat*, Consciousness – that it can never let go. Fear (*tamas*) contracts. It makes the mind small, limited and afraid. For the body, death means return to the elements – *tamas*. For the ego, death spells the end of its existence. Sleep, like meditation, is a kind of death, and for it to obtain the ego must let go of the body-mind, surrender to *tamas* and the macrocosmic causal body – *Isvara*. A mind identified with ego and cannot sleep or be still is experience-oriented instead of oriented to who it really is – Consciousness.

focused on the future, Chased by the Past

A mind that cannot let go, focused on the future (projection/*rajas*), is chased by fear of the past (*tamas*). Its mental checklists of things it must do, avoid, accomplish or gain from people and situations is constant. It cannot rest, relax or enjoy itself, no matter what is going on – even when situations are favourable and it is getting what it wants. It is always afraid that it will lose what it is has gained, thus remains insecure. It is prone to jealousy, envy; lust; delusion; illusion; comparison of itself with others; greed; and anger – all symptoms of *rajas* and *tamas* working together.

Chapter 9

Why Everyone Needs God

THE GOD/ISVARA issue is a complex and contentious topic, and perhaps one of the most misunderstood. You may wonder why it comes into the discussion again at this point, since we have already touched on how Vedanta sees God and have unfolded the forces that create our psychology (the three *gunas*) as they relate to the ultimate solution to all life's problems, Self-inquiry. But the teaching on God encapsulates all the teachings and stages of Self-inquiry, so I end this first book in the Lifestyle trilogy with a more in-depth look at God-devotion according to Vedanta.

Though Self-inquiry is not affiliated with any religious or philosophical thought, I have bad news for people who have an aversion to the word or idea of "God," which is often the case with those qualified for Vedanta and ready to move beyond the idea of God as a parent. God is unavoidable, and must be understood if you really want a happy life, and especially if you want Self-inquiry to work for you. In Vedanta, the teachings on what or who God is are the subtlest, and for many inquirers a stumbling block. But to take your identity as the Self and free from limitation will not obtain without the assimilation of this teaching.

One Truth That Stands for All at All Times

Is there such a thing as truth that stands true for everyone in all situations? Most available literature and wisdom teachings through the ages, while inspirational, invariably leave us with more questions than answers. Seeing as nobody can stop bad things from happening, what gives us the grace to walk through despair without ever losing peace of mind? Blind faith in a powerful and external deity brings comfort to many. Vedanta is definitely not against the idea of a religious God, and in fact encourages a devotional attitude as essential to Self-inquiry. One of the meanings of the word "religion" comes from the Latin *religare*, meaning "to bind," and faith in God binds one to truth. But in traditional religious traditions, religion means to have faith in God by whatever name as a dualistic, paternal, bigger, better albeit "divine" person, separate from you, whom you must obey or else.

Some people believe that Vedanta is atheistic, but that is very far from the truth. In Vedanta, God is referred to as *Isvara* and not as a dualistic, external, personal God who hangs out somewhere above and beyond. *Isvara* is the all-pervasive, impersonal, non-dual principle, one with the Self, therefore one with us as individuals and as the Self. God is the Creator and governor of the Field of Existence, an intelligently designed universe that runs on natural laws and in which everything works perfectly, all appearances to the contrary notwithstanding. But to get to that understanding requires a particular and refined intellect.

Are We Matter or Spirit?

Today we live in particularly challenging times, and humanity is at a collective crossroads in many ways. Life would be a lot simpler if all we had to contend with was our physical survival. The human being is a combination of self-reflective, discriminating intellect/mind (spirit) and body (matter). This faculty developed early in our history as we increasingly needed answers to how to relate to our environment to survive physically and thrive psychologically. What differentiates human beings from other animals is the capacity for self-reflection. While self-reflectivity is all very wonderful, and without it we would still be swinging from trees, it does have a downside.

Spirit or Matter: Does It Matter?

For better or worse, self-reflectivity grants us "free will" and the ability to make reasoned choices. Thanks to this, we consider ourselves the "roof and crown" of sentient beings, capable of transcending the limits of being merely human. But along with the capacity for choice comes doubt. The doubting function is important because it gives us the ability to discriminate. It is vital for our survival because nothing in the world is what it appears to be. The downside of the ability to doubt, however, means we live in the twilight zone between ignorance and knowledge. We make mistakes and suffer because we are always confused about what the truth is, particularly the truth about what or who we are. Are we spirit or are we matter? How can we tell?

Animals have a much easier time because they are not self-reflective, so being blissfully ignorant that self-doubt or concern about the meaning of existence never occurs to them. They have only rudimentary intellects, and their power to think is only in terms of their instincts and desires. While we can also apply this description to many humans, animals differ from (most) of us in significant ways. They do not need to interpret their environment other than for physical survival, such as ideal times to hunt or when to hide from prey, whereas understanding our environment for our physical and mental well-being is imperative for us. Animals act purely according to their God-given program, from which they cannot deviate. We humans, however, can deviate from our program, usually much to our detriment.

Preprogrammed Behavioural Determination

Because of preprogrammed behavioural predetermination, animals do not feel incomplete or separate. They are incapable of worry, because they accept reality as it is. They do not chase objects to complete themselves, because unlike humans they have no concept of being incomplete or inadequate. Unable to conceptualize either the future or death, they fear neither. While animals experience physical fear as a protective mechanism, they do not have the capacity for rational evaluation. Therefore they do not suffer psychologically from the things that happen to them, in them or around them.

Animal-lovers will protest and claim that animals do have feelings and suffer emotionally. It's true that domesticated pets or animals who come into close contact with humans are positively and negatively affected, and develop strong bonds with us. Many animals seem to display human-like emotions and tendencies, such as sadness, love, affection, loyalty to and care for young and members of their group as well for humans. Even wild animals such as elephants show a marked capacity for meaningful connection and empathy. But this does not make animals self-reflective. As much as we tend to project our humanity and neuroses onto them, no animal can break out of its program. And no animal is going to write a book or give a talk on the meaning of existence anytime soon.

The Ones That Worry

Making bad decisions or breaking the rules of life, fear of inadequacy, of death, of what might or might not happen in the future, are solely expressions of the nature and plight of human beings. We are what the Vedic scriptures define as "the ones that worry." Moreover, and perhaps most importantly, because animals have no free will, they cannot break *dharma*, the natural laws that govern the Field of Existence. So there is no *karma* for them. They are exempt from the moral and psychological human order of existence, whereas everything that happens in the Field affects us psychologically and we pay a big price for breaking the natural laws of life.

Animals are not attached to results and do not suffer when they do not get what they want. It's not that they do not act for results, because obviously they do. For instance, a hungry lion chasing a zebra is not just having fun or seeing how fast it can run. It definitely wants to kill and eat the zebra. But if it does not catch its zebra dinner, the lion will not get depressed or beat up on itself. It won't need to book an appointment with its therapist to discover why it failed or stay awake at night worrying if it will ever catch a zebra. The lion does not care or suffer from self-doubt, and will try again the moment the opportunity presents itself.

On the other hand, human beings, caught in the twilight zone of doubt, care very much if they don't get the results they want. Not only that, but we evaluate ourselves mercilessly based on our success and failure at doing so. Our happiness and suffering boils down to whether we get what we want or avoid what we don't want. The results of our actions, however, are value-neutral, and above all not up to us. Humans do have *karma* because we can make choices that often result in suffering for ourselves and others.

Karma Is Only Meaningful When Evaluated

Everything in life is *karma*, or results, either in the form of thoughts and feelings, action or inaction. *Karma* becomes meaningful only when we learn to evaluate it. We either like our *karma*, don't like it or are indifferent to it. While we have a choice as to how we relate to our *karma*, we cannot avoid it. One of our greatest challenges is to learn to navigate life free of the psychological and physical suffering that ensues when we don't understand what's going on, make bad decisions and don't get what we want. To do this, we must develop the ability to assimilate the meaning of experience so that we can learn and grow from it. We cannot do that unless we understand the logic of existence, which entails a threefold process: (1) understanding who we are; (2) understanding the natural laws that govern the Field we are a part of and live in; and (3) understanding how we relate to it. For that, we need God-knowledge because God and the Field are synonymous.

The History of Spirituality

Almost the entire history of human spirituality is one long interconnected ever-evolving and remarkably cohesive effort to fashion God in our own image. We find the only exception in Vedic scripture, the planet's oldest extant texts on existence. Predating most religions by thousands of years, these scriptures made it clear that God and the Field are non-different and impersonal. At heart, however, religion is an attempt to make sense of the Divine – and how we fit into the picture – by projecting onto God our emotions and our personalities by ascribing to it our traits and desires, our strengths and our weaknesses. In short, religion conceives of God as an infinitely superior, invisible and untouchable version of us. Thus, whether we are aware of it or not, and regardless of whether we're believers or not, what most of us envisage when we think about God is a divine portrayal of ourselves: a human being but with superhuman powers and attributes.

The Anthropocentric God

The Mesopotamians, Egyptians, Greeks, Romans, Indians, Persians, Hebrews, Arabs and the plethora of more recent religions all devised theistic systems in human terms and with human imagery. The same holds true for non-theistic traditions, such as New Age counterculture, pagan and indigenous belief systems. Even Jainism and Buddhism conceive of the spirits and *devas* that populate their theologies as superhuman beings who are, like their human counterparts, bound by the laws of *karma*. Though for the most part Islam deems it sacrilegious to depict the Divine in form, this does not change the fact that the Islamic God, like all the others, is ascribed superhuman qualities.

Now it seems the personified God is in trouble. The problem with seeing God in human terms is that if God is a magnified and superior version of us, he (it's almost always a He) must also share our flaws and limitations, but on an even greater scale. Unable to reconcile this limited and gender-centric view of God, growing numbers now reject religion on the grounds that it is not rational and just does not make intellectual sense. How or why are we supposed to worship a capricious and fickle God who created us as flawed beings, yet demands perfection from us in a flawed, ever-changing, unpredictable, unfair and perilous world where the odds are stacked against us?

Do We Really Need God?

This raises some important questions. Do we even need religion?

Or God, for that matter? While rejection of the notion of a petty tyrannical God is a good idea, if we say that we don't need God at all and throw God out, what will give humanity a moral compass to sustain us through dark times, let alone the normal challenges of life? More importantly, who are we without God, how do we relate to our environment, and how do we understand ourselves and life if we reject the intelligent cause behind it all? There is no way to make sense of life without including an intelligent creative force.

Scientists, atheists and thinkers may understandably deny the existence of an almighty yet flawed humanoid God. But, although most people have never thought about it, if we apply the simple logic of inference, we can legitimately infer that there must be an intelligent conscious cause behind the Creation. You cannot deny that you exist and are conscious, because you must exist and be conscious to deny your existence/consciousness. Therefore you cannot deny that God exists, because without God as cause there would not only be no existence, but no logic to existence. Whether we know it or not, we all seek God because we want to be happy. Being happy involves understanding our mind and being in tune with our environment.

Programmed to find Answers

To say there is no God relies on nihilistic thinking and the principle of infinite regress or random chance, all of which lack logic. As self-reflective beings, our program hardwires us to search for and find the meaning of our existence. We are impelled to find answers to questions such as: How did we get here? Where do we come from or go to? What sets off infinite regress or causes randomness, and how can consciousness arise from matter? Nobody can ignore this fundamental drive, not even the committed atheist.

It makes no difference if in our search for the meaning of existence (or release from it) we find religion, drop out in India and chase *nirvana*, turn to science, rely on work and worldly success, sport, sex, entertainment, drugs or the bottom of a bottle. Wherever we seek and whatever we choose to call it, we are looking for God, period. Whether we realize it or not, the lightning storm of the brain's endless activity is all about evolving to find God. This is because finding God is not a choice. It is a necessity. Those who do not find God (or a suitable substitute) do not fare well in this world.

We Need a (New) God Narrative

Perhaps the problem is not God, but our narratives about God. We need a new narrative that is not anthropomorphic but impersonal. The propensity to see God in human terms is what binds man and God to the smallest common denominator – the inadequate limited human. While God and man have different functions in the Field of Existence, we share the same essential nature, which is neither human nor divine. Our shared nature is eternal, all-pervasive, unlimited and ordinary Consciousness, the non-dual essence and source of the Field of Existence. We add the adjective "ordinary" because if something is all there is, it cannot be extraordinary, because there is nothing to compare it to.

A Paradigm Shift

To come to a different view of God, we need a paradigm shift in our thinking. This will allow us to conduct an inquiry into the Creation that is independent of personal views and beliefs, one that includes intelligent cause and frees us from limitation. We experience Consciousness as our Existence all the time, whether we realize we do or not. Even though this knowledge is at the heart of more enlightened modern-day physics and neuroscience, the "old guard" stubbornly clings to its outdated views.

Some scientists still insist that the universe is random. Its origin, they purport, was an explosion that came out of nothing, and consciousness evolved from dead matter. The synapses in our brains somehow fire up like spontaneous combustion and create consciousness. Now, that's a bit of a stretch, even for most scientists, because everyone knows the brain is just meat without consciousness, and nothing comes from nothing. How is it possible for inert matter to create consciousness? And if you still insist that consciousness comes from matter, where does matter come from? There had to be something that the Big Bang "banged" from. What was there prior to objects to make them manifest?

Many believe that the current struggle between science and spirituality will shape our future. Many of our pioneering scientists were actually mystics, Nikola Tesla, for example, a thinker and inventor heavily influenced by Vedic philosophy. He said: "The day science begins to study non-physical phenomena, it will make more progress in one decade than in all the previous centuries of its existence."

Max Planck, the physicist who has been credited with originating quantum theory, for which he won the Nobel Prize in physics in 1918, famously said: "I regard consciousness as fundamental. I regard matter as derivative from consciousness. We cannot get behind consciousness. Everything that we talk about, everything that we regard as existing, postulates consciousness."

Yet mainstream science lags behind, and despite its noble cause, is aggressively limited to and dominated by materialism. Science may have explained many things on the material plane, yet nothing it has come up with frees us from the limitations of being human. Scientists proclaim that it is not their job to provide answers to the meaning of existence, and generally deplore the unmeasurable and murky world of spirituality, which is fair enough. We cannot blame them for such a myopic view. But as much as its proponents try to stay away from the topic of consciousness because of the metaphysical implications, science has reached a point where certain basic mysteries it has grappled with for a long time cannot be solved without resolving consciousness.

Chemically Determined or Random Process

The scientific world view traces all activity, all physical processes in the brain, including our imagination and creativity, to either chemically determined or random processes, depending on which strain of materialism you confront. A century after the quantum revolution in physics, scientists still cannot agree that matter and energy both emerged from a timeless state that is either an empty void (which no one accepts) or a field of infinite possibilities, a veritable womb of creation, which almost everyone is beginning to accept. And as much as many scientists find it offensive and religious types contest it, the world's ancient sages and spiritual teachers knew about this timeless domain long before religion appeared or physics arrived with its exact measuring devices and methods.

In the beginning,
There was neither existence nor non-existence,

All this world was unmanifest energy…
The One breathed, without breath, by its own power
Nothing else was there…

(Excerpt from the *Rig Veda*, one of the oldest known religious texts, circa 1700 BCE)

Existence and Non-Existence Have No Location

The Vedic seers knew that neither existence nor non-existence can be located, since that applies only to things with a beginning and an end. Existence (or Consciousness, if you prefer) does not begin or end. Physicists refer to what came before matter as a singularity that exploded into being in a blinding flash of light: the Big Bang. But because the pre-Creation "state" did not happen in time, it must still be "there." No matter how many Big Bangs bang and universes expand across billions of light years only to collapse on themselves and withdraw into the void, nothing will change or can change on the pre-Creation level. This "level" has no location, no boundaries and is unchanging because it is not in time or space, i.e. not in duality. It is non-dual and omnipresent. It is not a "state," because all states exist in time and therefore come and go. It is the unchangeable knower of all states.

Science proceeds perfectly in everyday affairs without tackling the thorny issue of "metaphysics" as materialists like to call all things related to God and spirituality. But as reality is a shared concern and not to be left to "specialists," the issue of where the cosmos came from matters a great deal to us because the answer reveals not only where we come from, but who we are. We cannot avoid the question "Is the universe conscious?" If it is, as it clearly must be, then our minds are embedded in the cosmic mind – it cannot be any other way. What this cosmic mind is, and what it says about who we are, are neither specialist, scientific nor even necessarily religious questions. They cut to the heart of what God is, and by extension what man is and is not.

Which Came First?

If we ask which came first, consciousness or matter, we need to ask another question: Which stands alone? There is no debate here, as it's clear that living organisms are dependent on Consciousness, because they are inanimate without it. But it's not so obvious that inert objects are also made of Consciousness. However, if we investigate matter scientifically, it breaks down into increasingly smaller particles and then into space – and – the most important factor which few take into consideration: the knower of particles and space. Science calls this the "observer effect" because it has demonstrated that the act of observation can alter scientific results. But it does not know that the Consciousness in the scientist is the non-experiencing observer itself: the knower, the known and the source of all that is known. It is a dispassionate "all-knowing eye in the sky": always watchful, always aware and never not present.

We Cannot Stuff the Infinite Into the Finite

The arguments in the scientific community over the nature of consciousness are heated, and the prevailing view assumes that alternative hypotheses are all "pseudoscience." Not long ago, no self-respecting scientist would even dare raise the subject for fear of being labelled a crackpot and thus seriously undermine their credibility. Isn't that amazing? How persuasive ignorance is! It's almost funny. The material scientist who seeks a material equation will never grasp Consciousness, because, being non-dual and not *in* this universe but the *source* of it, Consciousness is not subject to any of the natural laws of physics that run the whole Creation. The materialist scientists try to make Consciousness fit into what they think and know, which will never work. How can a finite mind, applying finite logic, stuff the infinite into a finite theory? It is impossible, no matter how good the mathematics.

And yet, although quantum physics is a thorn in the side of science, it is the closest science has come to proving that reality is not what it appears to be, and verges on the mystical. As a scientific theory, quantum physics has been bad news for scientists since it first emerged some one hundred or so years ago. It destroyed all convoluted theories designed to preserve scientific ideas of reality prior to it, and it won't go away. Even today, to paraphrase the famous saying by the scientist Werner Heisenberg that quantum physics is not only stranger than we think but stranger than we can think, holds true. Though quantum physics has invaluable practical applications (such as telecommunications, upon which our electronic and computerized world depends) and allows us to understand many things about how our world works, like light or how the sun burns, it's almost as though science knows what quantum physics can do, but not why it can do what it does. The only thing predictable about it is how unpredictable it is.

Maddeningly for the materialist, quantum mechanics shows that quantum properties simply do not exist independent of their observation (measurement). Objects are only "real" from the observer's point of view. They have no actual substantive reality, but dissolve into the substratum, which science calls the unified field, and we know as the ground of being, Consciousness. Scientists just don't realize that the observer *is* Consciousness – big

"C." Even so, quantum physics only operates within the Creation and is not capable of explaining Consciousness; it can only reveal probabilities of different realities. It does not destroy the notion of duality, even though it points to non-duality.

Consciousness Never Gets Switched On or Off

Furthermore, though materialists may balk, what quantum physics shows is that while matter is dependent on Consciousness, Consciousness depends on nothing, because it is the observer whose very observation makes the observed possible. It exists with or without matter, because it is eternal, the one and only constant factor. Consciousness is not something that gets "switched on" at the moment of observation, because if that were so, the scientist would get switched off when Consciousness switched off. Science would begin and end as does everything else, including the scientist. But science, which is the quest for knowledge, is eternal.

Consciousness is not something that is there only when we are aware of it, because without it our conscious awareness would be impossible, and we would not exist. All matter, including the body-mind, comes and goes, but Consciousness, the knower of matter/the body-mind, does not. Consciousness is the real you. As Consciousness we are eternal, unborn, undying, unchanging, whole and complete, always present, never not here. We call Consciousness the Self – capital "S" – to distinguish it from our reflective, or individual, consciousness.

Only the Body Dies

You might say this is unprovable, and you would be right if you take yourself to be the body, because the body ends permanently at death. In spite of the Christian claim of the resurrection of Christ, nobody has ever come back from death to confirm that you do not end after the death of the body, though many near-death experiences (NDEs) confirm it. Scientists try to debunk them because they can't explain them. It's also true that those who experience an NDE often don't understand or assimilate the real import of their experience, because they are still identified with the body during the experience.

If you are identified with the body-mind, you are in duality, and from that position there is no way to prove anything but duality. Anything can be true or false, not to mention finite. Deductive reasoning will only get you so far. Science is all about the rational approach, but it does not use pure reasoning or logic as the essential part of its methods. Its epistemology is the five senses. Science calls knowledge gained from the senses that it can verify through established scientific methods "empirical" knowledge.

Consciousness Is Not an Object of Knowledge

But the senses function in duality and only work for knowledge of objects. Consciousness is not an object of knowledge, because it is not in duality. We cannot measure Consciousness, because it is the measure of all things. The knower of all objects, it is that which makes knowing anything possible. The mind/senses are the effect, or the object, and as such are not capable of knowing or understanding Consciousness, because it is the cause, the subject. The effect can never understand the cause, because the cause is subtler than the effect. And the subject is subtler than the object.

Consciousness exists in "another order" of reality: non-duality. Non-duality and duality never meet, though they are not in opposition to each other, because nothing opposes non-duality. Non-duality allows everything to be because it is free of everything. If this were not so and duality could impact non-duality, there would be no possibility of freedom from it.

Duality Is Persuasive

Duality, however, is persuasive when we identify with the body and look at the world from the sensory perspective. And most of us are hardwired to do just that. The age-old philosophical and religious takes on what reality is or the nature of God are not much better at finding solutions than materialist atheistic science is. It is a big leap from the dualistic view of God as something separate from and infinitely better than me, or from denial of the existence of God, to the logical, non-dual, "non-different from me" God. When we are identified with the body-mind, we are limited to experience of the world through our senses, which are constrained and programmed to function only within a limited range.

From this perspective, there seems to be no other option but to deny or personify and objectify a Creator God, that is, until we have evolved to assimilate non-dual God-knowledge. Religion reinforces this view, as it creates an external, almighty, invisible God that we must fear and implore. Science fares no better, with its materialistic arguments that seemingly prove the non-existence of God. Vedanta has no quarrel with science, but the difficulties modern science has in understanding Consciousness or the origin of the universe show how counter-intuitive non-duality is.

Perception Is an Object Known to Consciousness

Western religions do not approach God as Consciousness, the

ground of being, though some Eastern religions do, particularly Vedic religion. Material science knows about consciousness, but it cannot make the obvious connection of matter and Consciousness, because it relies on perception and inference as its means of knowledge. Scientists do not realize that perception is an object known to Consciousness in the form of the scientist itself and that perception is dependent on Consciousness. Science can reason up to the point when Creation began — but it cannot tell us what happened before it began, and it never will. Though scientists are scrambling around with many speculative theories to explain what happened before the appearance of particles — the most popular being inflation theory — they cannot come up with a cohesive hypothesis because of the huge gap in their understanding.

The Science of Non-Dual Consciousness

That gap will never be bridged with current scientific methods, because beyond the Big Bang theory of Creation there is no information from which to reason. Inference does not work here. The only means of knowledge that works at this point is non-dual knowledge, because the Creation originates from non-dual Consciousness. "Non-dual" means "not two or more." While we say that all is one, technically non-duality does not mean only one either, because one implies two. If it is non-dual, there are no objects, no time, no space and no experience. Non-duality means "nothing other than." How do you measure that?

Vedanta is a science of non-dual Consciousness, but scientists and many atheists and intellectuals invariably dismiss non-duality as metaphysical nonsense. Yet, even if science were to accept non-dual Consciousness as the ground of being, it won't remove our suffering unless we accept our non-dual identity as Existence/ Consciousness. A purely intellectual understanding of Consciousness is not enough to break the hold duality has on the mind. You can approach Consciousness with the intellect, but you will only get to the doorway of non-dual knowledge and no further until the mind has evolved to want different things and the intellect has been trained to think differently. If we are too conceited to accept that our thinking may be flawed or lacking, and so vain that we think we can wrestle the ultimate answers from this world solely with our intellect, we will remain stuck in the world of duality, which is tantamount to conflict and suffering. We will never get through the doorway of non-duality to enjoy freedom from fear and limitation.

There Is Nothing More Fundamental

Life, the Field of Existence, duality — our universe — may well have begun with a bang and may end with one. Or maybe we will just float off into nothing in an ever-expanding universe. Nobody knows. But we do know it will end. Where does it go? It becomes unmanifest and disappears into non-dual Consciousness from whence it came. Scientists know that there is a fundamental substratum that cannot be negated, which is called the unified field, among other names. But what they do not know is that the fundamental substratum is non-dual Consciousness, the ground of being. The word "fundamental," like the word "unique," cannot have a comparative or a superlative, because if it did, it would void the meaning of those two words.

There is no such thing as "uniquer" or "uniquest" or "more fundamental." If something is the ground of being, that is the end of the line. But in duality, the world of the senses, we can never be sure that what we take to be the fundamental qualities of the world will stay fundamental for very long. Truth in anything, even in science, is always provisional. In fact science can sidestep the idea of truth altogether. There is only what is truer than what is currently known to be true. Progress in science might even be understood as the certain knowledge that there is always some as yet undiscovered quality that is more fundamental and "truer."

We Are Always Stepping Out of Duality

Our saving grace is that because Consciousness is not "in" duality, we can step out of duality. Even though the senses can trap the mind in duality without non-dual knowledge, we step out of duality all the time without realizing it. To find out who you are, there is no need to take a trip to India and sit in a cave in meditation for twenty years, chant *mantras*, take a trip on acid or court any other mystical "out-of-body" experience.

You can override sensory input by asking yourself just a couple of simple questions: Who or what is looking out of your eyes? Religion says that God is invisible and untouchable. We say that God is not only the one looking out of your eyes, it is all that is visible and what allows us to see it. Our vision cannot help but be organized around light, and we cannot see anything without it, so we could say that God is both light and that which makes light possible. The same brain responses that enable us to see a tree or a person as a tree or a person, instead of a ghostly swarm of buzzing atoms, also enable us to experience God every time we open our eyes. We just have to know what we are looking at.

If that doesn't help, let's once again ask, how do you know what you know? We have already established that you cannot be what you know, just like you can't be what you see, right? What you know and what you see is known to you. Who and what is that? If you say it is your mind that sees and knows objects outside of yourself, are the objects or your thoughts and feelings not known to you? Yes. Do they know you? No, they do not. Your thoughts and feelings and the objects you are looking at are not conscious. But you are. The only thing we need to determine is who that "you" is. And then the trick is to live that truth as your primary identity.

To function in this world, the senses relay information from the Field to our mind, which then interprets it through our intellect, thoughts and feelings. But there is some ever-present factor that always knows what we are seeing, thinking and feeling. Therefore you cannot be your mind. Your mind is another object known to you. Even in deep dreamless sleep, when there is no information exchange between the Field and the mind, consciousness must be present or you would not know you slept when you wake up. And in fact you would never wake up again. If you accept this – and how can you not? – you must agree that Consciousness cannot be negated, for two main reasons. Apart from the obvious fact that you could not be here reading this if you are not conscious, as we have said, there must be Consciousness present for you to deny its existence, as is demonstrated in the following true story.

Can You Step Out of Consciousness?

An alternative-thinking scientist was giving a lecture at the Max Planck Institute, the High Church of quantum physics, on the topic of the unified field and consciousness.

A very irate member of the audience, a well-known physicist, got up and challenged the speaker. His outrage concerned the fact that the speaker equated the unified field with consciousness.

So the speaker asked him: "Are you conscious?"

"Of course I am," the audience member replied.

The speaker asked, "Well then, could you please tell me how you step out of consciousness?"

The scientist had no answer. You cannot step out of Consciousness. You cannot step out of God. You cannot step out of your Self.

God Is Consciousness

The crux of the matter is then, what or who is God? Are God and Consciousness the same thing? We say yes, but what that means requires a different kind of thinking which is not religious or scientific in the way we usually understand those terms. We agree with the scientific method of establishing truth independent of personal views and opinions. What Vedanta teaches is neither "spiritual" nor materialistic. It explains the relationship between spirit and matter – how God/Consciousness and all sentient and insentient beings share the same essence. This teaching is counterintuitive and needs to be properly unfolded because the mind tends to interpret data according to its own ideas, which may or may not stand independently.

We teach that God is not only not "supernatural" or divine, but the only natural "thing" there is. In fact God is ALL there is, and not some remote extra-cosmic superhuman deity beyond our reach who doles out good and bad *karma*. You cannot divorce yourself from God, no matter how much you try. So the bad news is, if you want to deny God, you will have a hard time. And the good news is, if you are looking for God, you can't miss. We say that God is the essential part of the equation without which life makes no sense. Without an intelligent source, our existence has no foundation at all.

Denial of God Is a Cruel Waste of Joy

Denial of this is a waste of time, energy and of joy. The only sane way to live is to embrace God. Resistance is futile, so why try? If you don't or won't love God because you think you are so smart and God is a childish fantasy or a deluded religious fiction, God won't be hurt or even notice. But you will. God neither needs nor seeks our love, but cannot not love us, as God is intelligent and unlimited because God is non-dual Consciousness. Our refusal to love God is ignorance: a kind of masochistic refusal to love ourselves. As a result, we end up the only losers.

To Know God You Need Knowledge, Not Beliefs

To know God, you need God-knowledge, not religion. God doesn't make sense as a belief, because by saying God is a belief you're stating that God may or may not exist. All religions are based on beliefs, and because all beliefs lack certainty and can be negated, they must be defended. If your relationship with God is based on non-negatable knowledge instead of belief, there is no need for defence or beliefs.

The test for something that qualifies as non-negatable knowledge is this:

1. It stands alone, independent of my beliefs.

2. It is true in all time frames (past, present and future) and all

three states: awake, dream and deep sleep.

3. The knowledge is true to the subject, regardless of my beliefs and opinions (e.g. if a black cat appears in front of me, I will see a black cat and not a grey cat, even though I hate black cats and love grey ones).

If "your" knowledge fails on any of these three factors, it is subjective and not objectively true, thus can be negated. So when people say they don't believe in God, it's usually the religious subjective God they're referring to, whether we are talking about the Christian, Jewish or Muslim "God." In other words, they are saying they don't believe in a Big Daddy who sends people to heaven or hell depending on how many "Our Fathers" they recite; *adhans*, or calls to prayer, they heed; or *tefillahs*, prayers, observed; not to mention God is pretty unpopular these days, considering all the violence, confusion and corruption He has inspired for so long. Eastern religions like Buddhism and Hinduism do not have this problem, as their understanding of God is pantheistic. But to understand God for disenchanted and understandably critical Westerners like us, we need to clean the muddied slate and start from scratch.

How to Define God

Let's try to define God in a way that makes sense to a twenty-first-century-tuned intellect's view.

If you have trouble getting on board with the ideas presented so far, let's try defining God in a way that makes sense even to a jaded intellect. Through the process of logical, impartial, independent as well as empirical reasoning, we can show that the source of everything is unborn, changeless, limitless, non-dual Consciousness, in other words, that everything resolves into Consciousness and, most importantly, this is your own unexamined experience.

What is it that brought you into this world? It was not your mamma and papa, because though your mamma and papa know how to have sex, they have no idea how to biologically create a human being. What is it right now that is circulating your blood, keeping your heart beating, telling you to eat or drink and putting thoughts in your head? What is it that's growing everything: the grass, the flowers, the trees and the hair on your head? You could say it is nature and that is what brought you here. If so, what is nature?

God Is the Cause and the Effect

If we put all religious connotations of God aside for the moment, let's say nature is the effect and God is the cause. God is responsible for all the objects, including you and me. In short, God is the cause of everything and because its effects are the cause in a different form, everything is God. A good analogy is milk (cause) and cheese (effect). Cheese is not cheese without milk; it has changed its state, but it's still fundamentally milk. Its form has changed but the essential nature has not. The essential nature of anything is that without which a thing is not a thing. If we remove milk from cheese, it is not cheese anymore – just as if we remove sweet from sugar, salty from salt and heat from fire, we will no longer have sugar, salt or fire.

Or looked at another way – take, for example, a spider spinning its web. Is there a difference between the spider (cause) and the web (effect)? Yes and no. There is no web without the spider, and though the web is not the same as the spider, it is not different either, because it is made from the spider. Likewise, God is the essential nature, the universal intelligence, the energy and material behind all creation, and it is the Creation too. Therefore we cannot remove God from the equation, because God is our essential nature. Though we do not have God's powers as individuals, we share the same identity.

The End of God as Parent

God isn't a person with human qualities like a bearded old man doling out rewards and punishments according to our good and bad deeds. God is the power in and behind the Creation, an impersonal principle like gravity. For many, hearing that God is impartial and impersonal is a great relief because it lets them off the hook. For others, it is the worst news. It sounds so nihilistic and bleak – the big bad void. An infinite God that is nowhere and everywhere cannot be found and is of no use, if you are identified with being a person – i.e. identified with the body-mind.

If all you are after is God's "stuff," we understand this difficulty. Religions developed around the idea of a dualistic God who is there to protect, uplift and take care of us, but who also punishes. If you are not after God's stuff but after God, you are ready for Self-inquiry. We must warn you though that non-duality does away with the dualistic parent-God you must obey and placate. So if you are attached, it's best to stay where you are.

But if you have matured beyond the need for a parent-God, non-duality gives God back to us in a very different way. There is no need to seek this God, because it is you and everything around you. The non-dual God is not a nurturing or punishing parent. It does not ask anything of us and does not judge, nor does it tell us what to do (or else!).

Yet the non-dual God gives us everything we need, including the complete freedom to mess up. What's more, it offers us freedom from the messed-up version of who we think we are. It explains the laws (*dharma*) that operate in this world and how to manage our mind with Self-knowledge so that we don't mess up anymore. This God is in charge of rewards and punishments only according to the nature of our actions, which depend on whether we follow *dharma* or not.

The Field Runs on Natural Laws

The Field of Existence runs on natural, universal and immutable physical, psychological and moral laws that we cannot contravene without consequence. We call these laws universal *dharma*, which manifests as the Field of experiences that present themselves to us moment to moment. Physical laws exist to ensure that fire is always hot, sugar is always sweet, gravity is always gravity, etc. Psychological laws exist so that certain circumstances, like feeling loved, leave the mind peaceful, while others, like exposure to violence, leave it agitated. Moral laws exist so that lying, stealing or hurting others feels wrong, and being helpful, cheerful or showing compassion feels right.

The Law of Non-Injury

The law of non-injury is innate for most of us. If you doubt this and have a low opinion of humanity, research has shown that most people react instinctively to help a stranger in trouble without thought for themselves. This fact became so evident with the advent of the Covid-19 pandemic that many people surprised themselves and were surprised by humanity's innate connectivity and capacity to care. We may be a pathetic lot as humans in many ways, but it is only a very small minority who actually actively set out to cause harm. Nonetheless, while we all understand intuitively that there are universal laws, very few people understand that to live a relatively peaceful life all we need to do is follow them, assuming we want to be happy!

Universal Laws

Dharma basically comes down to the following: do no harm; respect nature, yourself and others; manage your thoughts and feelings for peace of mind (and don't take either too seriously); act appropriately and timeously; contribute to life. In short, don't be a jerk. If you follow these rules, your life experience (*karma*) will respond accordingly. *Karma* takes two forms: (1) it is any action, thought or word, and (2) the ("good" or "bad") results of any action, thought or word.

Your *karma* shows whether nature, or God (the Field), is currently on your side. Sometimes we follow *dharma* (or think we do) and get the opposite of what we want. There is always a lesson in this, regardless of whether we know what it is or not. But if we violate *dharma*, nature/life will cut us down and make us feel pain sooner or later. Nobody escapes *karma*. Just as a bullet once fired from a gun cannot be stopped, your *karma* will unerringly find its target. God never makes mistakes.

Clean up your *karma* by following *dharma*, and for the most part it will be smooth sailing. God isn't watching you. God is just handing out *karma* – the results of your actions. It's all impersonal, but it's the opposite of bleak and depressing. The non-dual God takes away all fear of lack, loss and death, and gives back to us our inviolate, unchanging and inherent wholeness. God's laws are built into the system. Therefore it's good to know the rules and live by them, because without God-knowledge you're a rudderless ship blown from trough to crest on the unpredictable, treacherous ocean of duality. Sooner or later, you will be smashed on its rocks.

Duality Is an Apparition, Not Reality

I have stated in many places in the last chapters that most of us experience the world as a duality: you are there, and I am here. Believing that they are separate from everything and everyone else, and identified with the body-mind, most people thus live in worry and fear. But duality is only an appearance, an apparition, and not reality. In fact all is one and there is no separation, because reality is non-dual. There is only one of us here appearing in seeming multiplicity. Duality tricks us and reverses the data we receive through our senses, putting us under its "spell."

Non-dual knowledge of God reverses that reversal so we can see life as it really is. It's like we have been standing on our heads our whole lives, and for the first time we are standing on our feet. Feet are what "stand under us," and it is the same when we understand and assimilate non-dual God-knowledge. We stand firmly as the Self, and not the limited, incomplete and fearful individual. So for now let's assume that all experience is non-dual, despite the scientist's world view that reality is a duality.

From your individual point of view, if we strip away the body-mind-sense complex, your story and every limb or part that you call "me," what remains? Just Consciousness – the essence of who you are. As we have determined many times in this book, I don't have to ask you if you're conscious, because it's obvious. From God's point of view, take away all of God's stuff – everything in the universe – and what remains is also just Consciousness.

Inference Is a Valid Means of Knowledge

We say the universe, God, is conscious. The universe isn't random. If it were, scientists wouldn't be able to, for example, do any calculations. It's only because of consistent natural laws and patterns that we can navigate the world at all. We can infer the intelligence behind all Creation because we are intelligent, and inference is a valid means of knowledge. Everything here is just knowledge made manifest. How else do you get a towering oak from a small acorn? Or a fully formed baby from an egg and sperm invisible to the naked eye? For this reason, we say the universe is intelligent.

Vedanta does not recognize the Bible as valid independent means of knowledge, because much (though not all) of what it holds as truth is based on beliefs and opinions of the people who wrote about the supposed events. But intelligent design is an area where we're in agreement with the Bible, as are some of the alleged comments ascribed to Christ which are non-dual in nature. So up until now we've learned that God is a figurative entity – a name for Consciousness plus various powers, including the knowledge, energy and matter to make stuff. We'll call these powers "*Maya*," a Sanskrit word that means "that which makes the changeless (Consciousness) appear to be changing" by spinning the dream of life as we know it.

Consciousness Plus *Maya* Equals God

From this we're able to state: Consciousness plus *Maya* equals God, the Creator. Okay, so we've defined God. But how about a person? Consciousness plus a body-mind-sense complex equals a person, the creature. Interestingly enough, God, the person and the Creation all include Consciousness. Everything just resolves back into Consciousness, even God and God's stuff. It may seem implausible, but the essence of the universe isn't dark matter; it's pure, attributeless, non-dual Consciousness.

Are We the Same as God?

We are and we are not the same as God. We share our essence with God, Consciousness, just like all clay pots are made of clay, gold rings are made of gold, all cheese is made of milk and all spiders' webs are made of the spiders who wove them. Is a ray of sunshine really that different from the sun? Yes and no.

Obviously as individuals we cannot wield God's powers, as we aren't omnipresent or omniscient. Only God, the creative principle, has total knowledge of everything in the Field. As individuals we only have knowledge of the world we have contact with. Whereas God creates everything, we only create our own subjective realities. Relative to the person, God is unlimited. As people we are limited and live in a limited Field. But we are God from the perspective that we are a product of God and by the fact that we share the same identity – Consciousness.

How you relate to these statements will depend on who you think you are. Are you the limited person or limitless Consciousness? Whichever it is, let's not diminish the fact that we share the same source, which is really cool. Knowing this reminds us that we are not small and limited, the scourge of the earth as religion would have us believe. We are unlimited, beautiful and whole. Moreover, acceptance of our true identity as universal eternal Consciousness does not eliminate us as a finite individual. It is liberation from our primary identity as a limited individual, and gives us freedom from and for the individual, in other words, freedom from the suffering imposed by duality when we are identified solely with the body-mind.

God's Stuff Is the Tricky Part

It gets tricky when we look at all God's stuff. We say God's Creation is beginningless because it exists in Consciousness. Consciousness is a causeless cause without beginning or end. Consciousness just is and has no limitations, because if it did, it wouldn't be whole, complete, changeless and non-dual. We say Consciousness is real, and all objects, including thoughts, are only apparently real because "real" is that which is always present and never changes. Can you come up with a better definition for "real"? Think about it. Objects – and that includes your thoughts, emotions and feelings too – are always changing and unreliable, so they don't qualify. Nothing in this world, including the world, is not subject to change, except for Consciousness.

All objects are also made up of other objects or parts, unlike Consciousness, which is whole, complete and independent of parts. Thus the only "thing" that is real is you, Consciousness, the knower of the body-mind-sense complex and its story that arise in you. Now it gets more difficult. You could argue that matter is also eternal because all matter reverts to energy that constantly recycles within the Field, which is true. Because matter cannot be destroyed but changes form, all objects are beginningless too, though they are not always manifest in form. Furthermore, all objects are fundamentally Consciousness, which is real. Something that is real can never be born. Only something that is not real can be born. When objects manifest in form, though their essence is non-dual Consciousness, they manifest as reflected consciousness, not pure Consciousness. Everything you are looking at is reflected consciousness, including your body.

Although Consciousness does not have eyes, what is looking out of your eyes is pure Consciousness looking at itself, just like you would look at your image in a mirror. Your reflection is you, but is not the same as you. We are not saying the reflection in the mirror (all objects) does not exist. Objects exist, because we experience them. But because they are always changing into something else, objects are only apparently, not actually, real, just like your reflection in a mirror is not real. But because duality fools us, we mistake the reflection for the real thing.

The Snake and the Rope

It's like the story of the guy who goes to the well at dusk to draw water, and in the dim light mistakes a coiled rope for a snake. At the moment of his misinterpretation, to him the rope is a snake, and he jumps back in fear. It's not until the error is corrected that the "snake" becomes a rope again, and he sees his mistake. The "snake" existed only in his mind, but wasn't real, although his fear felt very real. Objects exist, because we experience them, but on closer examination they flunk the test. Even science confirms this, because everything breaks down to atoms, then subatomic particles, then invisible energy.

Objects Are Just Thoughts

I have already explained the description for objects in previous chapters, but repeat it here, as understanding the definition is central to Self-inquiry. Objects are ephemeral and fleeting, appear as something one moment and something else the next. When examined closely, objects are just a temporary aggregate of smaller parts, but really they are just thoughts. All objects exist as thoughts. Our sense instruments don't actually sense objects, just their properties – colour, shape, texture, taste, smell, etc. From the various sensory inputs, the mind automatically takes the properties, aggregates them and applies a name and form so that "wet and translucent" becomes "water," "yellow" is "hot," "crackling" becomes "fire" and so on.

We live in a thought universe that operates in very predictable programs created by the forces that run the Field, and interpreted by our five senses. Translational neuroscientists have established that the process of observation/experience is the same as what you experience during a magic trick, which is a series of "electrochemical signals going around a bunch of circuits in your brain." Because there are no windows in your skull, the only way you can get information into your brain is through your five senses.

A Grand Simulation of Reality

From there, your brain draws on memories and uses cognition to fill in the details (or gaps) and essentially forms what neuroscientists call "a grand simulation of reality." From this point of view, it is true that we create our own reality, because we do not experience the world as it is. Rather we experience everything through the filters of our subjective beliefs, opinions and tendencies. We experience the world as *we* are and think. Within this transactional reality (reflected reality), it's not that the world around you is not there. It's there, but you've never actually lived there. You've never even been there for a visit. The only place you've ever been is inside your own mind. Now that's a thought to give some pause!

Maya, the transactional reality, superimposes the illusion of duality onto non-transactional non-duality. Like a mirage of water on the desert floor, it appears real but isn't. You cannot drink the mirage water. *Moksa*, a neat Sanskrit word that means "freedom from the hypnosis of duality," is the ability to discriminate what is real and always present (Consciousness/non-duality/the real you) from that which is not always present and always changing (the Field/duality, the apparent person and their story, i.e. the reflection).

Duality's Gift

There is nothing wrong with duality. Just as we cannot get rid of God, we cannot get rid of duality, we can only negate it as only apparently real. Duality is only a problem when we don't know what it is and mistake it to be real, like the snake and the rope. We suffer because of the belief that we are small, limited and inadequate, and that we must chase objects to complete us. There is nothing inherently wrong with objects, but if we chase them or are dependent on them for our happiness, they ultimately fail us because objects are value-neutral and cannot make us happy for long. But when we know the joy is in us and not in objects, we can enjoy them free of dependence and the inevitable fear of loss dependence generates. We know that we are fine with or without the objects of desire. We can love with open arms, and neither grasp nor cling.

Duality's special gift is that it gives us the opportunity to hold and touch the ones who embody the love we are, to enjoy a great meal, a sunset, to make and appreciate great art, and much more. All our creativity, innovation and ingenuity is possible thanks to duality and God, who is the only doer. Duality is only cruel when we fall under its spell and believe ourselves to be limited doers who own things. Life is beautiful and benign when we know that we are full and complete, when we understand how things work here and follow *dharma*. Self-knowledge does not immunize us from the challenges and losses of life, but it gives us the tools to deal with both, and therefore frees us of fear.

Where Does God Come from?

In answer to the question "Where does God come from?" we can reason that because Consciousness is never born and never dies, Consciousness is eternal; and because Consciousness is eternal, so is God. Remember, the essence of God is just Consciousness, and because Consciousness is beginningless and God's stuff exists within Consciousness, God is beginningless. Since God has no beginning, God is not born. God simply is. But here's the catch: God isn't real either.

By our definition, only Consciousness is real and unlimited. God, or the Creator and the Creation (Consciousness plus *Maya*), only exists because of Consciousness. When *Maya* is added to Consciousness, it appears to be limited, "impure," or to have qualities. *Maya* is a power that exists in Consciousness or Consciousness could not be called unlimited. To qualify as unlimited, Consciousness holds the potential for all powers, including the potential to limit itself, although it is only an apparent and not an actual limitation. When *Maya* appears in Consciousness, this Creation and your personal story appear along with it, just like a reflection in the mirror or a movie on a screen. The screen is you, and the movie playing out on it comes from you, but it is not you. This whole show is only a show, a trick of light, with a predetermined end, after which it goes unmanifest, until it appears again.

You Are "Here" Before, During and After

You, Consciousness, are here before, during and after. You have always been "here" because there is "nowhere" you are not. Think of a photograph. When you look at it, you don't see the camera. But you know there is a camera by virtue of the photo's existence. It is the same with Consciousness. For there to be a world to experience, there must be Consciousness, but just like the camera exists with or without the presence of a photograph, so does Consciousness exist with or without the Creation.

Therefore, like the individual, God is dependent on Consciousness, but Consciousness is independent of God. God is only apparently real, just like all God's stuff, and only apparently unlimited. Nevertheless, as a person living in this world, we still experience God as unlimited. You can't just write off God or pretend the rules of life do not apply to you when you claim your identity as nondual Consciousness. You're still in this dreamscape whether you like it or not. Everything you have is given to you by God, even if it isn't real by our definition, and you had better understand and follow the rules or you will suffer.

Why Does God Create?

As humans we think there must be an answer for everything, if only we can figure it out. Why would God want to create anything?

There is no answer. Maybe God was bored? Or maybe God just wanted to know itself, so it created conscious beings with senses that allow God to see, smell, taste, touch and hear its Creation. When we know that we share the same identity as God, we no longer care about why. It's a redundant question. To know that we are God experiencing itself suffices. Yet we know it is an enduring mystery why anything exists at all.

The deeper you dive into this Creation, the more bizarre it gets. Open one door and there's another, and then another – an endless series of doors to open. It's rather like *babushka* dolls stacked one inside the other in ever-diminishing sizes, a puzzle folded within another puzzle, where the macrocosmic mirrors the microcosmic and vice versa. To comprehend reality is to see the ocean in a drop of water, the intelligence of Creation in a seed and infinity in the eyes of a baby.

Let Go and Let God

God's stuff comprises a set of patterns which appear everywhere, for God is very frugal. Ponder nature's fractals, for example. The veins under your skin appear like the veins in a leaf, which look like the branches of a tree, which appear like the river-made veins found on the surface of our planet. Nature is just a fixed set of laws and patterns applied repeatedly. From a few we get the many, just like from the twenty-six letters of the alphabet countless words are assembled. Or by virtue of the four nucleobases that make up our DNA multitudinous living beings are created. We are just explaining nature, but in a way that suggests there is Consciousness and intelligence behind it. God isn't about guilt, fear or asking for a new SUV. God is about life itself, so do not supplicate. Appreciate.

Once you know God and how God's Field of Experience works, you just let go and let God do your life. Whether you like it or not, you really have no choice anyway, because you are not in control of what happens. God is. By living your life with an attitude of complete acceptance, surrender and gratitude, you shed the load of existential anxiety and put this burden where it belongs – with God, the Field. And with that acceptance comes a huge sense of relief. There are only two things up to us: our attitude, and appropriate and timely action in accordance with what each situation asks of us.

Do I Create My Own Reality?

You may think that, because you have free will, you don't need to negotiate with God, and that you create your own reality. While it's true you create your own subjective reality, that's about it. Even when we take the right action with the right attitude, there is no guarantee that we will get what we want. Often we don't. There are no guarantees in this world; we win as much as we lose. This may leave you feeling like a failure, despondent and in despair. But when you act in the spirit of surrender and gratitude, you know the results are impartial and not up to you, and you take what comes with equanimity. God's laws are non-negotiable, because if they were, everything here would fall apart.

From our individual point of view, we do have free will and a certain degree of control; we can choose an apple over an orange, for instance. If this were not the case, success at anything would be impossible. But looking at the big picture, you are totally dependent on God, even if you don't believe in God. God is synonymous with the Field of Existence, and no action takes place without the blessing of everything else. So many factors need to be present for anything to happen that it should be obvious there's an intricate network of constant support in operation that is not our doing. We appear to be doers, but we don't see the infinite factors that had to be present and actions that had to take place so that we can do anything or for anything to happen.

Self-Reliance Is an Illusion

Many people take pride in self-reliance, but it's all just a big joke. If you think you are solely responsible for your achievements, even your failures or what you "own," you are only fooling yourself. How you respond to what the Field asks of you is up to you, but everything has been given to you – your parents, your body, your shelter, your education, your clothing, your food, your partner, your entertainment. Even the things that are taken away from you and the tough times are gifts, because it is in suffering that we turn inwards to find answers.

God Is the Only Doer

Nothing belongs to anyone, and no one is doing anything. God is the only doer, and everything is God's stuff. Everything we need is always given to us, regardless of what we are going through. God takes care of even the smallest and seemingly most insignificant life forms. Life is an embarrassment of riches. Gratitude is therefore the best and only appropriate attitude.

There's an old Zen monk who likes to say that he can see the whole universe in a single sheet of paper, and he's right. Look at everything that had to occur for even a single sheet of paper to manifest – the sun, the water, the tree, the lumberjack, the chainsaw, the truck, the factory, the salesperson, the retailer and on and on. The sheet of paper didn't manifest itself, and neither did we, nor any of what we believe we control or own.

Our sense of control is just an illusion, because all results come from the Field of Existence, even our ability to make decisions. How much control do you even have over your own thoughts?! No action takes place without the blessing of all things in the Field, which takes care of the needs of the total before our own. We have a problem with this and suffer when we believe that our likes and dislikes take precedence. We believe that we can do our own thing in order to get what we want, and subscribe to the illusion that we can control the outcome – but we never can.

What About Evil and Bad Things Happening?

Many people have a great deal of difficulty over the thorny question of evil and suffering, and it is a tough one. Materialists base their arguments for the non-existence of God on the fact that belief in God must include all the bad things that happen, such as accidents, plagues, illness, violent crime and so on. Their point is that if we accept an all-powerful God that is good, we must also accept an all-powerful God that is "bad," which cancel each other out.

We agree that God is not logical from a dualistic point of view. But we say the non-dual God is logical, even though it makes both good and bad possible. The Field of Existence, which is a duality, is there for us to work out our *karma*. In the Field nothing exists without its opposite. If that were not so, the game of life would be impossible. You cannot have heat without cold, sweet without bitterness or "beautiful" without "ugly." If God had to restrict us to only good, how would we function here? Therefore God must give us the potential for both good and bad, and everything in between. It's not God that causes the world's problems; ignorance of God does that. When we know God and follow *dharma,* we do no evil, because we understand the rules of life and of non-injury.

Under the spell of duality, people believe they are small and inadequate and act out of fear and desire, thus create suffering. Take away the hypnosis of duality and ignorance of the true nature of reality, and everything is totally fine. Even though as individuals we must still contend with the gains and losses of life, we can do so from an entirely different perspective as the eternal Self when we take Consciousness as our primary identity. Nobody has knowledge of the big picture, so we cannot say from our limited knowledge as individuals why bad things happen to good people or good things to bad people. "On the subject of *karma,* even the sages are perplexed" say the sacred texts. But we do know that everyone experiences what they need to at that moment for reasons only God knows.

A Zero-Sum Game

There are no accidents or victims in God's world. There is also no death, no disease and no suffering, because we are not the body, and this world is only apparently real. In the world of duality, there are no winners, and all appearances to the contrary, no losers either. It's a zero-sum game. Everything evens out eventually. We're all swimming in the same fishbowl. Vedanta just calls out what you and everyone else intuitively already knows. We might not be able to put our finger on it, so we come up with all kinds of names for it – God, *Isvara,* Allah, Jehovah, Him, Her, or Universal Force. Whatever you want to call it, it doesn't really matter. It's all as impersonal as the weather.

The Saving Grace of God-Knowledge

Despite all the religious overtones and baggage, there's great use-fulness to having God-knowledge. It helps us understand that everything is the way it is and couldn't be otherwise. Things are working out in a grand scheme of things that we can never fully understand from a personal perspective, but which, appearances to the contrary notwithstanding, somehow takes care of the whole. It changes the victim-blame game into one of sanity and common sense, of beauty even, and grace. It removes anxiety and fear of the unknown, especially the fear of loss and death. With non-dual God-knowledge, we can understand how the whole Mandala of Existence works. These are not small things. God isn't just a paci-fier or some bedtime story to comfort you when life doesn't give you what you want.

God-knowledge alleviates ignorance – the cause of suffering – and it promotes healthy habits, such as gratitude and the ability to let go, two of this world's best remedies for stress. We could argue all day and night whether or not God exists or what God is, but you cannot deny your experience, even if you are oblivious to it, that everything you're witnessing right now is simultaneously created, maintained and recycled by a power greater than you. Call it nature, the Field, or Life if you will, it makes no difference.

Vedanta is neither for nor against any religion. As the science of Consciousness, Vedanta provides us with a valid and independent means of knowledge for both "small" self-inquiry and "big" Self-inquiry. It removes ignorance of our true nature as Consciousness and produces the ability to discriminate between the two orders of reality: duality and non-duality. It ends existential suffering, because it removes all doubt about who you are, how you relate to and need to function in the Field of Existence, and how to manage your mind.

A Religious Attitude

Vedanta advocates the need for a "religious attitude" to life as essential to happiness and a meaningful life. God is to be worshipped, not for God's benefit, but for ours. Worship of God is not about ritual or self-abnegation, it is about living intelligently because we understand the gift of life. It is about practising gratitude in whichever way works for us. If that is lighting a candle, chanting, sitting in silence, walking in nature, surfing a wave or revering a symbol of God meaningful to us, it matters not. God is not fussy, because everything is God. Though we should definitely not fear God, we need to respect life and live in harmony with it, because we aren't in control. We can try to live without God, but how impoverished our lives are without appreciation for God's bounty. How sad and joyless is a life without God!

The Four Stages *of* God-Knowledge

We need to understand the definitions of God according to Vedanta gradually and systematically until we can see the full vision, or the whole Mandala of Existence. The way in which I define (or deny) God will determine my life experience and devotion. Each level of my understanding of God produces its own kind of devotional attitude. The first three stages are personal devotion and involve free will, which is why these stages are called dualistic worship. The purpose of these stages of worship is that these practices reduce subjectivity and neutralize likes and dislikes, as well as negate the doer and manage and neutralize the childish ego. The fourth and last stage of devotion, non-dual devotion, takes place once the egoic doer is permanently negated by Self-knowledge.

Stage 1: Dualistic God-Knowledge and Worship

God-knowledge has three levels of dualistic devotional practice that develop as my understanding of God matures. Stage one is not essential, but it is a stepping stone to the next stage of devotion. In the first level of understanding, where all religions originate, my understanding of God is as a personified and "personal" deity, a He usually, a father figure who takes care of me and listens to my problems. It is a parent-child relationship. In this stage, most believers are after God's stuff rather than God. As a devotee I want something, so I supplicate God to get the desired results.

My devotion to God is informal, undisciplined, emotional, subjective and "heart-based." My desire is to serve and worship according to the qualities that condition the instrument of love: the mind and heart. If the heart/mind is dull (*tamasic*), superstition and fear inform one's worship; for example, fear-based religious worship. If the heart/mind is passionate (*rajasic*), desire informs one's worship. At its worst, it leads to sectarianism, fundamentalism, fanaticism and dogmatism, which give rise to all religious wars. It makes people feel self-righteous, that they have "God on their side" and can act out whatever they believe "in His name," that they are better than others and their way is the only way. On the other hand, it also offers the benefits of religion as mentioned previously, such as connection to others, the support of the community through the comfort of rituals, emotional/psychological support and coping systems or therapy.

Stage 2: *Karma Yoga* and Worship

My understanding has progressed somewhat beyond seeing God as a parent to seeing God in all of life. My devotional practice is emotional but also intellectual, and I start to develop the desire for God, not so much God's stuff anymore. I start to practise *karma yoga*: I surrender the results of actions to the Field (or God) with an attitude of consecration and gratitude because I have realized that the results of actions are not up to me, which helps neutralize the idea of doership. *Karma yoga* lessens the pressure of success or failure and offers me the tools to objectify my thoughts/emotions.

If my heart/mind is pure (*sattvic*), I love for the sake of the object/beloved (God) and for the sake of love itself, such as the ecstatic rapture of saints and mystics, who are often found in this stage. But even a pure mind sees the beloved as an object – as "other than." There is a doer, a lover. This doer/lover loves something or someone other than himself or herself, even though in all cases, whether one knows it or not, it is for the sake of the Self that one loves. A mature devotee knows that he or she is the Self and worships all as the Self. But a dull (*tamasic*) or extroverted (*rajasic*) devotee remains unaware of this fact, because they feel incomplete and love an object in order to feel complete (God or some other symbol of divinity) because it makes him or her feel more secure, more complete and "happier." There is usually, however, a sense of separation from the object.

The advantage that a *sattvic* (pure) devotee enjoys over a *tamasic/rajasic* devotee is that the object of worship (God in whatever way it is conceived) is always available to reciprocate, whereas if you see God as a person or a thing, your love is not always available or receptive. But the lover of God as Consciousness/Self is never far from the beloved, because God is Consciousness and Consciousness is unfailingly responsive. No matter how the Self is invoked, it responds lovingly because Consciousness is love. It does not matter whether you see Consciousness as the religious God or as another kind of symbol: an idol, a person, nature, a practice or ritual or as life itself. Consciousness does not discriminate, because it sees everything as itself. There is a beautiful saying in the *Bhagavad Gita*: Krishna speaking to Arjuna says, "In whatever way you worship me [i.e. the Self, or Consciousness], I will come to you to make your faith strong."

Stage 3: Objective God-Knowledge

This stage is also compulsory for Self-inquiry; here devotion is still dualistic, but much less so. Vedanta calls this *upasana yoga* (meditation, contemplating or keeping the mind focused on the Self). It is where worship of God becomes objective: purely impersonal and intellectual. Knowledge of God and the Creation start to crystallize. There is still duality and you see God in special forms (for example, in icons or beauty), but gradually, as your knowledge becomes firm, this progresses into seeing and worshipping God in all forms, the good and the bad.

Stage 4: Impersonal God-Knowledge, or Self-Knowledge

In the final stage of understanding, I transcend my idea of myself as merely a person. I see myself and God as the formless essence of all, both manifest and unmanifest, as Consciousness. My devotion is non-dual and therefore impersonal, beyond subjectivity and objectivity, i.e. free from the limited small self, the person and their story. With non-dual vision, you see everything primarily as the Self, and secondly as the person, and never confuse the two again. You still live as the person, obviously, and follow *dharma*, your own and universal *dharma*, which requires following the rules of the Field of Existence, or God, automatically. You continue with your devotional practice, except it is no longer dualistic in that you know that everything is you, Consciousness. You have permanently discriminated between what is real, i.e. what is always present and unchanging, and what is apparently real, or what is not always present and always changing – the body and the world.

The final stage does not negate the previous three, it simply completes the full picture. When we appreciate God as both form and formless, and as sharing the same identity as ours, we can see God as a "personified" deity if we choose to or in any symbol that is meaningful to us. Or we can see God as the totality of nature, as the Field. It does not matter at this stage of understanding, because my God-knowledge cannot be negated and has become firm Self-knowledge. Just as quantum physics does not displace Newtonian physics, both understandings are valid at their respective levels.

www.ingramcontent.com/pod-product-compliance
Lightning Source LLC
Chambersburg PA
CBHW051816090426
42736CB00011B/1505